CULTIVATING
THE ROSEBUDS

CULTIVATING THE ROSEBUDS

The Education of Women at the
Cherokee Female Seminary,
1851–1909

DEVON A. MIHESUAH

UNIVERSITY OF ILLINOIS PRESS
Urbana and Chicago

Illini Books edition, 1998

© 1993 by the Board of Trustees of the University of Illinois
Manufactured in the United States of America
1 2 3 4 5 C P 5 4 3 2 1

This book is printed on acid-free paper.

Library of Congress Cataloging-in-Publication Data

Mihesuah, Devon A. (Devon Abbott), 1957–
    Cultivating the rosebuds : the education of women at the Cherokee Female Seminary,
1851–1909 / Devon A. Mihesuah.
        p.   c.m.
    Includes bibliographical references and index.
    ISBN 0-252-01953-9 (cloth : acid-free paper). ISBN 0-252-06677-4 (pbk. : acid-free paper)
    1. Cherokee National Female Seminary. 2. Cherokee Indians—Education.
    3. Cherokee Indians—Women.   I. Title.
    E97.6.C35M54 1993
    376'.089'975—dc20   92-5845
                                                                             CIP

Digitally reprinted from the first paperback printing

UNIVERSITY OF ILLINOIS PRESS
1325 SOUTH OAK STREET
CHAMPAIGN, ILLINOIS 61820-6903
WWW.PRESS.UILLINOIS.EDU

To my parents, Thomas James and Olyve Hallmark Abbott,
and to my aunt, Billie Mills, and my sister, Taryn Abbott

The Seminary our garden fair
And we, the flowers planted there . . .
Like roses bright we hope to grow,
And o'er our home such beauty throw
In future years—that all may see
Loveliest of lands,—the Cherokee.

Wreath of Cherokee Rose Buds
4 August 1855

Contents

Map and photographs follow page 50.

Acknowledgments

Over the past six years, many individuals have provided invaluable assistance with my research on the Cherokee Female Seminary and the preparation of this book. I extend my appreciation to Joyce Martindale, Brenda Barnes, William Farrington, Rosalie Bell, Robert Larramore, Audrey Vanderhoof, and Hugh McDonald of the Mary Couts Burnett Library, Texas Christian University. Thanks go also to Jennifer Carlson and Melissa Burkhart of the Department of Special Collections at the library of the University of Tulsa; Jacqueline K. Grieb, Linda Vann, and Tom Mooney of the Cherokee National Historical Society, Tahlequah, Oklahoma; Mary Lee Boyle, William D. Welge, Robert P. Nespar, Kay Zahrai, and Judith Michener of the Oklahoma Historical Society, Oklahoma City; and Kent Carter and Margaret Hacker of the Fort Worth Branch of the Federal Archives. I am grateful for the help of Elaine Trehub and Patricia Albright of the Williston Memorial Library, Mount Holyoke College, South Hadley, Massachusetts; John Mack Faragher, Linda Morgan, and Iona Crook at Mount Holyoke College; Nathan Bender and John R. Lovett of the Western History Collections, University of Oklahoma at Norman; Richard Madaus, former dean of the John Vaughan Library, Northeastern State University, Tahlequah; and Linda Beaverson and Delores Sumner, also of NSU. In addition, I thank Don Coerver, Kenneth Stevens, Jamie Gleason, and Margaret Farmer of the history department at Texas Christian University; R. David Edmunds, Indiana University;

Robert Trennert, Arizona State University; Mike Green, Dartmouth College; Rayna Green, Smithsonian Institution; Terry Wilson, University of California at Berkeley; Virginia Duffy McLoughlin of Providence, Rhode Island; and Neil Kunze, Maxine Campbell, Sarah Hillyer, and Sanda Luthy, Northern Arizona University.

I extend my deep gratitude to the Ford Foundation and to the Office of Fellowships and Grants at the Smithsonian Institution for their generous research support, and to Phi Alpha Theta and Westerners International for their inspiring dissertation award. Financial support came as a result of the efforts of several administrators at Northern Arizona University. These include Karl Webb, dean of the college of arts and sciences; Henry Hooper, associate vice president of graduate studies; and Cary Conover, grant administrator of organized research.

I especially want to thank Victoria Sheffler, head archivist at Northeastern State University, who has assisted me for six years on this study; Theda Perdue of the University of Kentucky, whose suggestions helped to change my outlook on many aspects of my topic; Curtis Hinsley of Northern Arizona University, who provided editorial comments, continuing friendship, and encouragement; and William McLoughlin of Brown University, Peter Iverson of Arizona State University, Tempe, and Joseph Boles, director of women's studies at Northern Arizona University, all three of whom offered helpful editorial advice. Other people at NAU who provided valuable help include my research assistant, Nancy Cannon, who ordered research materials and tirelessly helped with the seemingly endless alphabetizing and cross-referencing of the names of the seminary students, and Bob Baron of the Historical Climate Records Office in the Center for Colorado Plateau Studies at Northern Arizona University, who assisted in developing the statistical programs I have used.

My warm regard and gratitude go to my friend and former dissertation advisor, Donald Worcester, professor emeritus of history at Texas Christian University, for his enduring friendship and gentle criticism.

I thank my parents, Tom and Olyve Abbott, my sister, Taryn, and my aunt, Billie Mills, for their love and support throughout my academic career. Finally, I thank my husband, Joshua, who has shown patience during my ordeal of writing and who helps me to keep all things in perspective.

Terminology

The terms fullblood, mixed-blood, traditional, conservative, progressive, white, Cherokee, and Indian appear throughout this study. Because of the variables in each of these terms, a word of explanation is in order.

I use fullblood and mixed-blood to refer to physiology, while I use traditional, conservative, and progressive to refer to cultural adherence. (I do not use half-breed or mixed-breed, both of which seem more appropriately applied to dogs than people.) The lines separating the fullbloods, mixed-bloods, traditionals, and progressives cannot be drawn easily, if at all. The fullbloods were not always poor and uneducated; nor were they always conservative, that is, wanting to cling to traditional Cherokee culture. (Indeed, the idea of what is traditional has changed over time.) In this study, a traditional or conservative Cherokee is one who prefers to speak Cherokee, practices Cherokee religion, and resists white culture (although some have given it a try via education). Many fullbloods were affluent, educated, and "progressive," adopting the values of white society at the expense of losing their traditional Cherokee culture. Mixed-bloods, on the other hand, were not always wealthy, educated, or progressive. Many were quite poor or illiterate; some knew more about Cherokee culture (for example, language, dress, religion, and medicine) than did the fullbloods.

While it is certainly desirable to refer to American Indians by their tribal names and to point out individual tribal traits, it is not feasible to do so when discussing the tribes in general. Therefore, unless noted otherwise, the term Indian will refer here to all American Indians (a reference that I prefer over "Native American," which, in my mind, also applies to anyone born in the United States).

I use Cherokee to refer to anyone with Cherokee blood, while I use white to describe a person without Indian blood, excluding blacks, Asians, and Hispanics, although many of the latter adhered to "white culture." It is obvious that people of European descent are a diverse group. Germans are different from the French, and Swedes are different from Italians. But for lack of a better term, I also use "white" to denote a way of life and a person or persons who look "Caucasian."

Introduction

A forested area four miles south of the Western Cherokee Nation's capital, Tahlequah, in present-day eastern Oklahoma, is the location of the Cherokee Heritage Center. Also known as TSA-LA-GI, this cultural museum in the small town of Park Hill is the site of performances of *The Trail of Tears,* an outdoor drama that traces the cultural and political development of the Cherokee people. In front of the modern heritage center stand three brick columns, physical remnants of what was once the pride of the Cherokee Nation, the first Cherokee Female Seminary. Completed in 1851, the school educated several generations of young Cherokee women to adapt to a world and way of life quite different from that of their tribal past.

Fire destroyed the first seminary building in 1887, but two years later a new, larger seminary was completed. Located closer to Tahlequah than its predecessor and provided with a better water supply, the seminary functioned until 1909, when it was sold to the state of Oklahoma and became Northeastern State Normal School. The building eventually became the nucleus of the campus of Northeastern State University, where it is known today as Seminary Hall.

The nondenominational Cherokee Female Seminary was a unique institution. The school was established and maintained by the tribe, was open only to Cherokees, and offered students a course of study patterned after that of Mount Holyoke Seminary in South Hadley, Massachusetts. Like other schools during the early and middle decades of the nineteenth century, Mount Holyoke was called a seminary rather than a college. While Christianity was stressed at such a school, the term seminary actually referred to any institution of higher learning that also trained its students for employment in other fields. As at Mount Holyoke, the curriculum at the Cherokee seminary did not include any aspect of Cherokee culture. Despite this omission, the school was filled to capacity with Cherokee students almost every year. Many alumnae later graduated from colleges and universities around the country, becoming physicians, businesswomen, educators, and prominent social workers.

The seminary was created during a particularly tumultuous period in Cherokee history. A decade before, the tribe had been removed from its homelands in the East and resettled in southern Indian Territory, later Oklahoma. By mid-century, tribal members were attempting to reestablish their nation in an area surrounded by lands occupied by whites and by numerous other tribes. Because of the continued influx of "white blood" and white values into the tribe, the Cherokees' consciousness about race, class, and culture became more pronounced, causing cultural changes to accelerate and intratribal political and social rifts to reemerge, as they had existed in the East. There was much cultural ambiguity among the Cherokees. While the tribe consisted in part of individuals who resisted white culture and attempted to cling to tradition, it also was comprised of Cherokees who knew nothing about Cherokee culture, who looked Caucasian yet were acutely aware of themselves as Cherokees. Out of this confusion came the Cherokee Female Seminary, its student body made up of young Cherokee women who represented these different factions.

The Female Seminary exerted a positive influence on many of its pupils, but evidence suggests that the social atmosphere at the school contributed to a rift between Cherokee girls from progressive, mixed-blood families and those from more traditional, uneducated backgrounds. Although many of the girls were from traditionalist families, the seminary did nothing to preserve or reinforce Cherokee customs among its students. Modern-day education, not retention of ancestral Cherokee values, was one of the primary objectives of the school.

Over the course of forty academic years, almost three thousand young women attended the Female Seminary.[1] The physiologies and personalities of the students were quite varied and they adhered to traditional Cherokee culture to varying degrees, which makes it difficult to generalize about the student body. For example, some students were fullbloods, while others were blond, blue-eyed women of only 1/128 Cherokee blood. Some were from affluent, educated families, while others were from poor families whose members could neither read nor write English.[2] The seminarians' diverse backgrounds greatly influenced the way they viewed each other and the way they interpreted the purpose of the seminary. Unfortunately, the more traditional girls did not leave behind memoirs, which makes it difficult to know their viewpoints on education and on the progressive Cherokees.

One of the Cherokee National Council's rationales for establishing the school was to train the young women of the tribe in order to make them educated, dutiful, and "useful" wives for prominent Cherokee husbands. "Women's values" and the ideal of the "true woman" are often assumed to be a part of the white woman's world exclusively. But a number of Cherokee females were economically, socially, and physiologically nearly identical to Victorian society's white women, and many seminary students subscribed to the same value system as whites even before they enrolled. One question this book will explore is whether or not the alumnae of the seminary could realistically aspire to the ideal of a "true woman," inside or outside of the Cherokee Nation. Could they achieve that ideal if they looked "Indian," or was it possible only for those who looked white?

Another goal of the National Council was to educate Cherokee women who would in turn instruct the "uninformed" or "common" Cherokees, that is, children from the lower economic class who were often taught traditional Cherokee customs at home. From 1851 to 1856, there was a written entrance examination that only educated children (affluent mixed-bloods, with a few exceptions) were able to pass, thus excluding many Cherokees who wanted to attend. The result of this selective enrollment (and the expensive building maintenance that diverted tribal funds from agriculture) was that the seminary and its students were labeled as elitist, and intratribal debates raged over the practicality of a curriculum that included Latin and English literature instead of farming.

In 1872, because of pressure exerted on the council by the less affluent, disgruntled Cherokees who wanted their children educated at the school, seminary administrators began admitting the poorer, "indigent" children to the school. This move in effect created a class system along socioeconomic lines within the seminary.

Acculturated students and teachers took tremendous pride in their education and their physiology. Mixed-blood students frequently scorned those girls who had a lesser proportion of white blood and even other mixed-bloods who had darker skins, despite their acculturation and education. It was the consensus of the mixed-blood students and teachers—both white and Cherokee—that the fullblood girls were "a little bit backward," although a few progressive fullbloods also belittled those who had a minimal understanding of "white ways."[3]

These same divisions along socioeconomic lines were present throughout the Cherokee Nation. However, although many mixed-bloods referred to the uneducated, Cherokee-speaking fullbloods (and some mixed-bloods) as backward, unenlightened, and even immoral, that is not to imply that the fullbloods were cowed by the more affluent, educated Cherokees. Indeed, while poor fullbloods may have preferred not to live in poverty, they decided for themselves the cultural mores to which they would adhere. They possessed a strong political voice and were vital members of the tribal government. Utilization of what the seminaries had to offer was only one avenue Cherokees used to adapt to the changing world, and the fullbloods chose for themselves whether or not to send their children to the white-oriented schools.

Within the seminary domain, however, the dominant group was unquestionably the affluent, white-oriented, and often Caucasian-looking students. Any child who wished to graduate from the school had to adapt to the seminary lifestyle. Even the most emotionally secure traditionalist child would find herself becoming less sure of herself after being repeatedly reminded that her culture was an inferior one.

Another issue that is crucial to understanding the seminarians of the mid- to late-nineteenth century deals with identity. These young women held a variety of cultural beliefs—Cherokee, white, or a combination of the two. Their skin, hair, and eyes represented a broad spectrum of color. The issue of identity is made more complex by the fact that all of the students considered themselves Cherokees. At the same time that the progressive, light-skinned girls were desperately trying to adopt white ways and to find their place in the emerging American industrial society, the students from traditional backgrounds who had decided to try to graduate from the seminary were confused about how they—with their "Indian" appearance—would fit into the white society (or the progressive Cherokee society) for which the seminary had prepared them.

Because of these cultural and physiological differences among these students, some important questions emerge: Did the seminarians separate race from culture? Could there be more than one Cherokee culture?

One of the most striking aspects of the history of the Cherokee Female Seminary is that the school was established by the Cherokees, not by the federal government. The government, of course, had attempted to force education upon Indians throughout the country by taking Indian children from their homes and placing them in oppressive boarding schools. But the Cherokees built their own schools—including two expensive high schools—demonstrating rather dramatically that many of them had a mind-set that was different from that of other American Indians. Why was this so? Were all Cherokees supportive of the seminary's establishment, or was it created by and for a particular element within the tribe? Were those Cherokees connected with the seminary attempting to redefine what it meant to be a Cherokee while others preferred to maintain a more traditional lifestyle? Why didn't the Cherokees simply send their children to white schools in the East where they would receive almost the same education?

This book explores one school and one group of Cherokee females who shared the seminary experience; it focuses mainly on the mixed-bloods, since they left behind the documentation of that experience. However, it is not a social history of the seminary based solely on student accounts,[4] nor is it the political, social, or demographic history of the entire Cherokee Nation. (I refer those interested in the latter topics to the works of William McLoughlin, Russell Thornton, Theda Perdue, James Mooney, Bernard Strickland, and others.) Rather, this book examines the reasons the school was established and discusses its administration, curriculum, health care, social life, and faculty; it investigates how the students related to each other and records what some of the alumnae accomplished after leaving the seminary. Because the seminary was closed from 1856 to 1872, Chapter 3 focuses on the early years (1851–56) and the first few years after the school reopened in 1872. This time period can stand by itself because the value systems of most Americans in regard to the woman's sphere were different prior to the Civil War than they were after 1870; and after the seminary reopened, its student body was much more varied along socioeconomic lines than it had been in the 1850s.

The main text concludes with an epilogue that poses questions for further study. This is followed by several appendixes in which I have incorporated as many students' names, nicknames, and husbands' names as possible, although I regret that it was not feasible to include them all. In the appendixes, as in the text, the female students' eventual married names are given in parentheses. Two of my informants requested anonymity, and so I have given pseudonyms to all interviewees and the sites of the interviews.

Many people have a hard time grasping the concept that all Indians are not alike. They fail to recognize that within each tribe there were traditional and progressive elements and that the cultural traits of each tribe changed over time as a result of exposure to other Indian and non-Indian societies and in response to warfare, disease, genocide, forced relocation, and loss of land—all of which caused severe emotional stress. Movies and literature more often than not convey a stereotypical image of Indian people. Schools do not usually teach that each tribe had its own name for itself, along with a unique language, religion, economy, and world view, or that a tribe developed particular gender roles or methods of adaptation to the outside world. The compilation of the history of just one tribe would require a close investigation of the social, economic, physiological, and psychological factors at work in that tribe. A study of the Cherokee Female Seminary cannot address all of these aspects of the Cherokees' history, nor even the entire history of Cherokee women. It will, however, show that, historically and today, Cherokee women are especially complex individuals, different from one another and from women of other tribes. Many tantalizing issues remain to be explored.

1

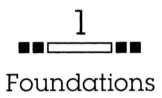

Foundations

On a sweltering day in late June 1827, the Reverend Samuel Austin Worcester leaned back in his chair as he listened to the young Cherokee students of Tennessee's Brainerd Mission reciting their daily lessons. In the front row, eager to give their recitations, sat boys and girls of white or mixed Cherokee-white lineage. Farther back, and much less vocal, sat the Cherokee fullbloods, children whose parents also wanted them to learn about the white man's religion and way of life. Attempting to please the missionaries, who often considered them inferior, some of these shy, fullblood children had exchanged their Cherokee names for new, Anglicized ones. They attempted to keep pace with classmates who were already fluent in English, but they read their lessons haltingly and with little confidence, as if they were already intimidated by their more acculturated peers.

Rev. Worcester took pride in the young Cherokees' ability to read Bible verses aloud, solve simple arithmetic problems, and write short essays. But he was concerned about a declining enrollment among the fullbloods. In 1821, more than half the student population at Brainerd had consisted of fullbloods, but in subsequent years the percentage had fallen markedly. As the fullbloods' enrollment declined, the number of mixed-bloods and whites increased.[1]

Established in 1816 near modern Chattanooga, Tennessee, Brainerd Mission was founded by the American Board of Commissioners for Foreign Missions, an organization dedicated to Christianizing the entire world. The missionaries realized that before the Cherokees could be converted they would have to learn English. What the missionaries did not foresee, however, was the opposition to their work from many mixed-bloods who already could speak English and who were more interested in seeing their children educated than "reborn," as well as from traditional fullbloods, who had little interest in anything the missionaries had to offer.[2]

Perhaps the decline of fullblood enrollment at Brainerd—and at other mission schools throughout the Cherokee Nation—can be attributed to Sequoyah's completion of the Cherokee syllabary in 1821.[3] Some Cherokees must have questioned why they should learn English when they could now read and write in their own language. Yet the declining enrollment cannot be explained totally by the development of the syllabary, since even some staunchly conservative Cherokees championed literacy in the belief that it would facilitate preserving the words to their sacred songs and ceremonies for future generations. Other factors were at work in the declining enrollment at mission schools. Some tribesmen feared that the missionaries would take Cherokee lands as payment for their labors. Others resented the missionaries' lack of respect for Cherokee culture or complained about their failure to employ Cherokee-speaking instructors.[4]

By all accounts, the missionary effort among the Cherokees helped widen the gulf between mixed-bloods and fullbloods, creating resentment and accentuating tribal factionalism. While the men of God inspired some Cherokees to pursue more advanced education, their crusading zeal alienated others. Yet even though the discord within the tribe grew more intense, all Cherokees realized that they faced the same problems: forced removal from their homeland and the disruption of all aspects of their culture.

Before their removal to Indian Territory, the Cherokees' domain included northern Alabama, northwestern Georgia, northwestern South Carolina, southwestern North Carolina, western Virginia, and most of eastern Kentucky and Tennessee. When the American Revolution erupted, the tribe sided with the British, but in 1777, Cherokees living in the "Upper Towns" of North Carolina, Georgia, and eastern Tennessee negotiated an uneasy peace with the Americans. The part of the tribe known as the Chickamaugas, or "Lower Town" Cherokees, was more resistant to white influence and remained at war with the Americans for two more decades.[5]

All Cherokees were determined to keep their traditional homeland, but the intrusion of white settlers and the resulting land cessions to the Americans had diminished their territory. Between 1721 and 1785, the Cherokees lost more than half of their original land. In 1785, following the Revolutionary War, the Cherokees signed the Treaty of Hopewell with the United States.[6] The agreement included a promise by the government to protect the remaining Cherokee homelands, but other treaties over the next thirty years resulted in the loss of two-thirds of the territory guaranteed in the Hopewell treaty.[7] By 1800, only twenty-four of the sixty-four Cherokee towns that had existed ten years earlier remained. Despite Cherokee protests and the federal government's assurances of protection, the incursion of non-Indians continued, and more territory was lost.[8]

The Cherokees were continually pressured to move farther west. By 1818, two thousand to three thousand of the fifteen thousand members of the tribe had moved across the Mississippi River to reestablish themselves in Arkansas Territory. Known as the "Old Settlers," these conservative western Cherokees asserted their autonomy. A treaty signed in 1828 required them to emigrate even farther, to the northeast portion of Indian Territory—an area that today is included in the state of Oklahoma. A smaller band of Cherokees settled in east Texas under the leadership of Chief Bowles, but in 1839 the group was violently driven out, some members moving to Indian Territory and others to Mexico.[9]

The Cherokees had cultivated small garden plots for centuries, but the depletion of their tribal hunting grounds forced them into intensive agriculture and the raising of livestock. In 1791, the Treaty of Holston included a provision for the federal government to help develop husbandry in the Cherokee Nation. The tribe was supplied with farming tools, equipment for constructing gristmills and sawmills, and white blacksmiths and artisans to train Cherokee apprentices. Although the Cherokees were less than pleased with the treaty (it required them to cede parts of their northeastern lands), some did show interest in this "Civilization Program."[10]

The acquisition of European goods combined with the pressure to cede lands had a profound effect upon traditional Cherokee culture. The tribe had long maintained close contacts with Europeans, thereby

acquiring customs and viewpoints other than their own. Cherokees
first contacted the Spanish in the mid-sixteenth century, but by the late
1600s most of their ties were to the British. Cornelius Dougherty, an
Irishman, had traded with the tribe in 1690, and James Adair, an English
merchant, settled among the Cherokees in 1730. By the 1790s, English
traders, German artisans, Tories, Scots, and Irishmen had established
themselves among the Indians. These Europeans intermarried with the
Cherokees, producing a population of mixed-bloods who often adopted
the value system of their white fathers or, to a lesser extent, white
mothers.[11]

Traditional Cherokee customs diminished as more tribespeople learned
to speak English, more Cherokee women married white men (and their
mixed-blood offspring married whites or other mixed-bloods), and many
Cherokees began to adopt the principles of capitalism. Although tribal
lands were held in common, many Cherokees preferred separate home-
steads over communal living. The new value system caused the break-
down of the tribe's political structure and of the established roles for
men and women. Religion once had permeated every aspect of Cherokees' lives and had given the tribe stability, but interest in traditional
ceremonies and dances began to wane. Men ceased to hunt and moved
into the fields to work (traditionally the women's role), taking the place
of women who now learned to use spinning wheels and looms. The
deer herds diminished and boys were no longer trained by their fathers
and uncles to be hunters and warriors. By the early nineteenth century,
the Cherokees' traditional matriarchal system had faded in favor of
the patriarchal family, which recognized males as leaders of the social
order. Many mixed-blood children adhered to the whites' view of
women as submissive homemakers instead of individuals of political
and economic importance.[12]

While many fullbloods attempted to adhere to the old ways and
wanted their children to become educated according to the teachings
of traditional Cherokee society, most mixed-bloods appeared to have
little interest in Cherokee customs and aspired to have their children
receive a white man's education and to become Christians, thus altering
the definition of "Cherokee" and "Cherokee education." The progressive Cherokees gained access to high positions in the tribal government
and controlled the annuity payments from the federal government for
past land concessions. They purchased black slaves, developed the best
farms, and amassed personal wealth. They were economically suc-

cessful because they were acquisitive, educated in the ways of white society, and aware of the importance of long-term planning. Furthermore, because of their appearance and ability to speak English, the mixed-bloods could better communicate with whites.[13]

Many mixed-blood Cherokees inherited wealth and learned business methods from their white parents. James Vann, a mixed-blood Cherokee National Council member and leader of the Cherokee Lower Towns, inherited trading posts, ferries, a gristmill, a distillery, two farms, and a large plantation.[14] Other tribespeople cultivated corn, wheat, cotton, and fruit trees, wore European-style clothing, and lived in one- or two-story log cabins or brick houses.[15] A few lived in plantation-style mansions and kept black slaves to cultivate the crops.[16] At the end of the 1820s, the tribe boasted 22,400 head of cattle, 40,000 swine, gristmills, sawmills, blacksmith shops, ferries, public roads, and a turnpike. A library society organized by tribe members had collected enough books to fill substantial libraries. In 1825, one-quarter of the Cherokee population was composed of mixed-bloods.[17]

The acculturated Cherokee was probably best exemplified by Elias Boudinot, coeditor of the Cherokee Nation's first newspaper, the *Cherokee Phoenix*, and by John Ross, principal chief of the Cherokee Nation from 1827 until his death in 1866. Boudinot, born Buck Watie, was a mixed-blood who adopted the name of a New Jersey philanthropist while attending the Cornwall Foreign Mission School in Cornwall, Connecticut.[18] A firm believer in education and acculturation, Boudinot remarked in 1826 that all tribes, not just the Cherokee, had little choice but to strive to adapt to the whites. They could "either become civilized and happy [or] become extinct."[19] Ross was only one-eighth Cherokee, but despite his predominantly white ancestry and urban lifestyle, he proved an effective spokesman for the rights and welfare of all Cherokee people.[20]

Although some Cherokees lived quite comfortably, not all could or even wanted to live in opulence. Most fullbloods and traditional Cherokees preferred to live in relatively isolated areas and had little interest in learning English, keeping slaves, or becoming Christians (although a few fullbloods did all of these things). Their traditional Cherokee society, with its system of clan revenge, division of labor by gender, and strong sense of community, was deteriorating, yet they continued to practice their religious ceremonies, speak Cherokee, and teach their children Cherokee rituals and language. In turn, many mixed-bloods and nontraditional Cherokees looked upon the less acculturated tribes-people with disdain. Inevitably, friction developed between those who struggled to preserve the traditional Cherokee lifestyle and those who wished to emulate white society.

In response to the changing conditions, a new governing body, the Cherokee National Executive Council, was formalized in 1809 for the purpose of resisting further removals and land cessions and uniting the Upper and Lower towns.[21] Also, the traditional custom of clan or blood revenge was outlawed, and a "Light Horse" brigade was created to enforce the peace.[22] By the 1820s, the tribe had organized a republican form of government and designated a capital city, New Echota, in northern Georgia. The Cherokee Nation was divided into eight districts, each with its own judge and marshal, and with rangers to find stray livestock.[23]

In 1827, the Cherokees adopted a constitution that was modeled in part on the Constitution of the United States, with articles pertaining to every aspect of their society. It divided the tribal government into three branches—legislative, judicial, and executive. The legislative branch was further divided into two sections: the National Council, consisting of three elected citizen representatives from each district, and the National Committee, composed of two elected representatives. The judicial powers were vested in a Supreme Court, which had the power to "ordain and establish" circuit and other courts throughout the Nation. Chosen by election, the principal chief held "supreme executive power" in the Cherokee Nation. He could approve or veto bills and, together with the Executive Council—appointed by the National Council—could "order and direct the affairs" of the Nation, including all recommendations and laws pertaining to education. Whites could not participate in tribal elections, but their mixed-blood male offspring could vote and hold office.[24]

Although fullbloods retained a voice in the affairs of the Cherokee Nation, the governing body was increasingly responsive to the needs of the mixed-bloods. The Executive Council controlled annuities, which perhaps accounts for the affluence of some of its members. The tribal lands remained "common property," but the constitution permitted "improvements" to be made on an individual's holdings—provided that he or she had no "view of speculation." The size of an individual's estate was limited only by the amount of money he could amass.[25]

To preclude rebellion—such as White Path's resistance to acculturation (1823–27)—the National Council passed a law in 1828 prescribing one hundred lashes for any member of the tribe found guilty of holding "unlawful meetings to encourage rebellion" against the Cherokee government. Indeed, those who formed that government intended to control the Cherokee Nation without interference.[26]

Despite the tribe's acculturation, Georgians would not tolerate another nation within the boundaries of their state. And when gold was discovered in Dahlonega in 1828—the worst calamity that can fall upon Indian lands—the Georgia legislature passed a series of laws designed to establish state control over the Cherokees. The state surveyed the tribal lands and raffled off sections to whites before resident Cherokees could remove their belongings from their homes. The state prohibited tribespeople from digging gold on their own property and even from submitting their grievances to any state or federal court. Cherokees of all classes, especially the poor fullbloods, were hard-pressed to survive.[27]

Tribal factionalism, which had continued after the 1828 removal of the Old Settlers, intensified over the question of the surrender of eastern Cherokee lands and the removal of the Cherokees to Indian Territory. Some tribesmen, such as Elias Boudinot, insisted that Cherokees should remove to the west. Others, including many fullbloods, were determined to stay on their traditional lands no matter how difficult the struggle. On 26 October 1829, the National Council, in an attempt to prevent removal, revitalized a Cherokee law condemning to death any tribe member who agreed to sell lands to whites without permission of the council.[28]

In defiance of the law, on 29 December 1835, a group of Cherokees, including Major Ridge (a fullblood), his son John Ridge, and Elias Boudinot and his brother Stand Watie, signed the Treaty of New Echota, which provided for the removal of the entire tribe to Indian Territory. The following year, these leaders and thirty followers of what was known as the Treaty Party relocated to reestablish themselves among the Old Settlers.[29]

The vast majority of Cherokees, however, denounced the treaty and proclaimed their refusal to leave their homeland. This faction, known as the Ross Party, was championed by Chief John Ross. Except for some small groups that stayed in the forests of North Carolina, however, the Cherokee removal was inevitable. From September 1838 through March 1839, approximately twelve thousand Cherokees began the long journey west over the "Trail of Tears" (also known as "The Trail Where They Cried"). This tragic trek to Indian Territory cost thousands of Cherokee lives. Among the casualties was Quatie Ross, the wife of Chief Ross.[30]

Bitterness over removal persisted after the survivors reached Indian Territory. The Treaty Party had found relative contentment in the west, but with the arrival of John Ross and his followers a contest for political leadership resurfaced. Violence erupted, and on 22 June 1839, Cherokees resentful of the removal treaty murdered Elias Boudinot, Major Ridge, and John Ridge. Stand Watie escaped. He killed James Foreman, a member of the Ross Party, and then organized his own armed force to counter John Ross's Light Horse police regiment. Over the next decade, more Cherokees were murdered, including Thomas Watie, Stand Watie's brother.[31]

In an attempt to reunite tribal members and reestablish peace, representatives of the warring factions came together during the summer of 1839 at the Illinois Camp Grounds in northeastern Indian Territory for an "Act of Union." On 12 July, the Ross faction adopted a new constitution, reaffirmed John Ross as chief of the Cherokee Nation, and proclaimed the renewal of the Cherokee government as it had existed in the East. The Treaty Party and the Old Settlers, however, did not acquiesce until the signing of a peace treaty in 1846. Factional differences were for the most part subordinated, at least until the Civil War.[32]

When the removal ended, almost eight thousand Cherokees and their slaves had relocated in the new Cherokee Nation. By 1840, the Cherokees had begun to recover from the devastation of removal. They had long since buried those who succumbed to illness from the long, arduous journey west, and they now attended to the business of building homes, clearing and plowing fields, planting crops, and settling into daily routines. Soon, over a thousand farms were in operation.[33]

On 4 November 1840, the Cherokee Council divided the Cherokee Nation into eight districts: Saline, Delaware, Tahlequah, Going Snake, Skin Bayou, Illinois, Canadian, and Flint. Each district had its own sheriff and district court. Following procedures established earlier in Georgia, every two years male Cherokees eighteen years of age and older in each district elected two citizens to the National Committee and three to the National Council.[34]

In 1841, the National Council proclaimed Tahlequah the capital of the Cherokee Nation. Located in a wooded valley three miles from the Illinois River, Tahlequah soon flourished as a business town. Along its main street stood grocery and dry goods stores, mechanics' shops, taverns, hotels, and boardinghouses. Churches, mills, schools, and homes also were built.[35] In 1843, the *Cherokee Advocate* was declared the Nation's newspaper, and the Cherokee Bible Society was organized.[36] A post office was established in May 1847, and by 1850 the Supreme Court and Masonic Lodge buildings had been completed. Two years later a chapter of the Sons of Temperance was formed.[37]

Although many Cherokees had lost their fortunes during removal, there was still an unequal distribution of wealth among members of the tribe. Many of the Old Settlers who had moved to Indian Territory in 1828 had built spacious homes, developed productive farms, and made substantial profits selling beef and produce to the government, army garrisons, and white settlers.[38] After the remainder of the Cherokees moved west, the tribe found another source of income. The United States government owed the Cherokee Nation over five million dollars by the provisions of the Treaty of New Echota. In theory, the annuities were to be distributed evenly by the Cherokee government. But as visitors noted, some tribespeople—usually the mixed-bloods— seemed prosperous while others lived in utter poverty.[39]

In reaction to federal policies and under the influence of missionaries and intermarried whites, the Cherokees had manifested an interest in formal education years before their removal to Indian Territory. Some Cherokees had built their own schools. In 1799, Daniel Ross, the father of John Ross, had solved the problem of educating his children by hiring John Barber Davis to teach in the Ross family's private school in Kingston, Tennessee. A few Lutheran and Moravian (or Society of United Brethren) missionaries had unsuccessfully attempted to establish missions among the Cherokees in the latter half of the eighteenth century. But in 1800, the Cherokee National Council finally granted the Moravians permission to open a mission school in northwest Georgia, provided the students received a secular education.[40]

The Moravian school, named Spring Place, was established on the property of James Vann in present-day Murray County, Georgia. The student body consisted of a "respectable number" of fullblood Cherokees, whites, and members of the mixed-blood Hicks, Ridge, and Watie families. Among the converts was Charles Renatus Hicks, a

Cherokee mixed-blood who served as second principal chief from 1810 to 1827 and as principal chief in 1827.[41]

Throughout the nineteenth century, other religious and lay groups attempted to establish schools for the Cherokees. In 1803, Rev. Gideon Blackburn, a Presbyterian, opened three mission schools in Tennessee. Staffed by lay teachers, the curriculum of his schools consisted of reading, writing, and small doses of religion. But Blackburn's schools ultimately failed, in part because of the barriers of language and culture that existed between the fullbloods and the missionaries, and in part because of Blackburn's alleged misappropriation of funds.[42]

In the 1820s, other Presbyterian, Baptist, Methodist, and nondenominational schools opened throughout the Cherokee Nation. Financial difficulties, lack of interest, and general political upheaval forced the closing of many schools, although the Methodists and Baptists successfully converted many Cherokees to Christianity. By the decade during which removal took place, there were at least a thousand Cherokee Methodists, including Chief John Ross; between 1830 and 1838, the number of Baptist Cherokees increased 500 percent. Some mission schools established by Cherokee citizens for their children remained in operation, but enterprising whites who wanted to open private academies usually met with disappointment.[43]

The first educational institution among the Cherokees west of the Mississippi River was the American Board's Dwight Mission, founded by Cephus Washburn and Alfred Finney in 1819 in west-central Arkansas. Dwight Mission was somewhat sympathetic to fullblood students, meeting with such success that it had to turn students away for lack of room. In 1829, the mission was moved twenty-five miles west of Fort Smith, Arkansas, in Indian Territory. There, Dwight operated a substantial farm and raised cattle, which helped to defray the costs of boarding its students and also provided funds for building the dining hall, classrooms, chapel, and dormitories.[44]

Other schools soon followed. The Moravians opened a day school near the Illinois River in 1830, and another at Beatties Prairie, forty miles north of Tahlequah.[45] The Catholics opened one school despite the tribe's general disinterest in Catholicism, and the Reverend Thomas Berholf, a Methodist minister, directed a day school in northern Going Snake district.[46] In 1844, the Baptists were operating three day-schools.[47] Twenty miles northwest of Dwight Mission, Dr. Marcus Palmer opened a branch of the mission, the Fairfield day school, a relatively well-equipped institution that primarily served mixed-blood children. Another branch, called Forks of the Illinois, was opened northwest of Dwight.[48] Other mission schools in the western Cherokee Nation were established at Park Hill, Breadtown, New Springplace, Elm Springs, and Tahlequah.[49]

Many Cherokees proved as persistent in their desire for education as the missionaries were in their pursuit of converts. Most Cherokees were able to read and write in their own language, but in 1830 only a moderate number—usually mixed-bloods—could understand English. The prominent mixed-bloods championed a progressive educational system as a key to the enhancement of their political power in the tribe.[50]

In 1838, the Cherokee Nation Council laid the groundwork for the Nation's public school system. These schools flourished until Oklahoma achieved statehood, but it was the Nation's female and male seminaries that proved to be the ultimate expressions of the progressive Cherokees' desire for enlightenment and equality with whites.

2

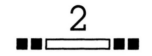

Establishing the
Seminary

After the Cherokees' removal to Indian Territory, the members of the
National Council took measures to keep Cherokee students out of the
mission boarding schools and to operate its own, secular educational
institutions. When missionaries began planning their schools and missions, the council enacted a law requiring that all proponents of education obtain permission from the council before any institution could
be established. A tribal ordinance, however, did allow non-Cherokee
teachers to live among the Nation's citizens for the purpose of educating
Cherokee children.[1]

Despite the Cherokees' emphasis on secular schools, they did not
intend to abandon Christianity. Two articles of the Cherokee Constitution of 1827 expressed their commitment to religion and to education.
One stated that "no person who denies the being of God or future
state of reward and punishment shall hold office in the civil department
in this Nation" and the other held that "religion, morality and knowledge, being necessary to good government, the preservation of liberty
and happiness of mankind, schools and the means of education shall
forever be encouraged in this Nation." Reflecting the values of their
white neighbors, the Cherokees also passed an act forbidding "any
person or persons whatever, to teach any free negro or negros not of
Cherokee blood, or any slave belonging to any citizen or citizens of
the Nation, to read or write."[2]

Another act, passed on 26 September 1838, provided for a committee of three persons appointed by the principal chief to prepare the educational system of the Cherokee Nation and "such laws for its establishment and promotion as may be necessary." In 1841, the council provided for eleven public, or common, schools to be dispersed throughout the eight districts according to need. Orphaned children were to be placed in the homes of families near the schools. The council also created the position of Superintendent of Education, whose responsibilities included the appointment of a three-member board of directors that hired the teachers, the supervision of the establishment of "good comfortable school houses," the preparation of annual reports on the schools' condition, and the accounting for all funds received by the superintendent from the Nation's treasurer for educational use.[3]

The first superintendent was Rev. Stephen Foreman, the son of Anthony Foreman, a Scot, and his wife, Elizabeth, a fullblood Cherokee. Prior to moving west with the tribe, the younger Foreman had studied at the College of Richmond in Virginia and at Princeton Theological Seminary, and he later served as assistant editor of the *Cherokee Phoenix*. In 1839, he arrived in Indian Territory and worked as a translator for Samuel Worcester after the death of Elias Boudinot. He also served as clerk of the Cherokee Senate and as superintendent of elections for the Tahlequah District.[4]

In 1843, there were five hundred students enrolled in the eleven schools and they were taught by two Cherokees and nine whites. That same year, the National Council authorized the building of seven more common schools. Noncitizens living in the Cherokee Nation were not allowed to attend Cherokee schools, but they could enroll in the mission schools. They also had their own "subscription schools," such as the private institutions of Dwight Hitchcock and Frederick W. Linde near Tahlequah.[5]

The success of many mixed-blood merchants convinced Cherokees who had been reluctant to send their children to school that education could help them rise from "ignorance to intelligence" and from "obscurity to distinction." Others believed that the white man's education would help their children become "qualified for any business in life, whether civil or political."[6]

The Cherokees' desire to have their children educated spread throughout much of the Nation, and their public school system proved popular, especially among mixed-bloods. In 1852, eleven hundred Cherokees were enrolled in twenty-one schools. Two years later, more than half of the teachers in the common schools were of Cherokee descent. The log schoolhouses in which instruction took place were equipped with fireplaces, stoves, benches, blackboards, and glass windows, and were said to be clean and comfortable. The course of study was basic; all students learned reading and spelling, while those with some educational background (usually the mixed-bloods) were instructed in geography and arithmetic. The Commissioner of Indian Affairs could report that "thousands of Cherokees could speak English" and "hundreds" were able to draw up contracts and deeds. Visiting missionaries who expected to need interpreters found that most Cherokees in the Tahlequah vicinity spoke English. Many of the traditional Cherokees, especially the fullbloods, however, still kept to themselves and refused to take advantage of the educational opportunities.[7]

Mixed-blood leaders had expressed their desire for "schools of higher learning" as early as the 1820s. Both Chief John Ross and Second Principal Chief Charles R. Hicks had been outspoken advocates of education. In 1823, Chief Ross pointed out the need for a Cherokee "national free school" for those who possessed a basic knowledge of English, arithmetic, geography, and history. Those members of the Treaty Party who negotiated the New Echota treaty of 1835 made certain to include a provision for funds to support a "national academy."[8]

After removal, the Cherokees were free from their dependence on the missionaries for primary schools. But by the 1840s the council wanted its own institutions of higher learning, apparently for several reasons. It is possible that the council feared that the "Indian" appearance of some of its youths would cause them not to be accepted in the white schools. After all, despite his education, name change, and "white" manner, Elias Boudinot had been hung in effigy in Connecticut for marrying a white woman. Even those progressive Cherokee children who looked Caucasian still felt more comfortable within the bounds of the Cherokee Nation and preferred to attend a good school close to their families.

It is also likely that the race-conscious progressive Cherokees, who were busily planning their high schools, establishing businesses, and publishing a newspaper, wanted to prove themselves distinct from other tribes. Despite the richness of the various tribes' cultures, whites of that day (and later, of course) believed themselves superior to all Indians and commonly referred to them as "uncivilized," "rude," "wild," and "heathenistic." The progressive Cherokees certainly did not believe themselves "primitive" and were determined to prove it by making their tribe a model of white society. These progressives wanted an educational system in order to "uplift" the entire tribe, including poor fullbloods and some mixed-bloods, whom they considered to be "unenlightened" and "uninformed."

There was another reason behind the council's desire to create its own high schools. The affluent councilmen and their wives subscribed to the value system of the upper class in the antebellum South, including the belief that women should be educated in order to lead the "social salvation" of their community (in this case, the Cherokee tribe) and to lend stability and solidarity to the population by instructing the young. In this regard, education would serve to reform or mold Cherokee society into a copy of white society, a goal that many Cherokees shared. Educated females would become pious homemakers and companions to their prominent husbands, whose self-esteem was undoubtedly elevated by placing women in a position that seemed exalted yet was subservient. Any school for females in the tribe would be controlled by men who espoused this ideology.[9]

The Fayetteville Female Academy in Arkansas especially attracted the attention of the wealthier mixed-bloods. Sophia Sawyer, from Fitchburg, Massachusetts, established the school in 1839. Sawyer and her faculty taught geography and ancient history, logic, natural philosophy, literature, astronomy, and social skills with the goal of raising the "female character in the Nation." She personally selected the students and required all girls over the age of twelve to present testimonials to their "good moral character." Not surprisingly, among her charges were the daughters of the affluent mixed-blood families — the Rosses, Ridges, Starrs, Drews, and Adairs. Sawyer was a dynamic woman of "spasmodic temperament" with a reputation for being strict and demanding, and her crusading zeal made her unpopular among the fullbloods.[10]

Another option for young Cherokee women was a school known as the Cherokee Female Seminary (a school that was distinct from the one that is the subject of this book), which was "connected with the Baptist mission" and established in Tahlequah in 1843 for the "improvement, subsequent usefulness, and ultimate happiness of the young ladies of the Cherokee Nation." Under the supervision of Sarah Hale Hibbard, for $1.25 a week the pupils received instruction in a "regular curriculum," plus civil and ecclesiastical history, Latin, natural science, and social and intellectual philosophy. Teacher training was also part of the course of study. In 1844, Hibbard had charge of fifty "very high-class students," all of whom were English-speaking mixed-bloods. The school did not last long, however, and closed in 1846 for lack of funds.[11]

In October 1846, Chief Ross submitted a proposal to the twenty members of the council (comprised at that time mainly of mixed-bloods) for the construction of two high schools. The council approved the request on 26 November, noting that "we are now in the possession of the means sufficient to carry out, to a further degree of maturity, the national system of education already commenced." It directed that "two seminaries or high schools be established, one for males, the other for females: in which all those branches of learning be taught, which may be required to carry the mental culture of the youth of our country to the highest practicable point." Money for building the seminaries would be provided by the Cherokee Nation's general fund and by the school fund established in the 1835 Treaty of New Echota.[12]

Other tribes in Indian Territory also established boarding schools around this time, such as Spencer Academy (Choctaw); Wapanucka Female Manual Labour School, also known as Wapanucka Institute or Academy, and Bloomfield Academy (Chickasaw); Tullahassee Manual Labor School (Creek); the Quapaw Boarding School; the Seneca, Wyandot, and Shawnee Boarding School; and the Osage Manual Labor School. The Cherokee boarding schools differed from the other tribes' schools in that the Cherokees did not include manual training, nor did they contract with missionaries to run the schools, although missionaries did indeed eventually teach at both the female and male seminaries.[13]

On 12 November 1847, the council passed an act creating the Board of Directors of High Schools in the Cherokee Nation, a five-member board appointed by the principal chief (who served as ex-officio president of the board) with the council's consent. The five men had the authority to hire and dismiss teachers, expel students, oversee the examinations conducted during each school session, and purchase school supplies and building maintenance materials. The board hired the seminary's steward (the title was later changed to Seminary Superintendent) and selected a clerk from its own ranks to keep all records and prepare an annual report.[14]

The first board members and their successors were all wealthy and politically active mixed-bloods. James M. Payne was Speaker of the council in 1843 and superintendent of education in 1845.[15] One of the Old Settlers, William Shorey Coodey, who had drafted the constitution of 1839, was president of the National Committee and in 1845 senator from the Canadian District.[16] David Carter was clerk of the National Council, and served as superintendent of education in 1843.[17] William Potter Ross, a graduate of Princeton University who was the first editor of the *Cherokee Advocate*, was chief from 1866 to 1867 and from 1872 to 1874.[18] David Vann served intermittently as treasurer of the Cherokee Nation between 1839 and 1851.[19] Henry Dobson Reese was the attorney of the Tahlequah District in 1845 and 1846, judge in 1875, and superintendent of education from 1853 to 1859.[20] John Thorn was superintendent of elections in the Canadian District in 1840.[21] Riley Keys was chief justice of the Cherokee Supreme Court in 1872.[22]

Members of the National Council and the seminary board had a personal interest in the seminaries. At least ninety-six female relatives of the 1846 council eventually enrolled in the seminary, and only one of the original board members did not have a relative who ultimately attended the school. More than twenty of Chief Ross's relatives — daughters, nieces, and nephews — were to graduate from either the male or female seminary.[23]

The council ordered that both seminaries be located within fifteen miles of Tahlequah at sites where there was "good water" and "sufficient timber." It also stipulated that no more than three hundred dollars could be paid for site improvements. In the spring of 1847, Chief Ross and the executive council selected the sites for the schools and contracted for the construction of both buildings. They decided to build the Female Seminary at Park Hill, two miles south of Tahlequah, and the male institution two miles to the southwest.[24]

After moving to Indian Territory from Arkansas in 1828, many of the Old Settlers had been attracted to the region's scattered forests, numerous springs, and green prairies. Although the climate was hot and humid in summer, game was plentiful, and many Cherokees believed in the healing powers of the springs. In 1829, Rev. Samuel Newton of the American Board had named the settlement (and the adjoining mission station) Park Hill. Like Tahlequah, Park Hill was home to a variety of economic classes. Visitors remarked on the beauty of the area, the "stately dwellings," and the large farms, but they could not overlook the "miserable homes of the indigent."[25]

The most conspicuous residents of Park Hill were members of the

Ross family. Chief John Ross owned a large plantation-style home, dubbed Rose Cottage because of the rosebush-lined, half-mile-long private road that led to his mansion, stables, dairy, blacksmith shop, guest house, and slave quarters. Lewis Ross, the chief's brother, lived nearby at an even more elaborate estate, Prairie Lea. William Potter Ross and his brother Daniel Hicks Ross established a sawmill near their large, two-story brick houses along Park Hill Creek, and the chief purchased an Old Settler home, the roomy Hinton House, for his daughter Jane.[26]

Perhaps the most impressive Park Hill estate was that of George Michael Murrell, a former Louisiana planter turned merchant. He had married Minerva Ross, daughter of Lewis Ross, and after her death married her sister, Amanda Melvina Ross. Known as the Murrell Home or Hunter's Home, Murrell's residence was the most sumptuous in Indian Territory, boasting chandeliers, large mirrors, brass fireplace fixtures, curtains, and furniture imported from Europe. Later, guests and students of both seminaries would stroll through the elaborate gardens beneath shade trees while listening to the songs of Murrell's one hundred pet canaries caged in the sitting room.[27]

Murrell operated a successful store in Park Hill, as did others, such as R. J. Meigs. Their advertisements in the *Advocate* offered such popular dry goods as silk hose and hats, black silk cravats, Leghorn and straw bonnets, red flannel, and Kentucky jeans. Another shopkeeper, Lorenzo Delano, a native of Canada, stocked his store with goods he brought in on his private steamboat, the *Santa Fe*. Even Chief Ross supplemented his income during the California gold rush by stocking a store with mining equipment, and Stand Watie operated a store about a mile outside of town.[28]

Among the Park Hill residents was Dr. Samuel Austin Worcester. Numerous other missionaries had moved to Indian Territory with the tribe, but Worcester was to leave his mark on the Cherokee Nation. Called the "Messenger" by the Cherokees during his tenure at Brainerd Mission, Worcester lived and worked amidst the tribe for over three decades, until his death in 1859. In 1832, along with two other missionaries, Dr. Elizur Butler and John Foster Wheeler, Worcester refused to comply with a Georgia law that required all missionaries living among the Cherokees to pledge their allegiance to the state of Georgia. Charges were brought against the men, and despite the favorable ruling in

Worcester v. Georgia, the three were sentenced to a Georgia prison for four years.[29]

While at Brainerd, Worcester had translated the New Testament and many hymns into the Cherokee language and had organized a Cherokee book society. Together with Elias Boudinot, he published the *Cherokee Phoenix.* Utilizing a special Cherokee-alphabet printing press, Worcester produced thousands of pages of almanacs, books, and pamphlets, all in the Cherokee language.[30] He brought his family to Park Hill in 1836 and immediately began expanding Park Hill Mission. The mission station soon consisted of a farm, schoolhouse, "book establishment," printshop, and Worcester's own two-story home.[31]

Worcester's assistants were experienced and dedicated. Elias Boudinot, despite his unpopularity in some quarters and over the objections of the Cherokee National Council, worked as Worcester's translator. John Foster Wheeler of Kentucky worked alongside his brother-in-law, John Walker Candy, and Edwin Archer, formerly of New York City, translating English works into Creek, Choctaw, Wea, and Cherokee.[32] After Worcester's eldest daughter, Ann Eliza, graduated from the St. Johnsbury Academy in Vermont, she returned to teach at the Park Hill school.[33]

Missionaries like Worcester still attempted to convert the Cherokees, but in 1846 only three thousand of the twenty thousand tribespeople were professed Christians. Worcester's Congregational Church at Park Hill boasted two hundred members—almost all the village residents.[34] But the influence of the missionaries was not limited to education and conversion. Spurred by the tremendous influx of illegal liquor into the Cherokee Nation, missionaries and four hundred abstemious tribe members formed the Cherokee Temperance Society. In 1844, the society's secretary, Stephen Foreman, reported that 2,000 of the 2,473 members were Cherokees. The remainder were soldiers from Fort Gibson and other whites living as noncitizens in the Nation. The Cherokee Cold Water Army wrote temperance songs, painted banners warning against the evils of imbibing, and advertised meetings throughout the Cherokee Nation. Students at the Male Seminary later became active members at the urging of their teachers, and the female seminarians would sing the praises of temperance on a daily basis.[35]

It was during this period of vigorous development of the Cherokee Nation, on 21 June 1847, that Chief Ross laid the cornerstone of the first Female Seminary. Among the twenty-seven items placed inside the cornerstone were copies of the constitution of the Cherokee Nation, Sequoyah's alphabet, and the Holy Scriptures printed in Cherokee; *The Cherokee Hymnbook;* an essay on "The Evils of Intoxicating Liquors with the Remedy"; 1847 editions of the *Cherokee Advocate* and the *Cherokee Almanac;* and examples of "Indian education": *The Cherokee Primer, The Choctaw Spelling Book,* and *The Choctaw Arithmetic Book.*[36]

To make certain that the seminary building would be similar to other schools in the East, the Cherokee Nation had hired Sheppard H. Blackmer, a contractor from Boston, to oversee the building of the seminary, and the firm of Brown and McCoy to supply the carpentry and joiner's work. Bricks for the seminaries were fired in a kiln on the outskirts of Park Hill. Although bad weather and the loss of workers to the California gold rush slowed construction, both seminaries neared completion in 1850. Each building cost more than $60,000.[37]

The main building at each school was two stories high and measured eighty by forty feet, with two forty-foot wings separated by an eighteen-foot passage. The west, south, and east faces of the structures were adorned with classical columns. In each structure, a hall extended from the west entrance all the way to the east side, while a large open court occupied the center. Upon completion, the seminaries were the largest and most attractive buildings in Indian Territory, each sitting on high ground and surrounded by a grove of trees. Augustus W. Loomis, in *Scenes in the Indian Country,* described the Female Seminary as a "large, handsome, well-furnished brick building. . . . One almost wonders what such a noble edifice is doing way out here."[38]

When the two buildings were almost completed, the board made plans to engage teachers and to devise a curriculum. But the Cherokees encountered problems in the search for qualified instructors. Until the first graduates of the seminaries were available to teach in the public school system, the district boards had to secure instructors from outside the Nation, and many whites were reluctant to teach in unfamiliar territory populated by Indians.

Because of the Cherokees' "high and exalted estimate of female character" (which included qualities such as piety), women taught only at the mission schools, and until the 1850s the secular public schools were taught by men, most of whom were alumni of colleges in the Northeast. The *Cherokee Advocate* even pointed out that "there are no inducements for female teachers to come to this country in quest of schools."[39] But with male instructors in short supply and the National

Council aware that schools for white girls outside the Nation were run by women, it enacted a law on 12 November 1847, requiring that the teachers of the Female Seminary be female and the teachers at the Male Seminary be male. The "Principal Teacher" of the Female Seminary should be able to teach "all the branches of literature and science commonly taught in the academies of the United States," and she was authorized to add assistant teachers when needed. A man, however, always filled the administrative position of seminary steward.[40]

The Cherokees turned to Mount Holyoke Female Seminary in South Hadley, Massachusetts, as a source of instructors for the Female Seminary.[41] Founded by Mary Lyon in February 1836, the school quickly became one of the leading schools for women in the East, and it was also the alma mater of the daughters of many Cherokee missionaries.[42] Elizur Butler, Stephen Foreman, and Samuel Worcester had sent their daughters to Mount Holyoke, and some teachers employed at the Fayetteville Female Seminary also had graduated from the Massachusetts institution.[43] Worcester's wife, Ann Orr Worcester, was a former high-school classmate of Mary Lyon at the Byfield School for girls. Mary Avery had attended Mount Holyoke from 1837 to 1839 before coming to teach at the Park Hill mission. Because of the New England connection, it was logical that the Cherokees would seek teachers and advice from the principal of the school they most wanted to emulate.[44]

The Cherokees were impressed by Mount Holyoke's stringent course of study and its emphasis on religion and teacher training, which prepared its students for jobs throughout the world.[45] Between 1839 and 1856, twenty-four Mount Holyoke alumnae taught among North American tribes.[46] More than four hundred graduates in the school's first century became missionaries to China, India, Turkey, and several Latin American countries.[47] Other female schools in the United States, such as the female seminary in Marion, Alabama, and the Monticello Female Academy at Godfrey, Illinois, also used Mount Holyoke as a model for curriculum development.[48]

In 1850, two prominent members of the Cherokee tribe, David Vann and William Potter Ross, visited Boston, Andover, and New Haven in search of teachers for the Cherokee Male Seminary. Since the abolitionist influence was strong in parts of the Northeast, the slave-owning Cherokees at first encountered difficulty in securing male instructors. But finally, Thomas Budd Van Horne, a graduate of Newton Theological

Seminary, and Oswald Langdon Woodford, an alumnus of Yale College and Williston Seminary, accepted the Cherokees' invitation.[49]

Vann and Ross traveled next to Mount Holyoke to observe its curriculum in operation and to hire some of the school's graduates as teachers for the Female Seminary. After talking to prospective teachers, the two men wrote to Mary Chapin, the principal of Mount Holyoke, requesting to hire two of her students, Ellen Rebecca Whitmore and Sarah Worcester, the latter the daughter of Rev. Samuel Worcester.[50]

Vann and Ross reminded Chapin that a new teacher must have "at least a good English education," be a "believer in the Christian religion," agree to live at the seminary, and accept a salary of six hundred dollars per annum, two hundred dollars more than the salary of the Cherokee Superintendent of Education. Although the new teachers possessed strong missionary zeal, they would be subject to the control of the Cherokee national government, not a religious denomination.[51]

Attracted by the opportunity to bring education to the Cherokees (and also by generous salaries that were comparable to those of male teachers), the young women accepted immediately. Accordingly, during the fall of 1850, Sarah Worcester, Ellen Whitmore, Oswald Woodford, and Thomas Van Horne prepared for the long journey to the Cherokee seminaries at Park Hill in Indian Territory.

3

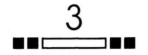

The Early Years:
1851 – 76

Teachers and prospective students began arriving in Park Hill in November 1850. Both the male and female seminaries were to have begun instruction the previous month, but the openings were postponed because of delays in construction and in the delivery of furniture. Many faculty members and students returned home, but others waited in Tahlequah until the schools finally opened seven months later.[1]

The Female Seminary was built to accommodate one hundred students, but to assure the school's successful operation, the National Council allowed only twenty-five pupils to enroll the first year. Each year thereafter, twenty-five more applicants would be admitted, until the enrollment reached one hundred. In theory, a quarter of the students would graduate by the end of the fourth year, and so the number of new pupils and graduates would remain constant thereafter. Both schools were to provide pupils with lodging, food, textbooks, lighting fuel, and laundry services, but students had to furnish their own linens, clothes, toiletries, and "comforts." In addition to money allotted for basic expenses, the National Council allocated eight hundred dollars to each seminary for books, paper, and miscellaneous "school apparatus."[2]

Applicants to the seminaries were required to be members of the Cherokee tribe (possessing any degree of Cherokee blood), to be proficient in the skills taught in the common schools, and to be prepared to remain for the entire four years of study unless they had attended other high schools and wanted to enter as students in the upper classes.

To assess prospective students' abilities, school officials administered English-language admissions tests, requiring applicants to demonstrate proficiency in reading, spelling, arithmetic, grammar, and geography. The first of these tests took place on 1 May 1851 and the "Flowers of the Cherokees" who passed the examinations were notified the next day.[3]

The National Council claimed that family wealth was not a factor in admittance because there was no tuition. But of the seventy-five enrollees in the 1850s, at least fifty were daughters of district sheriffs, councilors, senators, or judges, or of National clerks and treasurers. In addition, many of the girls were members of affluent mixed-blood families such as the Bushyheads, Rosses, Adairs, Candys, McNairs, and Mayeses. The majority of students who passed the tests were mixed-bloods with English-speaking, educated parents who could afford private tutors. These students contrasted sharply with many pupils in the public schools—predominantly fullbloods—who spoke no English and whose teachers could not speak Cherokee. Many of those children had no chance to learn even the rudiments of reading, writing, and arithmetic. The two fullbloods who were admitted to the seminary the first year had received thorough instruction at the mission schools, and they eventually graduated from the seminary.[4]

On 6 May 1851, the Male Seminary finally opened, and the next morning the female school began its classes with much fanfare. The military band from Fort Gibson played to the sizable crowd—many citizens of the Cherokee Nation had eagerly awaited the opening of their seminaries—and Chief John Ross spoke of the importance of education, recalling the days when instruction was not readily available to the Cherokee people. He correctly predicted that the day would be remembered by Cherokee youths who "should be so fortunate as to enter the temples of education."[5]

Following the advice of Mary Chapin, the principal of Mount Holyoke who, at the request of Chief John Ross, had designed the Female Seminary's curriculum after her own school's four-year course of study, the National Council divided the school year into two sessions of twenty weeks each, with classes five days a week, six hours a day. However, the ambitious plan was not immediately realized. Because of the oppressive humidity in August during the first year, the school closed after only thirteen weeks, seven weeks ahead of schedule.[6]

The female students were divided into four classes, and the curriculum was essentially the same as at the Male Seminary. First-year students studied geometry, Greek history, intellectual theology, and a course based on Paley's *Natural Theology*—the same work Mary Lyon used to impress the importance of Christianity upon her Mount Holyoke pupils. The second-year class studied algebra, physiology, Latin, and Watts's *Improvement of the Mind*. Third- and fourth-year students studied geography, Latin, and advanced arithmetic. The board also required seminary teachers to instruct students in vocal music. This course of study—which never included any courses on Cherokee culture—remained unchanged through the school's first five years. Unlike some schools, the seminary did not include any "home management" courses, following instead the Mount Holyoke philosophy that "home is the proper place for the daughters of our country to be taught [domestic science] and the mother is the appropriate teacher." Pupils did not cook any meals, nor did they wash their own clothes or linens. It is not known if Cherokee citizens were paid to allow their black slaves to work at the school.[7]

One of the newly recruited teachers, Ellen Rebecca Whitmore of Marlborough, Massachusetts, became the first principal of the Female Seminary, serving from 1851 to late 1852, even though she was still a year away from graduation at Mount Holyoke. Sarah Worcester, the tall, handsome daughter of Samuel and Ann Orr Worcester, acted as her assistant. Worcester had undoubtedly helped to convince Whitmore and the other new teachers, Oswald Woodford and Thomas Van Horne, of the safety and opportunities offered by the Park Hill area and had probably assured them of the level of acculturation among the Cherokees living there. Worcester had grown up with the Boudinot children before and after removal, and was well aware of the political rivalries within the Cherokee Nation. Eager to begin teaching the Cherokees, Worcester was dedicated to instructing her students in the "social graces" and "meticulous refinements of good breeding" as well as in academic disciplines. The women arrived in Park Hill on 13 November 1851, but since the construction of the seminary was unfinished, Whitmore spent the winter with the Worcester family. During those months she oversaw the completion of the building and prepared for the institution's opening in the spring.[8]

Another authority figure present at the seminary was the steward, a position that would always be filled by a male, possibly to offset the female teachers. The first steward, Dr. Elizur Butler, was a missionary of the American Board. He had worked from 1821 to 1824 at Brainerd Mission, had been a medical missionary in the Eastern Cherokee Nation, and had served as a physician with one of the removal parties that went west during 1838 and 1839. After reaching Indian Territory, Butler worked at Fairfield Mission, where Chief Ross appointed him the Cherokee National Physician. Butler accepted the position of Female Seminary steward in 1851, and he and his wife, Lucy, moved into the school the following May. They had the considerable responsibility of providing meals, maintaining seminary property, and overseeing the washing, ironing, and mending of clothing and bedding. Dr. Butler preached at the seminary each Sunday and also cared for sick students, but when any pupils became seriously ill, Dr. E. Poe Harris of Tahlequah assisted in treating them. Although the stewards' wives were always present and were known as "co-stewards," the women were not paid.[9]

Although Whitmore and Worcester had arrived at Park Hill determined upon careers as teachers among the Cherokees and had immersed themselves in their work, their terms at the seminary were brief. After only one year as principal, Whitmore resigned, and on 17 June 1852 she married Warren Goodale, a missionary, at John Ross's Rose Cottage. Shortly afterward the newlyweds moved to Hawaii to continue their missionary work. Worcester also married a missionary, Dr. Daniel Dwight Hitchcock, a graduate of Amherst and of Bowdoin Medical College. They wed on 15 February 1853 in the Female Seminary parlor. After Sarah's death at Park Hill just four years later, Hitchcock married her sister, Hannah.[10]

Although Whitmore's tenure at the seminary was short-lived, she evidently enjoyed her work. Before resigning on 16 March 1852, she wrote to Mary Chapin at Mount Holyoke, remarking on the "superior order" of the "society of the neighborhood" at Park Hill. She described the country as "delightful," the salary as "large . . . $800.00 a year." Although she alluded to being homesick, her said her seminary work was "the pleasantest field in which I have ever been called to labor. . . . I have found warm friends here whose unremitting kindness I can never repay." Whitmore seems to have socialized only with members of the Ross and Worcester families and the teachers at the Male Seminary, not with the fullbloods who lived in the vicinity of Park Hill.[11]

Whitmore urged Chapin to send a replacement who was a "dedicated, active Christian, one lovely and pleasing in her manners." She advised that the new principal should expect to stay at least three or four years, for if her health was good and she was as "happy as I have been," she would "not want to leave." Yet Whitmore warned that the candidate should not be too young since the position was not "free from trials." Indeed, as the first principal of a new institution, Whitmore had found herself under extreme pressure to make the seminary successful. Caring for twenty-five homesick adolescent girls was a demanding job. During the winter and spring months, cases of pneumonia and chills were common, and in the summer the heat was almost unbearable. Many girls who presented discipline problems were evidently agitated by the rigorous regimen. One student, Na-Li, complained, "I can't sit here all day and study; I want some running about to do." Other students behaved erratically, apparently because of the regular doses of morphine they took to counteract boredom.[12]

After Whitmore's resignation, Harriet Johnson of Sturbridge, Massachusetts, became principal. She was an experienced educator, having taught from 1848 to 1852 at Roxbury, Boston, and Mount Holyoke. But Johnson stayed in the Cherokee Nation only one year. She married the Reverend Robert McGill Loughridge in October 1853 and the couple moved to a mission in the Creek Nation.[13]

The principal's job was filled in late 1853 by Pauline Avery, an 1850 graduate of Mount Holyoke. Pauline's older sister, Mary, had taught in Tuscaloosa, Alabama, and in the Cherokee public schools in the 1840s. Their father, Deacon Joseph Avery, was a Mount Holyoke trustee from 1836 to 1855. Assisting Pauline Avery were Charlotte "Lotta" E. Raymond, a native of Philadelphia, and Eliza Jane Ross, the niece of Chief John Ross and the sister of the future chief, William Potter Ross. Eliza Ross had attended school at Cane Hill in Arkansas and had been enrolled in the Bethlehem Female Seminary in Pennsylvania for four years. Avery remained at the Female Seminary until 1856, when she wed Rev. Oswald Langdon Woodford, one of the original teachers at the Male Seminary, who taught there from 1851 to 1855. Pauline Avery Woodford died in 1858 in Grasshopper Falls, Kansas, after the birth of a daughter.[14]

Seminary principals were paid an annual salary of eight hundred dollars; the first assistants, six hundred dollars; and the second assistants, five hundred dollars. In addition to salaries, all faculty members were provided with room and board. Reflecting the importance placed on female education in the Cherokee Nation, Chief John Ross reported in 1855 that the instructors at the Male Seminary had complained about being paid the same as the women at the Female Seminary, but Ross dryly noted that the women had "never interposed any objection."[15]

Teachers and administrators conducted yearly public examinations at both schools, and all classes were periodically open to the public for observation. At such times, a representative from each class recited the events that had occurred during the year. Chief Ross reported with "unmingled pleasure" that the first evaluation was a success and that the "deportment" of the students was "in a high degree gratifying and satisfactory." At the 1852 evaluation, George Butler, an Indian agent, found that the seminary students showed vast improvement in "letters and morals" since the school's opening. Their conduct "fully met, or even exceeded the anticipations of the public," he said, and they had made "commendable progress" in all courses of study. This had been accomplished with relatively "little restraint" on those at the female school, but twenty students at the male school had been expelled for misbehaving. The Reverend William Schenk Robertson from Tullahassee Mission (the largest of the Creek Nation schools, which was located on the Arkansas River a few miles northwest of Muskogee) also attended the 1852 evaluation and wrote to his parents that "quite a number of teachers are here," and the forty-six girls present "appeared well, very well—all dressed in white with pink belts." Impressed by their recitations, he commented that they were "a credit to their teachers and their Nation may well be proud of them."[16]

No problems arose during the next two years, except for a ten-month delay in obtaining textbooks because low water levels in the Arkansas River prohibited boats from delivering supplies. The schools continued to prosper, and Principal Avery reported a "marked improvement, both in deportment and application to study." The following list (which shows some overlap in class periods) was prepared for the 1855 "Examination Day" and illustrates the regimentation of the seminary's class schedule at that time:[17]

Subject	Time	Supervising Teacher
Devotions	7:1/4 to 7:1/2	
Geography	7:1/2 to 7:50	Raymond
Latin	7:50 to 8:1/4	Avery
Arithmetic	8:1/4 to 9:00	Ross

Rhetoric	9:00 to 9:1/2	Raymond
Geometry and Star of Twilight		
Abou Ben Adem [sic]	9:1/2 to 10:1/4	Avery
Physiology	10:00 to 11:1/4	Ross
Recess	11:1/2	
Algebra	11:00 to 12:20	Raymond
Intellectual Philosophy	12:20 to 1:00	Ross
Dinner	1:00 to 1:1/2	
Natural Theology and "Merry goes the Time"	1:1/2 to 2:1/4	Raymond
Evidences of Christianity	2:1/4 to 3:00	Avery
Music—"We Plough the Fertile Meadow"	3:00 to 3:15	Avery
Paper and Marks; Singing—"I'm Going Home"	3:15 to 3:3/4	

Not long after its opening, the Female Seminary became the center for social events. In 1854, when the Methodist congregation of the Sehon Chapel lacked sufficient funds to complete its building near Park Hill, the seminary students gave concerts and donated the proceeds to the church building fund. Seminary students often visited Tahlequah to attend lectures, to dine, and to shop, and on New Year's Eve, boys from the Male Seminary attended celebrations at the girls' school. Teachers from both seminaries occasionally mingled for tea at the female school and took carriage rides together.[18]

The girls eagerly anticipated the Friday mail delivery (the parcels were left by the side of the road leading to the seminary to be delivered by anyone en route to the school)[19] and the weekly visit of Chief John Ross for Sunday services at the seminary. Maintaining his lifestyle as a wealthy Southern planter, Ross and his new wife, Mary Stapler, the daughter of a wealthy Philadelphia merchant, arrived at the seminary entrance in their elegant coach driven by their liveried black coachman.[20]

Religion played a primary role in shaping the values of the seminarians. The seminary was not associated with any religious denomination, but in accordance with the emphasis placed on piety among the Cherokees and at Mount Holyoke, the students' "Christian spirituality" was a prime concern of the National Council. In 1852, several tribal members formed the Cherokee Educational Association, an organization for promulgating a "wholesome Christian influence on the public schools." The board required students to attend church services of "their choice" on Sunday, although the selection was limited to Presbyterian, Baptist, Methodist, Moravian, or Congregational churches. Over half the fifty girls enrolled at the seminary in 1853 had attended Dwight Mission, but there is scant documentation as to which churches the seminary students actually did attend.[21] An excerpt from a letter that Sarah Worcester wrote to her brother John (as noted, their father, Samuel, was a missionary for the American Board of Commissioners for Foreign Missions [ABCFM]) in 1856 suggests that not many took part in Methodist or Baptist services: "John, the Methodists are growing worse and worse. The last Sabbath of last term they 'opened the doors of the church' to the scholars of the F. Seminary, saying they wanted to 'have their share.' They preach Methodism, instead of Christ. —I think that I can receive Baptists as cordially as I can Methodists, for the former do not reject any of the great truths of the Bible."[22] All the seminary teachers and administrators in the early years were members of the Presbyterian, Moravian, or Baptist churches.

Teachers and ministers were careful not to preach against slavery, even if they were abolitionists, in order to avoid being expelled from the Cherokee Nation. They were well aware that many of the students were from slave-holding families and that even Chief Ross owned at least forty slaves. Because of the clergymen's cautious approach, it is doubtful that most students had to go through a "crisis conversion" (pro-slavery to anti-slavery) in order to join the churches. The teachers and missionaries from the North were apparently more frustrated about the issue than were the students.[23]

In October 1854, George Butler indicated that the religious fervor among the Cherokees continued unabated. He wrote to his superiors that "the influence of the Bible [permeates] our common schools, our high schools, our temperance societies, and even our form of government." Samuel Worcester reported that several of the pupils at the seminaries had joined the Park Hill church, and others were expected to join the nearby Sehon Chapel upon its completion in 1856.[24]

Besides their interest in religion, the seminary students found an alternative to class work in publishing a school newspaper. The official newspaper at the Female Seminary in the 1850s was the *Cherokee Rose Buds*, which was published by the girls and sold for ten cents per copy. Making its first appearance on 2 August 1854, the paper was edited by seminary students ("co-editresses," they called themselves)[25] and was devoted to "the Good, the Beautiful, and the True." Measuring ten by twelve inches, each page consisted of three columns, with some editorials written in English and in Cherokee so all the tribe's citizens could read them. The paper contained notices of forthcoming events, editorials, engagement and wedding announcements of prominent persons, short stories, and poetry. In 1855, the name of the newspaper was changed to *A Wreath of Cherokee Rose Buds*.[26]

There is not enough evidence to reconstruct what the students were taught regarding their gender role and "Indianness," but the editorials and stories in the *Rose Buds* reveal that the race-conscious and ethnocentric students were attempting to define their roles as women and as Cherokees. The females who have been the focus of studies of domesticity and Protestant evangelism have usually been white, but like them, the Cherokee students of the Female Seminary were advocates of the "true woman" ideal. The seminarians were confident about the influence women could have on humanity, and the stories they incorporated in the *Rose Buds* declared their belief that women's responsibilities were important and distinctive. In the commentary "Female Influence," for example, student Qua-Tay asserted that "the destiny of the world depends on woman . . . [as] the appointed agent of morality . . . the inspirer of those feelings and dispositions which form the moral nature of man."[27] A student named Alice further elaborated on the grace of women, in her essay entitled "Beauty": "But man, himself, in physical beauty, excels in the works of God. What more admirable than the noble form, erect in God-like majesty, or the more perfect gracefulness of woman? Like flowers, the more they are cultivated the more beautiful they become."[28]

The seminarians adopted the names "Rose Buds" and described rosebuds (and, indirectly, themselves) as "beautiful," "fresh," "flourishing," and potentially "blossoming" into roses. The reference to roses was used by Indian agents, parents, and chiefs to refer to the girls, and it permeated the students' poetry:

> The Seminary our garden fair
> And we, the flowers planted there . . .
> Like roses bright we hope to grow,
> And o'er our home such beauty throw
> In future years—that all may see
> Loveliest of lands,—the Cherokee.[29]

Editorials and poetry in the Male Seminary's newspaper, *The Sequoyah Memorial* (dedicated to "Truth, Justice, Freedom of Speech and Cherokee Improvement"), praised women, reiterating the theme of roses:

> Though far away 'neath orient skies
> Where clouds come not, nor sweeps the storm,
> The maid may blush in roseate eyes
> Like hues upon the angel's form;
> The flashing light of jeweled fire
> That wealth may shower o'er neck and arm,
> Though soft, voluptuous, gay attire
> May heighten every dazzling charm,—
> Still, wanton Nature's dark-eyed child,
> Is far more dear to me—
> The sweetest flower that gems the wild,
> Is the Rose of Cherokee.[30]

Issues of the *Rose Buds* are filled with religious overtones. Music, for example, "is surely a gift sent from Heaven," stars are "holes in the floor of heaven, to let the glory through," and wind is "like the spirit of God omnipresent."[31] One issue focused on Catherine Brown, a mixed-blood who, almost thirty years earlier, had joined Brainerd Mission and was baptized. She remained devout the rest of her life, despite the missionaries' fears that she would be unable to adapt to the role of domestic female.[32] She made a strong impression on the missionaries, and later, on the female seminarians, who immortalized her in a poem (although they misspelled her name):

> Ah Cherokee! Where is the daughter of Brown?
> She is resting beneath the tall tree;
> But her spirit, so spotless, has silently flown
> Far away to Guh-lul-Inhdi-a-hi!
> Death marked her his prey in the blossom of youth,
> From his grasp no kind angel could save;
> And innocence, meekness, religion and truth
> All slumber in CATHARINE'S GRAVE.[33]

As with women in other parts of the United States, the religious female seminarians were understandably concerned about the flow of liquor into their communities and the effect of alcohol on their families. They never tired of attending the Sons of Temperance meetings or of discussing ways that they could better their society. According to student comments in the *Rose Buds*, the subject of intemperance "cannot be worn out. . . . Dissipation or intemperance is one of the greatest evils in our [Cherokee] Nation. . . . Ought we not all try to lend our aid in putting down this great evil? If we are young, we have an influence so let us one and all give our utmost influence for this noble cause."[34] The female seminarians may have been repressed by males in some parts of their lives, but by banding together and touting temperance, they were able to rebel against male dominance at least a little. Many of the male seminarians (some of whom were brothers of female seminarians) did in fact break their pledge of abstinence and were expelled from the school for being intoxicated. The female students felt that by attending weekly church services, the seminary's daily chapel services, and temperance meetings, in addition to using the *Rose Buds* to express their opinions, they were fulfilling their roles as "true women" and doing something worthwhile for society.

The seminaries were established fifty years before W. E. B. Du Bois espoused his philosophy of the "Talented Tenth," that is, the belief that "the Talented Tenth of the Negro race must be made leaders of thought and missionaries of culture among their people. No others can do this work and Negro colleges must train men for it. The Negro race, like all other races, is going to be saved by its exceptional men."[35] But the seminarians already subscribed to the philosophy that they had a duty to save their nation, and the *Rose Buds* reveals that the students were convinced of their superiority over the "unenlightened" members of their tribe. These attitudes reflected the growing class system within the tribe, based not only on differing cultural ideals between the progressives and the traditionals, but also between those who looked "Indian" (i.e., had darker skin) and the generation of mixed-blood children, who had lighter skin and hair. As time passed and more Cherokees intermarried with whites, the offspring appeared even more Caucasian. In 1899, the preponderance of mixed-blood Cherokees in Tahlequah was noted by Ora Eddleman, a writer for *Twin Territories*, who expressed dismay over the wealthy Cherokees and the "blond Cherokee women."[36]

Rose Buds editorials reflected the seminarians' deep-seated belief in their duty to "uplift" the Cherokee Nation and their inclination to monitor one another's behavior. One writer urged, "Let us begin now in new energy that we may gain that intellectual knowledge which will reward the hopes of our Nation, fitting us for doing much good among our people." Another warned, "Young people—do not forget a remark made at the [recent] temperance meeting . . . that your character is weighed by those around you." Other writings and poems addressed themes such as the "Power of Kindness," "Tardiness," "Patience," "Angry Words," and "Conscience" (who, "with her small voice, gives no rest for the wicked"). Another student writer, perhaps reflecting the girls' affluent backgrounds, espoused the idea that "however beautiful or wealthy we may be, it is but for a moment. . . . Beauty of the soul will, if properly cultivated, flourish long after the Earth with all it contains, has passed away."[37]

There are no records indicating that the Female Seminary subscribed to one of the premier women's magazines of that day, *Godey's Lady's Book*, but the students and teachers certainly adhered to the publication's philosophy that women were subordinate to men. The *Lady's Book* editors did take notice of the Female Seminary in 1857, however, calling the school "quite imposing" in a "Nation of red men."[38]

During the 1850s, there were only two fullblood Cherokee girls enrolled, prompting citizens of the Cherokee Nation to charge that there was elitism and prejudice against the fullbloods at the seminary. But in 1854, a progressive fullblood student named Na-Li staunchly defended her seminary by stating in the *Rose Buds* that "it is sometimes said that our Seminaries were made only for the rich and those who were not full Cherokee; but it is a mistake. . . . Our Chief and directors would like very much that they [full Cherokees] should come and enjoy these same privileges as those that are here present." Na-Li, however, had been adopted by a mission at an early age, had a thorough primary education, and could easily pass the seminary entrance examination.[39]

In further defense of her heritage and her skin color, Na-Li asserted that although her parents were "full Cherokees . . . belonging to the common class," she felt it "no disgrace to be a full Cherokee. My complexion does not prevent me from acquiring knowledge and being useful hereafter. . . . [I will] endeavor to be useful, although I sometimes think that I cannot be."[40] Apparently, the more Cherokee blood a seminary girl had, or the more "Indian" she looked, the more she felt she had to prove herself as a scholar and as a "useful" member of a society that she believed valued only those women who were white in appearance and attitude.

The early seminarians were indeed defensive about the color of their hair and skin. A popular theme of the anecdotes and stories published in the Cherokee seminary's paper was physical appearance, particularly blue eyes. For example, one story told of the consequences that young "Kate M." faced after plagiarizing a poem for literature class. "Fun and abundance," a student named Lusette wrote, "peeped from her blue eyes . . . and the crimson blush stole upon her cheeks." In the same issue, an author named Inez wrote about what her schoolmates might be doing in four years. One was described as a "fair, gay, blue-eyed girl" and another was a "fairy-like creature with auburn hair." Still another story by a student, Icy, was entitled "Two Companions" and paired Hope ("the very personification of loveliness") with a "tiny blue-eyed child" named Faith.[41] In an 1855 issue of *A Wreath of Cherokee Rose Buds*, offended seminarians complained in an editorial about the Townsend (Massachusetts) Female Seminary's paper, the *Lesbian Wreath*, which referred to the Cherokee girls as their "dusky sisters."[42] Evidently, seminary students believed that blue eyes were the epitome of enlightenment and civilization.

Students took pleasure in comparing the old Cherokee ways with the new-and-improved lifestyles of the tribe to show that many tribe members had progressed past savagery and were on their way to equality with whites. In an 1854 issue of *Rose Buds*, a student named Edith championed the virtues of nineteenth-century white society and boasted of the progress the Cherokees had made. "Instead of the rudely constructed wigwams of our forefathers which stood there [the Park Hill area] not more than half-a-century ago," she wrote, "elegant white buildings are seen. Everything around denotes taste, refinement, and progress of civilization among our people."[43]

The prolific Na-Li collaborated with another student in 1855 to illustrate their uneducated ancestors' backwardness, and more important, to emphasize the vast improvements the tribe had made. In "Scene One" of the essay "Two Scenes in Indian Land," Na-Li described a "wild and desolate estate of a Cherokee family" comprised of "whooping, swarthy-looking boys" and plaited-haired women, all of whom, she wrote, "bear a striking resemblance to their rude and uncivilized hut." She concluded that the poor imbeciles "pass the days of their wild, passive, uninteresting life without any intellectual pleasure or enjoyment," except, she added, to attend the green corn dance, a "kind of religious festival."[44]

"Scene Two," by a girl named Fanny, painted a completely different picture of Cherokee life. In her commentary, even the environment around the family's home has magically blossomed from the influence of the missionaries. "Civilization and nature are here united," she declared. "Flowers, music, and even better, the *Holy Word of God* is here to study, showing that religion has shed its pure light over all." The Indian lad, "in place of his bow and arrow, is now taught to use the pen and wield the powers of eloquence. The girl, instead of keeping time with the rattling of the terrapin shells [around her ankles] now keeps time with the chalk as her fingers fly nimbly over the blackboard." Fanny then professed her hope that "we may advance, never faltering until all the clouds of ignorance and superstition and wickedness flee from before the rays of the Suns of Knowledge and Righteousness."[45]

In these tales, then, there was the promise that the "wild Cherokee Indian" could be changed and become a new person. The seminarians were not shy in verbalizing their hope that their unsophisticated tribespeople would make the transition.

The attitude that the Cherokees needed a moral change was also illustrated in the *Sequoyah Memorial*, the newspaper of the Cherokee Male Seminary. One student wrote that "the bow and arrow have been laid aside," and until the Cherokees reached the "summit of civilization and refinement," they could never be "happy and contented"[46] A female student named Estelle exclaimed, "O! that all, especially among the Cherokees, could but learn the vast importance of a good education. This and only this will place us on equality with other enlightened and cultivated Nations . . . if we love our country, if we would have the name of a Cherokee an honor, let us strive earnestly to value education aright."[47]

The seminarians were convinced of their superiority over members of other tribes. After a group of Osage men visited the seminary in 1855, a student named Irene wrote a romantic essay—not unlike those of white authors of the day—about the "lofty, symmetrical forms, and proud, free step of these sons of nature just from their wild hunting ground." She found their war dance amusing ("those tall, dusky forms stomping and stooping around . . . making a wailing sound"). In comparing her tribe and theirs, she pointed out that the Osages listened to the seminarians sing "Over There" so attentively because, she assumed, at least the "wild and untutored Savage had an ear for music as well as the cultivated and refined."[48]

Other articles in the *Rose Buds* include anecdotes about "hostile Indians" out in the "wild and unknown regions" attacking peaceful Cherokees on their way to the California gold fields, and about "bar-

barous Camanches [sic]" living in their "wild wilderness." A student named Cherokee described a Seneca Dog Dance in which the drum "made a very disagreeable noise," and she observed, "what there was in such music to excite the Seneca belles is more than I can imagine." Although she judged the dancers to be graceful, she believed they "ought to have been at something better."[49]

No reference to blacks or slavery is made in any of the *Rose Buds* or *Sequoyah Memorial* issues, or in the memoirs of the early female teachers. The students' exact ideas on the subject are unknown, although most students' families did own slaves and dozens of male seminarians fought (and died) for the Confederacy. In regard to the slavery issue, life at the seminary was much calmer than in the rest of the Cherokee Nation. While the students were occupied with studies, the debates over slavery were much in evidence outside the seminaries. For example, late in 1860, Dr. Torry, supervisor of the ABCFM missions, was denied access to the Fairfield missions because of his alleged anti-slavery remarks, and John B. Jones, a Baptist missionary, was expelled from the Nation for promoting abolitionism. In 1859, the anti-slavery Keetoowah Society was organized within the Nation (its members were also known as "Pin Indians"), with the goal of preserving traditional Cherokee customs and traditions, but none of the seminarians at that time joined the group. After 1860, numerous male seminarians did become members of the Knights of the Golden Circle, an organization dedicated to the preservation of slavery. However, beginning in the early 1870s, many young people whose fathers were Keetoowahs did enroll in both seminaries.[50]

While a faction of the seminarians and faculty believed themselves superior to the unenlightened members of their tribe, to other tribes as a whole, and to blacks, these same girls and teachers felt somewhat inferior to whites, despite the fact that many of seminarians had far more "white blood" than Cherokee (especially those who were enrolled after 1870). The same *Rose Buds* issue that discussed the "elegance and civilization" of the Cherokee Nation also compared it unfavorably with Eastern states, noting that the new bride of Chief John Ross, Mary Stapler, admirably left her more civilized surroundings in Philadelphia in order to "dwell with him in his *wild* prairie home" (the editors' emphasis). Another editorial, commenting on the completed 1855 spring term, said, "We present you again with a collection of Rosebuds, gathered from our seminary garden. If, on examining them, you chance to find a withered or dwarfish bud, please pass it by . . . we hope for lenient judgment, when our efforts are compared with those of our white sisters." The article "Exchanges" acknowledged the newspapers received from girls' schools in New England. But the Cherokee seminarians did not send copies of the *Rose Buds* in return because, as an editor explained, "we feel ourselves entirely too feeble to make any adequate recompense. . . . we are simply Cherokee school girls." These students appear to have been much like the individuals E. Franklin Frazier later described as the "Black Bourgeoisie," those blacks who develop feelings of inferiority because they judge themselves by white standards.[51]

But the students can hardly be blamed for focusing upon skin color and the acculturative achievements of their tribe. Many had a parent who was white or at least of mixed blood. Even fullblood students still attempted to emulate whites who deemed themselves superior to blacks and other races. In addition, the works of Charles Caldwell, Samuel George Morton, and Josiah C. Nott, physicians who believed in the inherent superiority of the Caucasian race, were available in the seminary library for the students to read and fret over.[52] Considering the seminary's philosophy ("white is best"), the students' skin coloring (usually dark), and the "backwardness" of many Cherokees, it is little wonder that the seminarians berated themselves for falling short of the white ideal.

In February 1855, the Female Seminary graduated less than half of its first class. Of the twelve graduates, eleven were mixed-bloods. The other, Catherine Hastings, was a fullblood Cherokee whose English name had been given her by missionaries at the Dwight Mission. In comparison, because of unruly behavior and consequent expulsion, only five pupils graduated from the Male Seminary that year.[53]

The year 1855 marked a high point in the early history of the seminary, for in the next year the school's fortunes waned. Not only was the tribe facing financial difficulties, but arguments flared over the need for two high schools that served a small minority of the tribe. Critics of the schools charged that the seminaries were elitist and were racist toward fullbloods and traditional Cherokees. Because the seminaries' newspapers were sold not only to seminarians but also to the Nation's citizens, the viewpoints of the male and female students— who believed that those Cherokees who possessed lighter hair and skin were superior to the darker girls, and especially, to those who were traditionalists—were widely known and not always appreciated.

Agent Butler reported in September 1856 that the tribe had suffered several financial setbacks and that the Cherokee schools faced fiscal uncertainty. The financial collapse resulted from several causes, including a severe summer drought in 1854 in eastern Indian Territory that devastated many of the tribe's crops. The *Cherokee Advocate* suspended publication because of the shortage of funds. Although the schools were financed by a special fund for education, by 1856 nothing was left in it except the annual interest on the accrued capital, and this was not enough to support both the public schools and the seminaries.[54]

Some of John Ross's political enemies serving on the National Council (who had no relatives attending the seminaries) had pressured the chief to close the seminaries and channel the tribe's financial resources into the common schools their children attended. Even Agent W. A. Duncan was inclined to agree that the two expensive, academic high schools "were only producing intellectuals . . . [but] not everyone can become a professional . . . [or] live here without manual labor." He believed that ultimately the students not given vocational education would need to find employment (and marriage partners) in white society rather than within their own Cherokee Nation. At the end of the 1856 academic year, Chief Ross relented and the two high schools were closed.[55]

The National Council made several attempts to raise sufficient funds to reopen the schools. The 1835 Treaty of New Echota had given the Cherokees hegemony over 800,000 acres in the northeastern section of Indian Territory (now southeastern Kansas). By an act of the National Council on 1 December 1846, this area was named the "eight hundred thousand acre tract" and made a part of the Delaware District. Also called the "Neutral Lands," the land was used only for cattle grazing. White settlers had continually complained that the Cherokee Nation monopolized a vast, fertile area but neither paid taxes nor made productive use of it. The Cherokees had wanted to sell land to individual settlers, but they first had to attain United States citizenship. Until they were recognized as citizens, they could sell land only to the United States government, and since the Cherokees' price for the Neutral Lands included the original $500,000, in addition to the interest it had accrued over the years, federal officials were not interested.[56]

Most of the Cherokees favored selling the land, but they disagreed on what should be done with the money. Some opposed using any of it to pay the Nation's debts. Others wanted to pay the debt first, then invest a portion of the remainder to support education. The arguments continued, but the federal government still refused to buy the land, so the schools remained closed.[57] Upset over the closing, Chief Ross charged that if the federal government had purchased the Neutral Lands, the Cherokees could have maintained the schools despite their other problems. Convinced that all the Cherokees' "earthly interests are involved in the general education" of their citizens, Ross complained in his annual message on 3 October 1859 that the closing of the seminaries not only "checked the course of education, meted out a stinted pittance to every person engaged in public service, and defrauded the honest holders of public script," but also "disgraced the fair fame of the nation by an act of substantial repudiation." He further noted that closing the schools "disturbs the harmony of the people, excites disagreements and divisions," and "is insidiously sapping the foundations of the government."[58]

Although the two seminaries had been closed, the public schools continued to function, at least until the repercussions of the Civil War reached Indian Territory. In the late 1850s, the common schools enjoyed a surge in attendance, and Agent Butler reported that the Cherokee Nation's interest in education still continued in a "flourishing condition." By 1858, fifteen of the twenty-six Female Seminary graduates had been hired to teach in the Cherokee public schools that did not give instruction in the Cherokee language; only two teachers in the entire school system were not of Cherokee descent.[59]

By all accounts, the instructors in the common schools during the early years were competent, although some of the Nation's citizens were still skeptical about women teachers. Before teachers could be hired, they had to present a "certificate of good moral character" and pass an examination administered by a three-member testing board. Prospective instructors who passed the test received certificates of ability and could then be placed in teaching positions. The examination was waived for seminary graduates because of their advanced education.[60]

In 1859, because of the demands of every district, the number of public schools was increased to thirty, with over fifteen hundred enrollees. But owing to financial difficulties, texts printed in both English and Cherokee could not be provided and schoolhouses that needed repairs went without them. Citizens throughout the Cherokee Nation nevertheless continued to send their children to the common schools, hoping that eventually they could enroll them in the seminaries.[61]

By February 1861 the National Council finally raised enough money to reopen the Female Seminary and to operate it tuition free. Thirty-one students were enrolled, including girls of all ages and boys aged fifteen or younger. Joshua Ross, the nephew of Chief Ross, was hired as principal teacher. The younger Ross was an alumnus of the Fairfield Mission, the Cherokee Male Seminary, the Ozark Institute in Arkansas, and Emory and Henry College in Virginia. His wife, Jane, served as his assistant. Their terms were short, however, for the school was closed again five months later.[62]

The Civil War greatly aggravated the political factionalism that had plagued the tribe in the past. With the outbreak of war, Stand Watie, a political rival of John Ross and the leader of a faction of progressive mixed-bloods, sided with the South and was commissioned a colonel in the Confederate army in July 1861. At first, Chief John Ross advocated neutrality, but he was afraid that the tribe would be destroyed from within if the Cherokees did not agree on the issue, so in August 1861 he decided to ally with the Confederacy. But the tribe could not stay united. The majority of the men in a regiment of "Cherokee Mounted Rifles" led by John Drew (a nephew of Ross's) were anti-slavery fullbloods and ultimately deserted to the Union, thus widening the gulf between the two Cherokee factions.[63]

Soon after the seminary closed for the second time, Confederate troops appeared at Park Hill and Tahlequah. These visits frightened the residents, who feared attacks by vigilantes. After Union troops also appeared, the local people fled to Kansas or to Fort Gibson, a Union post on the Arkansas River.[64] Some families of the mixed-bloods who supported the Confederacy moved to Texas or Arkansas until the war was over. In 1863, A. G. Proctor, an Indian agent, reported that Park Hill was completely abandoned and that General Stand Watie and his Cherokee Confederate troops had burned the Rose Cottage of Chief John Ross. Farms throughout the Nation were overgrown and looked as "hopeless as can be conceived." Few schools were in operation by September 1863, and the abandoned buildings, including the seminaries, were either deteriorating or had been burned by Confederate guerrillas, as had many Cherokee homes and farms. Some Cherokees set up temporary schools in tents so their children could receive at least some education.[65]

The postwar period was also a time of troubles for the disunited Cherokees.[66] They lost their leader when Chief John Ross died on 1 August 1866 in Washington (his wife had died in 1861). As punishment for Stand Watie's support of the Confederacy, the Cherokees were forced by the federal government to relinquish part of their land and were hard-pressed to retain what was left them. At least seven thousand Cherokees had been killed, many tribespeople were homeless, one-third of the women were widows, and one of every four children was an orphan. The slaves had been freed, disrupting the Cherokee economy. The assistant chief, the Reverend Lewis Downing, temporarily replaced John Ross until October 1866, when Ross's nephew, William Potter Ross, was chosen principal chief. The new chief kept the factionalism alive by advocating the exclusion of all Confederate supporters from Cherokee tribal office.[67]

The Cherokees were determined to rebuild their shattered lives. The treaty signed in 1866 required that half of the proceeds from land sales be applied toward operating the Cherokee government, and the other half was to be divided between support of the common schools and other education ventures and support of orphans. Because money was now available, in 1867 the National Council reopened thirty-two public schools, and three years later thirty-two more had been built. White students resumed their education in mission schools at Tahlequah, Park Hill, Vinita, Prairie City, Locust Grove, Childer's Station, Webber's Falls, and Elm Springs. Although the seminaries were not in operation, a Moravian minister, Brother Mock, regularly held services in the Female Seminary dining hall for his thirty-nine-member congregation.[68]

Many citizens were eager to reopen the seminaries, but the schools could not resume operation without extensive repairs. In hopes of reuniting the various political factions, in December 1869 Principal Chief Lewis Downing (a fullblood elected in 1867) and the revitalized National Council approved an act appropriating over $3,200 to begin repairing the seminaries, to secure responsible persons or families to serve as caretakers at the schools, and to protect the buildings from trespassers. All the movable property of the male and female seminaries had been stored prior to the war, but the libraries were almost destroyed, and the second floor of the Female Seminary had been ruined by troops using it to store supplies.[69]

The council reopened the Female Seminary in May 1872, but administrators still faced monumental problems. The building remained in disrepair, the library was in shambles, and the furniture and most of the textbooks had been destroyed. The grounds were overgrown with weeds and bushes, and the entire building needed repainting.[70]

For the first time, a Cherokee woman, Mrs. Ellen Eblin, served as principal. The National Council appropriated $700 for her salary, but because of the dilapidated state of the seminary and the insufficient funding to repair it, she resigned in frustration after only five months. In October, she was succeeded by Ella N. Noyes, a native of Massachusetts and, like the first three principals, a product of Mount Holyoke. The *Cherokee Advocate* praised Noyes for her ability and excellent service, but she remained for only two years, resigning in 1875.[71]

The 1870s brought changes that would have a lasting impact on both the male and female seminaries. Although the National Council provided funds for the schools' maintenance, there was not enough money to support their operation. For the first time, students were required to pay for their room and board, although instruction was still free. Not surprisingly, the financially troubled schools suffered from insufficient enrollment, either because many students could not afford to pay the tuition or because prospective students feared that the school would not stay open and thus enrolled in the public schools. During the first two years after its reopening, the Female Seminary drew fewer than fifty applicants.[72]

Many Cherokee women were widowed during the Civil War, and although there was a renewed excitement about education after the war, young Cherokee women often stayed at home to help, rather than enroll in school. In order to attract more students, the school offered its services at bargain prices. Mrs. Jane Thompson, who supervised the lodging and food service, offered meals, laundry service, "lights, fuel, and all necessary expenses for $12.50 per month." If the students brought their own bedding and washed their own clothes, they paid Thompson ten dollars per month, about half the charge for board in Tahlequah. Thompson was even willing to "take supplies of any kind she need[ed] in payment at cash prices."[73] Even the modest charges proved too expensive, so the National Council set the tuition at $5.00 per month, lowered admission standards, and opened the school to girls from other tribes.[74] *Advocate* editorials urged its readers to enroll their daughters at the institution: "We do think that the citizens of the

Nation should take an interest in sustaining the Female Seminary. The rates are so low that anyone can afford to send, and if each one waits for the other they will never build up the school. . . . Send your daughter to this school, and be liberal with the noble women who are trying to build it up, and the time is not far distant when there will be a school there of which all would be proud."[75]

Late in 1873, the National Council revived the Board of Education and reaffirmed its authority to exercise control over both seminaries and all other educational facilities of the Nation. The council voted to establish a "literary institution for the education of indigent persons," and at least $75,000 was appropriated for a "primary department," grades one through five, and a "preparatory department," grades six through eight. The students in these two departments were collectively known as the "primaries," or "indigents" (and "beginners," by some students). As a compromise with those Cherokees who complained that the seminary was too expensive, fifty children were selected from the "Cherokee-speaking class" to attend school in the primary grades free of charge. These children did not live near any public schools, and preference was given to those lacking proficiency in the English language. Despite the legislation's requirements that they be "really indigent," however, by the late 1880s more girls from the Cherokee "upper class" than indigents were enrolled in the primary grades.[76]

Although no students graduated from the reopened Female Seminary until 1879, the school was back in "good running order" by 1876, and a total of 167 students were enrolled.[77] Thereafter, more students applied for admission, the curriculum was steadily diversified, and the building was enlarged and made more comfortable. After twenty years of hard times, the seminary had apparently recovered, but the reopening marked profound changes in the atmosphere of the school. From 1851 to 1856, the seminary had been a training ground for teachers and housewives, but in the 1870s, new teachers with broader ideas about the woman's sphere contributed to a shift in values at the school. During the 1850s, most of the controversies about the seminary had taken place outside of the school. But because of the inclusion of Cherokee girls from a variety of social and economic classes at the school after 1872, the clash of cultural ideals moved inside the seminary walls.

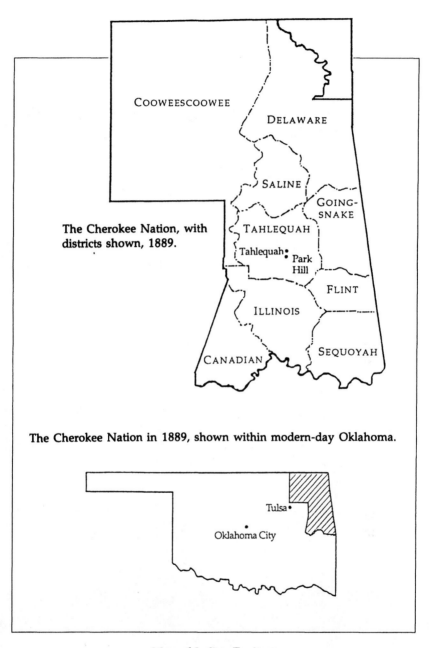

The Cherokee Nation, with districts shown, 1889.

COOWEESCOOWEE

DELAWARE

SALINE

GOING-SNAKE

TAHLEQUAH

Tahlequah• •Park Hill

FLINT

ILLINOIS

CANADIAN

SEQUOYAH

The Cherokee Nation in 1889, shown within modern-day Oklahoma.

Tulsa•

•Oklahoma City

Map of Indian Territory

Juniors and Seniors in front of the Cherokee Female Seminary, 1892. (University Archives, John Vaughan Library, Northeastern State University, Tahlequah, Oklahoma)

The first Cherokee Female Seminary, Park Hill, Indian Territory, opened May 1852 and burned April 1887. (Oklahoma Historical Society Archives and Manuscripts Division)

Chief John Ross and his second wife, Mary Stapler. (Western History Collections, University of Oklahoma Library)

Seminary students, 1854. (From a daguerreotype in the private collection of Virginia McLoughlin)

Seminary students playing "Indian," 1894. (University Archives, John Vaughan Library, Northeastern State University, Tahlequah, Oklahoma)

Seminary students and teachers performing in blackface, 1896. This skit was entitled "De dabatin' club." (University Archives, John Vaughan Library, Northeastern State University, Tahlequah, Oklahoma)

Ann Florence Wilson, principal of the Cherokee Female Seminary from 1875 to 1901. (University Archives, John Vaughan Library, Northeastern State University, Tahlequah, Oklahoma)

Each day the students cleaned the kitchen, parlor, classrooms, and bathrooms. Here, students sweep and mop the dining room floor, 1905. (University Archives, John Vaughan Library, Northeastern State University, Tahlequah, Oklahoma)

Students in the seminary parlor, c. 1900. The parlor was off-limits to students except when they had visitors, cleaning duty, or a photograph session. (University Archives, John Vaughan Library, Northeastern State University, Tahlequah, Oklahoma)

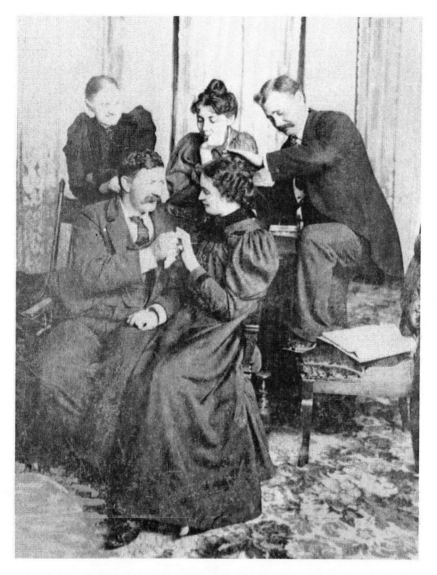

Teachers from the female and male seminaries performing a "mock wedding" for students in the Female Seminary parlor, c. 1899. Principal Wilson is in back row, left; Wilson's niece, Dora Wilson Hearon, is seated in foreground. Teacher Carlotta "Lotta" Archer is in back row, center. (University Archives, John Vaughan Library, Northeastern State University, Tahlequah, Oklahoma)

The students began rehearsing the annual Shakespeare production during the fall semester. Here, the actresses emote in preparation for the spring event, c. 1901. (University archives, John Vaughan Library, Northeastern State University, Tahlequah, Oklahoma)

Seminary students, 1904. Left to right: Betty Walkingstick, Elinor "Ella" Cookson, Rachel Wilkinson. (University Archives, John Vaughan Library, Northeastern State University, Tahlequah, Oklahoma)

Members of the junior class, 1898. (Western History Collections, University of Oklahoma Library)

Seminary students wore their finest clothes whenever they left campus or had their photograph taken. c. 1900. (University Archives, John Vaughan Library, Northeastern State University, Tahlequah, Oklahoma)

Students could attend class only with "every hair in place," and they spent hours on their hairstyles. (Courtesy of Richard Corley)

Mealtime, c. 1905. Two students from each table served the rest of their classmates. To make sure that students' table manners were correct, a teacher or upperclassman sat at each table. (University Archives, John Vaughan Library, Northeastern State University, Tahlequah, Oklahoma)

Students, c. 1902. (University Archives, John Vaughan Library, Northeastern
State University, Tahlequah, Oklahoma)

Sophomore class, 1903. For special events and photographs, students were allowed to wear the clothes of their choice, as long as they did not wear corsets or hoop skirts. (University Archives, John Vaughan Library, Northeastern State University, Tahlequah, Oklahoma)

Members of the class of 1903. Left to right: Leola "Lee" Ward Newton; Grace Wallace Richards; Caroline "Carrie" Freeman Baird; Laura Effie Duckworth Boatright. All four were 1/32 Cherokee. (University Archives, John Vaughan Library, Northeastern State University, Tahlequah, Oklahoma)

Class of 1905. (University Archives, John Vaughan Library, Northeastern State University, Tahlequah, Oklahoma)

Athletes, 1908. Seminarians played basketball, tennis, and occasionally, touch football. (University Archives, John Vaughan Library, Northeastern State University, Tahlequah, Oklahoma)

Class of 1908 (University Archives, John Vaughan Library, Northeastern State University, Tahlequah, Oklahoma)

Female Seminary building, c. 1900. (University Archives, John Vaughan Library, Northeastern State University, Tahlequah, Oklahoma)

4

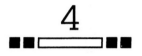

Teachers, Curriculum, and Administration: 1876 – 1909

By the mid-1870s, the Female Seminary had surpassed its pre–Civil War academic accomplishments. The fall semester of 1876 opened with 167 pupils, and that year most of the girls in the upper grades earned high marks in all their classes. Because so many students desired admittance, the National Council allotted more money to enlarge the building and to hire additional teachers and staff. Although many white families lived in the vicinity of the seminary, their children, with the exception of children of the white seminary teachers and local ministers, were still ineligible to attend it or any of the Cherokee common schools. But children with any Cherokee blood (even as little as 1/128) were welcome, as were children of other tribes who could pay the tuition.[1]

Wealth still gave students an advantage. Some students who failed courses semester after semester were continually readmitted—as long as they could pay the tuition of $5.00 per semester (later raised to $7.50 per semester).[2] The poor spelling and punctuation that appear in the following excerpt from a student's letter to her sister in 1889 reveal the lower standard sometimes applied to those who could pay tuition: "I seat myself this evening to right you a few lines to let you know that I am well at the present and hope this to find you the same I was glad to hear frome you this evening I haven't got but 2 letters frome home and one frome you and I have writen 6 letters since I have been here and this is the 7 I ain't rooming with no body yet here is a picture of the jail house. . . ."[3]

Although many students (especially those who graduated) were indeed from affluent families, wealthy students were in the minority. Most of the students were from middle- or lower-class backgrounds, and the indigents were quite poor. While it is true that the majority of students came from families who could manage to pay the tuition, they were not necessarily from the monied class. Also, each year dozens of primary-grade students went to the school free of charge. In fact, daughters of the wealthier families were sent to schools outside of the Cherokee Nation without ever attending the Female Seminary,[4] and some "ultra-feminine" girls may not have enrolled in any school. Other children were the offspring of white parents who, ironically, did not approve of their mixed-blood daughters attending school with Indians. One student stayed at the school for only one semester (in 1882) before moving East, because, according to her mother, "the west was too wild. . . . [It was] not the proper place for children."[5]

After 1876, the student population began to diversify and the administration changed as well. For twenty years the primary source of principals for the seminary had been Mount Holyoke. But in 1875, Ann Florence Wilson, a non-Indian native of Arkansas who graduated from New York's Oswego Normal School, was appointed principal teacher. While studying at Oswego, Wilson had been deeply influenced by her female mentors. Some had been educated in Europe and almost all had earned terminal degrees. Wilson clearly possessed a much broader view of women's abilities than had the previous seminary principals. While she accepted the traditional role of women as pious homemakers, she also advocated expanding the woman's sphere to include pursuing careers. For the next quarter century, this strong and uncompromising woman shaped the school's policies and curriculum, and she had a profound effect upon her students and teachers.[6]

Wilson was born 3 December 1842, in Washington County, Arkansas, the daughter of Thaddeus C. Wilson III, a Mississippi steamboat captain, and Eliza Jane McKisick. Because her parents died when she was two years old, Florence and her brother, Montgomery, were taken to Evansville, Arkansas, to be raised by their aunt and uncle. That couple died a few years later, and Florence moved into the historic White McClellan mansion at Cane Hill, Arkansas, with family friends.[7]

She began her formal education at Cane Hill Female Seminary in Arkansas, a school founded by a Mount Holyoke graduate, Laura Graham. In 1858, at the age of sixteen, Wilson graduated with honors from La Grange Female College near Jackson, Tennessee. Afterward, she served as a teaching assistant at a female institution in Russellville, Arkansas, until the Civil War. In 1872, she enrolled in the two-year elementary teacher's course at the prestigious Oswego Normal School in New York. Because of her training in the areas of curriculum development, student psychology, textbook selection, and teaching techniques, she was chosen as principal of the Tahlequah public schools, one of the first eleven public schools that the Cherokee Nation had established in 1841. In 1875, Wilson was hired as principal of the Female Seminary, and her training and experience enabled her to help the school improve its academic policies and its relations with the public.[8]

Wilson never married, but while teaching at Russellville she had been engaged to Pleasant Buchanan, a mathematics professor at Cane Hill College who was killed fighting for the Confederacy at the Battle of Prairie Grove. Although Wilson had subsequent offers of marriage, she preferred to devote herself to the seminary—a lifestyle that would later influence many of her pupils who remained single. She always maintained a hard-boiled demeanor, and she deliberately showed no favoritism to any faculty member or student, but she sometimes secretly permitted students of limited ability to retake examinations after failing them. Wilson also gave both encouragement and money to several indigent students, especially the fullblood girls, and she continually defended the traditional members of the tribe against the adverse opinions of the acculturated pupils.[9]

Wilson proved an intellectual inspiration to both students and personnel. She was a voracious reader and was particularly interested in literature and science. She studied the Bible daily, and she made certain that Bible verses were a part of the English courses. Wilson could not sing or play an instrument but she was an advocate of music and voice lessons for all students, and she encouraged everyone to participate in the seminary's dramatic productions. She was a member of the Daughters of the American Revolution, and although neither she nor any of her teachers or students could vote, she still required everyone to attend political rallies in Tahlequah regularly.[10]

In 1876, the year after Wilson became principal, the Board of Education established the position of Superintendent of Public Schools. Although it was an administrative post for men only, with duties that focused on the fiscal problems of the seminaries, the development of curricula, and the "conditions and wants" of the schools, the super-intendent depended on the advice of Florence Wilson and subsequent principals. The first superintendent was the Reverend Hamilton Balentine, an Irishman who died at the seminary a few months after assuming office. He was succeeded temporarily by his son William, who had been a student at Westminster College in Missouri. In 1876 the younger Balentine was replaced by the Reverend Timothy Rights; in 1877 Rights relinquished the position to the Reverend Joseph Thompson.[11]

In the years between 1876 and 1887, the seminary faculty included a growing number of young alumnae who were supported by many skilled white teachers, including Dora Wilson Hearon, Florence Wilson's niece. These non-Cherokees had no difficulty adapting to the seminary lifestyle, and they all made strong impressions (usually favorable) on the seminary students.[12]

Numerous Cherokees and blacks found temporary employment at the seminary. Furnace and wagon repairmen, laborers and woodcutters (sometimes convicts), piano tuners, carpenters, and roofers—many of whom were freedmen and women—were paid by the day, while sick-nurses, and black washerwomen, cooks, matrons, and porters were hired by contract for longer periods. Grocers in Tahlequah benefited from supplying the vast amount of food the seminarians required, and other local stores such as Levison and Blythe Stationery Company, Ed Lutz Metals and Sheet Iron, Fire Dust Company Extinguishers, Arthur Jones Carpets, and C. J. Brockman's Flowers regularly served students and faculty from both high schools.[13]

The National Council expressed its concern that the Cherokees would be left behind if the seminary's curriculum did not keep pace with the course of study offered at other women's schools in the United States. For example, at one annual May picnic celebrating the opening of the seminaries, William Potter Ross, a former chief who advocated acculturation, expressed fear that his people would be outdone by other tribes in Indian Territory. "While our neighboring Tribes and Nations are pressing forward in the pursuit of knowledge, let not the Chero-kee . . . be second in the race," he said. The last thing his tribe needed, he warned the seminarians, was "lazy and useless men," and "slouchy and slip-shod women."[14] And to make it clear that the Cherokees still had not reached the summit of equality with whites by 1884, Chief Dennis Bushyhead spoke earnestly of the importance of praying at the same altar with "our whiter and stronger brothers [giving] our common thanks to God . . . [that they] will show magnanimity and justice to their weaker brethren."[15]

In response to a growing enrollment and a need for laboratories and classrooms, in 1877 the National Council authorized a three-story addition to the seminary building, increasing the total number of rooms to at least eighty, with accommodations for about 150 students. The basement of the addition held storage areas, laundry facilities, and a furnace. The first floor contained the auditorium, dining hall, guest rooms, and the library, which doubled as a "recitation room." Also on the first floor was the parlor filled with "typical, old fashioned furniture." It was used by teachers, guests, and visiting parents, but the students were not permitted in the room except for visits with relatives. On the second and third floors were the living quarters of the matrons, pupils, and teachers. Window ledges were adorned with planter boxes, and each dining room and parlor table was decorated with wild flowers.[16]

The curriculum in all the grades had also been expanded and diversified between the late seventies and late eighties. Students in the elementary and middle grades studied (at various levels) penmanship, phonetics, geography, arithmetic, reading, composition, grammar, and "object lessons." High-school freshmen devoted their efforts to a more intensive study of the basic subjects. Sophomores studied English history, geometry, chemistry, natural philosophy, rhetoric, and the writings of Julius Caesar. Juniors read the works of Cicero, Ovid, and Thucydides as well as English and American authors. Students also enrolled in courses in political economy, moral philosophy, trigonometry, analytical geometry, botany, geology, French, and German. During their final year, seniors continued the earlier disciplines, but added "English criticism," "mental science," "mental philosophy," logic, calculus, surveying, and zoology. They also studied the works of Virgil, Livy, Homer, Goethe, and Molière.[17]

The school year began in late August, and because of the uncomfortable humidity, physical exercises were scheduled according to the weather. Each school year ended in late May, before the weather became too hot. The students followed a precise schedule — with some alterations over the years — which apportioned their school day as follows:

AM	PM
Students Rise 5:30	Recitations 2:00 to 4:00
Study Hall 6:00 to 7:00	Exercises 4:15 to 4:45

Breakfast and	Supper 5:00
Detail 7:00 to 8:30	Study Hall 6:45 to 8:45
Chapel 8:30 to 9:00	First Retiring Bell 9:00
Recitations 9:00 to 12:00	Second Retiring Bell 9:15
Noon 12:00 to 2:00[18]	

The girls were supervised during meals. The dining room was located in the northeast corner of the building and was furnished with long tables covered with white tablecloths. At mealtimes the dining-room matron rang a bell, and when all the students had reached their assigned seats she tapped the bell again as a signal for them to sit down. Two girls from each table served the rest of their classmates, and to make sure that their manners were correct, a teacher or upperclassman sat at each table. After everyone finished, the bell was tapped again, and the girls were expected to leave the room in as orderly a manner as they had entered it.[19]

Despite the barrier against non-Indians enrolling at the seminary and in disregard for the number of traditionalist girls in attendance, the curriculum still contained no courses focusing upon tribal history, religion, or any other aspect of Cherokee culture, and the official language at the school remained English. This was not so unusual, however, since none of the tribal schools in Indian Territory—and certainly none of the federal boarding schools—included tribal traditions and languages in their curricula either. Many of the primary-grade students who spoke Cherokee had to be taught English (by teachers who spoke no Cherokee), and they also had to wait until they returned home for the Christmas holidays or summer vacation in order to take part in traditional Cherokee religious ceremonies. Since tribal traditions were of little interest to the faculty or administration, they were rarely discussed with the students. Teachers did, however, keep the girls abreast of Cherokee tribal politics.[20]

The routine of school and the peace and calm of Easter Sunday 1887 were disrupted by what Chief William Potter Ross described as "a calamity hitherto unknown in the history of the country," when the seminary burned to the ground. The fire was allegedly started by a "fanatical" visitor, Louis McLain (or McLane), who tried in vain to take the girls into the woods to "preach the gospel" to them. Later, while leaning against the northeast corner fence-rail, he dropped some embers from his pipe, which somehow were supposedly carried through the hollow rail into a nearby open window and onto the curtains. Principal Wilson ordered the students to evacuate the building, and a few teachers climbed to the cupola to ring the bell but found the rope gone. Upon seeing smoke from the burning building, the male seminarians left their church service and ran the three miles to the site, collecting articles of clothing blown by high winds into the fields after the girls threw them out the windows. By the time the boys and the townspeople arrived, the building was engulfed in flames and the fire was out of control.[21]

The girls had quickly evacuated the building, some carrying the smaller and sick students, and none had been injured. Some personal items, furniture, and books had been saved, but since the school had no fire-fighting equipment, the entire facility, including most of the school records, was lost. A well had been started outside the seminary a few years before, but the project was soon abandoned since the cost of digging was charged to the school. Evidently, the well was not deemed as important as curriculum development.[22]

After the National Council conducted preliminary investigations and read the eyewitness testimonies of J. A. McKenahan, superintendent of the seminaries; Judge J. M. Walker, the seminary steward; and Herman Migge, a cook, the council concluded that the administrators and workers had failed to do all they could to save the school. Water was stored in the third-floor tanks, and the council believed the quantity was sufficient for the men to have extinguished the fire. The seminary faculty, however, argued that the wind was too high and the fire spread too quickly for anyone to stop it. Ultimately, no one was punished, and the council appointed a seven-member committee to begin preparations for building a new seminary.[23]

Meanwhile, after spending a sorrowful night at the Male Seminary in a room next to the superintendent's office, or in the homes of Tahlequah and Park Hill residents, most of the girls had returned to their families and enrolled in neighborhood common schools. Many would not enroll in the new school when it opened two years later. The three members of the Female Seminary's graduating class of 1888 (Rachel Caroline "Callie" Eaton, Elizabeth "Lizzie" Bushyhead McNair, and Addie Roche Ross) received their diplomas at the Male Seminary on 28 June along with the ten boys who graduated.[24]

Parents of the seminary students campaigned to have the new seminary built nearer to Tahlequah. They purchased a privately owned lot on the outskirts of town and donated it to the Cherokee Nation as the site for the new school. Enthusiastic about the new school, the National Council advertised its construction plans in the *Cherokee Advocate*, the *Kansas City Times*, the *Fort Smith Times*, and the *St. Louis Globe Democrat*, and it subsequently awarded the building contract to W. A. Illsley and Son (C. E. Illsley) of Kansas. The original construction bid was $54,000, but almost $4,000 more was needed for alterations such as strengthening walls and foundations, the addition of a smokehouse for curing and storing meat, and an elaborate wrought-iron fence that some of the girls believed Principal Wilson wanted in an effort to limit their contact with the boys from the Male Seminary.[25]

The new building was constructed on higher ground than the old one, with an improved water supply and good drainage. Because of the distance from the building site to the railroad in Muskogee, only parts of the structure that could not be produced locally, such as windows and hardware, were shipped in. The bricks were made from local limestone and clay, and the lumber was cut in local sawmills. In contrast to the old school, the new facility featured water heated by steam, which was pumped to the kitchen, baths, basins, slop sinks, and water closets. A separate tank supplied water for baths in the sick wards located on the third floor. An elevator was installed to lift heavy furniture and trunks, and a dumb waiter reached the third floor. By 1904, the seminary had acquired electricity, and the girls no longer had to rely on coal oil. The building had a central heating system, but the students' rooms were also provided with fireplaces or pot-bellied stoves. Students often complained about having to tend their own fires, especially on freezing winter evenings when they had to carry wood from the pile behind the school.[26]

The main part of the seminary measured 246 by 96 feet, with an eastern wing measuring 70 by 100 feet. Each dormitory room was large enough to accommodate four girls, but on occasion, six sisters or cousins preferred to stay in one room. Most of the beds, curtains, nightstands, chairs, desks, china bowls, and pitchers were furnished by the school, but the more affluent parents provided their daughters' furniture. The high-school girls brought their own linens, wall hangings, and other decorations.[27]

The first floor housed the chapel (which doubled as the study and recitation hall), classrooms, dining room, kitchen, parlor, music rooms, and administration offices. On the second floor were the library, more music rooms, and quarters for the teachers and students. The third floor included six infirmary rooms and more student quarters. Many students later recalled being overwhelmed by the size of the building, by the length of the halls, and especially by the indoor bathrooms. The total cost of the new seminary was $78,000, but a reporter for the *Kansas City Times* commented that the seminary looked like "a $200,000 institution." After the new seminary opened on 26 August 1889, more than 250 girls applied for admission, but because of limited space only 232 were admitted.[28]

With such obvious support for an advanced education, the course of study at the seminary was broadened even further after 1890. Pupils entering the primary department could expect eight years of thorough education before entering the high school. Their texts included White's *Elementary Geometry*, Milne's *Elementary Algebra*, and Powel's *How to Talk*. Added to the curriculum were courses in geometry, advanced geography, physiology, business writing, "national vertical penmanship," and "morals and manners." Graduating seniors were more intensely exposed to literary masters such as Hawthorne, Eliot, Shakespeare, Bacon, and Tennyson. They were also required to write compositions, to translate Latin prose into English, and to study the culture of the Romans. The most dreaded assignment came at the end of each year, when students were asked to rewrite stories (from memory) they had read, such as *Ivanhoe*.[29]

Literary clubs, such as the Minervian, Germanae, Sodales, Netrophian, Philomathian, Utopian, and Hypathian societies, gave students an opportunity to develop their "literary, musical and dramatic talents" and to learn the important qualities "necessary to a pleasing appearance before the public." By 1893, the Hypathian Society had grown so large that the students organized an offshoot of it, the Excelsior Society.[30]

All students were expected to understand the structure of the United States government as well as the organization of their own Cherokee national government. For an additional five dollars per month, students could enroll in music courses, and after they completed the eighth grade they were eligible to join the prestigious Glee Club. Pupils in the science courses collected plants and insects for identification and conducted physics and chemistry experiments in the well-furnished laboratory. Students also made educational visits to the electric plant, ice factory, flour mills, and central telephone exchange in nearby Tahlequah.[31]

The new seminary library reflected the general improvements in the institution. Few books had survived the 1887 fire, but by 1904 the library had been increased to thirteen hundred volumes, including encyclopedias and other reference books, poetry, fiction, and classics. Also available were thirty-two of the leading magazines of that day, and newspapers such as the *Saint Louis Globe Democrat*, the *Indian Chieftain*, the *Telephone*, the *Indian Arrow*, the *Capitol*, and the *Oklahoman*. The library also contained letters from Cherokee statesmen in Washington and copies of speeches made by politicians campaigning in Indian Territory. Textbooks were supplied by dealers such as Robert D. Patterson and Company of St. Louis, the American Book Company, and Farquhar and Albrecht of Chicago. School supplies were purchased from J. B. Merwin School Supply Company, Levison and Blythe Stationery Company, Tahlequah Arrow Bookstore and News Stand, and other stores in Tahlequah.[32]

Students were required to assist in the building's maintenance. Duties were assigned to all students, even pupils in the primary grades, who were put on the dining-room detail. Those in the other grades swept and dusted the parlor, library, classrooms, and hallways. Every Saturday the girls received their cleaning assignments for the coming week, and all hoped they would get the parlor duty, since they were allowed in the room only on special occasions. These activities were intended to teach the girls the "art of handling the broom" and the "science of the dust cloth." Students also worked at the circulation desk in the library in addition to the two hours of study time they spent there during the week. These regular duties were limited to one hour each day, but in the warmer months students were also required to care for the campus lawn and flowers. The school maintained a garden divided into twelve plots, one for each grade, and the faculty expected the girls to tend them and to acquire "a knowledge of insect life and of seed, plant, blossom, and fruit."[33]

In response to the "professionalization" of housework by the turn of the century, the Department of the Interior's annual report for 1899 regarding the seminary stated that instead of "being taught the domestic arts [girls] are given . . . Latin and mathematics while branches of domestic economy are neglected. The dignity of work receives no attention at their hands." Because of pressure exerted by John Benedict, the new superintendent for the tribes of Indian Territory, the seminary administrators made certain that by 1905, the school's "Domestic Science" department included lessons in cleaning (dusting and making beds, although a laundress washed students' clothes) and sewing (usually to mend torn clothes; only a few girls became skilled seamstresses); there was also a modest agricultural program that featured botany, gardening, and flower arranging. One of the most popular courses among students and parents was "Household Chemistry" (cooking), which was taught in the school's "splendidly equipped home kitchen" located in the domestic science department, housed in a small building outside the seminary. Parents had been pushing administrators to teach their daughters the "most essential qualities that are so important to good housewivery," so the girls learned the basics of sewing, and some of their "fancy needlework" was displayed. Primary-grade students were encouraged to work with beads and baskets, while older girls produced embroidery. All students, except those with "defective eyes," were required to spend a period of time each Saturday mending and darning their clothing. It was supposed that such "charming" duties would "indelibly impress" on the minds of the future homemakers the importance of immediately addressing the problems that might arise in "otherwise well-regulated homes." Ironically, the only students who had laundry and cooking duty were the older indigent girls, who were required to work for their board.[34]

Religious influence remained strong. Unless the girls' families lived in the vicinity and the students went home on weekends, the girls were still required to attend (with an accompanying teacher or senior) the church of their choice. The seminary held Sunday school as well as its own church service in the afternoon. Each Sunday morning, the students spent one hour preparing for their Sunday school lessons. Students were also required to attend daily morning devotionals, which consisted of scripture reading, singing, and prayers led by seminary teachers on a rotating basis. By all accounts, daily chapel was one of the students' favorite activities. Callie Eaton and Bluie Adair, two assistant teachers in 1876, had founded a branch of the Young Women's Christian Association, which offered an additional weekly Sunday prayer meeting at the school. The teachers regularly discussed the temperance issue, as did visiting lecturers, such as Emma Malley of the Women's Christian Temperance Union of Ohio, who spoke to the girls on the evils of alcohol in 1884.[35]

The course of study at the Female Seminary was indeed demanding, the discipline was strict, and those girls with weak academic backgrounds had to work diligently to meet the institution's standards. If any girl was caught cheating on an examination, she was immediately sent home. Although study hall was mandatory, teachers pressured their pupils to study as much as possible during their free time. To give them a head start, on Saturday mornings students received their assignments for the coming week.[36]

Although most of the pupils and parents were relatively content with the course of study, not everyone in the Cherokee Nation was pleased with the high schools. In the 1850s, some Cherokees had wanted to send their daughters to the school, but often the girls could not pass the entrance examination; after the school's reopening in the 1870s, many could not afford the tuition. But some fullbloods opposed the seminaries and did not send their children to them even when they had the money. Prejudice against traditional Cherokees continued to be the main argument against enrollment, as it had been in the 1850s, but there were also doubts about the practicality of the school's curriculum. The schools met the expectations of the National Council, the teachers, and most of the Nation's citizens, but some Cherokees— perhaps echoing Booker T. Washington's enthusiasm for industrial education for blacks[37]—protested that the academic curriculum was not applicable to the needs of all the students.

This attitude was expressed in a letter from "Bood Guy" (probably "Good Guy") to the *Cherokee Advocate*. The writer stated that "what our youngsters ought to be . . . are farmers and stock raisers." He doubted that the students heard "the words 'farm' or 'farming'" during their years of instruction. Preferring practical training over traditional academic courses, the writer asked, "What sense or good is there in preparing our youth for their [whites'] business?" He concluded that both seminaries were merely "pieces of imitation, with the high schools of the United States for models," and therefore served no practical purpose in a nation comprised mainly of farmers. The education they receive, he believed, "ought to conform to, and fit them for, what they expect to become."[38] In 1880, out of a population of approximately 25,438, 3,550 Cherokees adults were farmers. Of the 859 parents of seminarians whose type of work could be ascertained, 85 percent were farmers, although some farmed as a supplement to their other professions.[39] Because of the desire for vocational training among its citizens, the National Council was pressured into giving the Board of Education permission to declare the boarding schools "industrial or manual labor boarding schools."[40]

Within the next few years, principal chiefs Dennis Bushyhead and Joel B. Mayes were concerned that the seminaries were not accomplishing all they should. While Bushyhead acknowledged the "gratifying results" of the seminaries' curricula, in 1881 he advocated using more of the tax revenue for a mandatory "system of manual labor" for the primary-grade students (who were usually from poor farming families), a system that would be "optionary" for upper grades. In the 1890s, Chief Mayes tried in vain to persuade the National Council to purchase Fort Gibson for use as an industrial school but the council was not receptive to the idea.[41] Many councilmen and seminarians (many of whom were children of councilmen) were strongly influenced by the emerging industrial American society that began encroaching into Indian Territory. The theory of Social Darwinism ("survival of the fittest" in regard to business and social activities) became popular, as did Horatio Alger stories ("rags to riches" via hard work). The seminarians, while still maintaining a strong Cherokee identity, were at the same time attuned to the idea of garnering individual wealth and status. Indeed, many seminarians — female and male — later would take advantage of the tribe's oil, timber, and coal resources for personal gain. Because most of the councilmen's children attended the seminaries and they had no intention of becoming laborers or farmers exclusively, the seminaries never became manual labor or industrial schools.

Another idea that emerged in the early 1900s came from officials at the coeducational Cherokee Orphan Asylum. They suggested that perhaps a single seminary might better serve the Nation, and the *Advocate* editorialized in favor of such a system. According to the *Advocate* it was better to have the male and female students, under the supervision of teachers, "mingle while at school and discuss subjects relative to the sciences, arts, literature or language," than to "wait until they are grown and have them meet at church or at cotton-pickings and dances." But conservative tribal officials and many citizens continued to reject the idea, and the seminaries remained segregated according to sex.[42]

The controversy over coeducation passed, but outside forces began to have an impact upon the Cherokee Nation and the seminary. Despite the strong objections of the tribes in Indian Territory, who were determined to retain their sovereignty, on 28 June 1898 Congress passed the Curtis Act, which was designed to assimilate the tribes of Indian

Territory into the emerging state of Oklahoma. Tribal affairs were to come gradually under the joint control of both the tribal councils and the United States government. Meanwhile, Cherokees were forced to submit to the policies of the General Allotment Act (also known as the Dawes Severalty Act), which stipulated, among other things, that the secretary of the interior would control all the Cherokee schools, school property, and school funds. United States citizenship would be bestowed upon the Cherokees (and other Indians of Indian Territory), Cherokees would add their names to the Dawes Roll (based on the 1880 census), and they would receive a portion of allotted land. Those lands not allotted to Indians would be sold to whites. Fortunately, forty acres for each of the two seminaries were set aside from the lands to be allotted.[43] Thus, surrounded by whites, and faced with impending Oklahoma statehood, all Cherokees—not just the seminarians—realized it was necessary to protect their tribal interests.

At least the tribe maintained a modicum of control over its schools. The secretary of the interior appointed a Board of Education for the Cherokee Nation, with two of its three members recommended by the principal chief. This board worked in conjunction with the superintendent of schools for Indian Territory (who had jurisdiction over all tribal schools) and each tribe's supervisor of schools. The first superintendent was John Downing Benedict, an experienced educator who was instrumental in increasing the number of schools throughout Indian Territory and in paving the way for a transition from tribally controlled schools to schools controlled by the county and the state. The supervisor of the Cherokee schools was Benjamin Seebohn Coppock, also a former teacher. Coppock worked with both Benedict and the Cherokee government to ensure high-quality education at all the public schools. He was an advocate of industrial training, not academic subjects, at the seminaries, which caused some friction with seminary administrators. But the tribe relented and allowed a few industrial courses to be added to the curricula.[44]

One of the first problems Benedict and Coppock had to deal with was the quality of primary education across the Cherokee Nation. Some districts boasted good schools but in others, students suffered because of nepotism and inadequately prepared teachers. When these younger students were admitted to the seminary, they were ill prepared for the rigorous course of study. An analysis of Ann Florence Wilson's "Great Leather-Bound Record Book" shows that many of the girls from common schools who were admitted to the high school between 1876 and 1903 were poorly prepared and had not even mastered the primary subjects. While the administration did indeed readmit students year after year if they could pay tuition, even though they repeatedly failed, the students had to have good marks in all classes in order to graduate.[45]

In 1898, reports reached Cherokee officials that teachers in some districts were so poorly prepared that they were bribing school superintendents in order to keep their jobs. In response, Benedict, Coppock, and members of the Nation's school board visited schools across the Nation, then decided that a series of summer "normal schools" should be instituted to provide better-trained teachers. The Female Seminary was chosen as the site for these institutes, and the first four-week program began in June 1899. Over 140 teachers were enrolled, including both applicants and those instructors already employed in the common schools. New teachers were tested for their competency, while experienced instructors received course work that reviewed academic material. Teachers who failed to attend the program were denied employment in the fall.[46]

The summer normal school held at the Female Seminary in 1901 included 154 teachers and prospective teachers. Each enrollee was required to take a course on the "Theory and Practice of Teaching," and those desiring a position at the high-school level were required to take psychology as well. Supervisor Coppock reported that the experienced teachers at the normal school were enthusiastic and "showed the spirit of those who believe industry and merit will win." Of those taking exams, 105 were certified to teach. Because the summer normal institutes increased the number of qualified teachers, the seminary was able to employ even better-prepared instructors than in previous years.[47]

Depending on their level of qualification, instructors were issued one of two certificates. Those desiring a Class A certificate had to pass examinations in algebra, arithmetic, civil government, geography, grammar, orthography, penmanship, physiology, primary work, reading, and United States history. Class B certificates were given to those passing courses in all the aforementioned subjects except algebra, physiology, and civil government. Because of the broad requirements of the Class A program, administrators preferred teachers from this group and selected them for employment at the seminaries.[48]

During the seminary's last decade, both Cherokee and visiting government officials repeatedly praised the seminary teachers and their students. A graduate of the seminary, Ida Wetzel (Tinnin), later recalled that the needs of the students—"physical, mental, moral, spiritual, and social"—were adequately met. There were no professional counselors, but the girls were always "subtly but firmly" guided by the regular faculty members. Tinnin noted that every teacher at the seminary had a part in "steering us in the right direction." The *Advocate* also reflected the tribe's pride in the seminary's accomplishments. According to one article, it would be difficult for anyone to "witness without emotions of satisfaction the exercises of the school, and the graces and accomplishments attained by all." Observers commented on the beautiful locale, the adequate furnishings, and the academic achievements that made it a "first-rate institution."[49]

The Board of Education noted that much of the seminary's success resulted from its excellent faculty. After the 1887 fire, Florence Wilson returned to Oswego for further education, and in January 1888 she graduated from the advanced English course. She then taught again at the Tahlequah National School until the seminary reopened in 1889, when she returned as principal.[50]

In 1900 Wilson celebrated her fifty-eighth birthday having spent most of her adult life associated with the seminary. She was proud that, as the twentieth century dawned, her assistant teachers, Lillian Alexander, Patsy Mayes, Mary Ann Duncan Shelton, Mary Llewellyn "Lelia" Morgan, and Ella Mae Covel (the latter two, seminary graduates), were all Cherokees. The same was true for her teachers the next year—Araminta "Minta" Ross Foreman, Dannie Ross, and Sallie G. Pendleton. In order to reduce expenses, the National Council passed an act limiting the number of workers (such as nurses, laborers, and cooks) the seminary superintendent could hire. The teachers found, therefore, that their responsibilities had increased. All the assistant teachers were paid $450 per year, but Principal Wilson received $900, and the first assistant, Mae Shelton, was paid $675.69.[51]

Principal Wilson was not the only teacher to leave a lasting impression upon her students. Alumna Polly Nelson (Hancock) distinctly remembered science teacher Minta Foreman (Ross) as being "tall, straight and haughty looking," and "when she'd walk down the hall, it would scare me to death." Pupil Evelyn Suagee (Maheres) also recalled Foreman as enthusiastic but dignified, and that she especially liked the outdoors and "field work." While other teachers were popular with the students, most of the girls "wanted to be like Minta Foreman . . . standing tall in her Indian eloquence" (the seminarians were not opposed to using stereotypical language).[52]

Reflecting the tribe's gratitude to Florence Wilson for her contribution to the seminary's success, and in "obedience to the confidence of the mothers who unhesitatingly commit their daughters to her care," in 1900 the Cherokee National Council unanimously appointed her principal for "as long as she may wish to receive it [the appointment]." The National Council commented that she had "devoted thirty years of her life to the advancement and culture of our wives and daughters and has placed the crown of her success upon the womanhood of this country." Indeed, Florence Wilson had received the support and encouragement of all seven principal chiefs of the Cherokee Nation during her tenure as seminary principal.[53]

But the tribe's decision to extend that tenure was overturned by a presidential veto on 28 December 1900. The precise reason for President William McKinley's veto remains unknown, although Wilson was politically outspoken and possibly a member of the Democratic party. The partisan McKinley may have refused, therefore, to appoint her for political reasons. However, it is more likely that by 1900 most officials realized that the Cherokee Nation would soon be absorbed into the emerging state of Oklahoma, and McKinley may have been reluctant to endorse any permanent appointment in a school system that would soon be controlled by the new state. Apparently, McKinley was determined to keep long-range decision making out of the Cherokees' hands.[54]

Whatever McKinley's true motives, his action had a devastating effect on Florence Wilson. Distraught, she resigned her post at the seminary following the 1900–1901 school term and moved to Springfield, Missouri. She lived there for two years before accepting a teaching position at Willie Halsell College at Vinita, Oklahoma. She was well liked by her students, but her heart remained with the Cherokee Female Seminary and she had little interest in her new job. After one year she resigned to share a home with her sister in Little Rock, Arkansas. On 13 August 1909, she died in self-imposed exile at Armstrong Springs, Arkansas, of "stomach and liver problems."[55]

Wilson's influence on the seminary remained strong despite her departure, and she was a topic of discussion among students for years after she left. In 1914, the Florence Wilson Memorial Column was erected in front of the seminary building. The largest dormitory on the campus of Northeastern State College (now Northeastern State University) was named after her. At least a dozen seminarians named their daughters Florence. In 1902, Etta Rider of Iowa was appointed as Wilson's successor, and she retained most of Wilson's curriculum, policies, and teachers, many of whom were seminary alumnae.[56]

Etta Rider resigned in 1903 and was replaced by Eleanor Allen, who served as principal for the next five years. Like Wilson, Allen was stern and strict, and according to students she had a "look that would shrivel us." Once after Alta Ward Nolton requested permission to have her "busted" shoe sole repaired at the cobbler's in Tahlequah, Allen replied, "Busted, busted, busted . . . the word is bursted!" and then sent the surprised pupil to her room. She even wanted her girls to have "military instruction," so she asked teachers from the Male Seminary to lead drill exercises for the seminary girls each afternoon. During Allen's tenure, a three-foot-high stone wall was erected along the eastern side of the campus by students, who were required to pick up stones around campus on their way back from their daily walks.[57]

During this period, enrollment at the seminary grew and the faculty was increased to nine, including Ida Virginia Mosser, a Vassar graduate. Students fondly remembered their cook, Paden Banks ("a little 5 by 5"), as being as stern as Principal Allen, but also generous. During mealtimes, as the older girls pushed their way to the front of the line, Banks would make them move back by scolding, "Let little honeys [the primary-grade students] get their biscuits first."[58]

In its final years the Female Seminary continued to be successful. During the late 1890s the Cherokee Board of Education praised the school as "the best system on earth" and reported that "there is no country under the sun so blessed with educational advantages as large as are the Cherokee people." In 1901, Benjamin Coppock noted the increased attendance and the amount and quality of work done at the school. After attending the seminary's commencement exercises, he remarked that the students seemed "better prepared," and that the orations, presented to the audience of "intelligent and cultivated people, [were] well pronounced." At the 1902 commencement, Coppock asserted that, "I can not learn that these schools were ever in a better condition than at this time."[59]

On 16 November 1907, Oklahoma became the forty-sixth state. The students seemed resigned to the reality of statehood and no celebrations were held at either seminary. Although the Cherokee Nation's tribal schools were absorbed into the Oklahoma state system, the Female Seminary continued to function as usual until the end of the 1908–9 school year. In March 1909, the Oklahoma state legislature passed an act providing for the creation of a teacher-training institution, the Northeastern State Normal School. The act also provided for purchasing the Female Seminary from the Cherokee tribal government for $45,000 to serve as the first building of the new school. Because many parents still wanted to send their children to a Cherokee high school, the Male Seminary was made coeducational in the fall of 1909.[60]

The new coeducational seminary opened on 14 September 1909, with an enrollment of 92 boys and 74 girls, a decrease from the enrollment of over 200 students at each of the seminaries the previous year. Obviously, not everyone was pleased with the concept of a coeducational boarding school. A few disgruntled older boys preferred not to enroll in the Northeastern State Normal School rather than share "their school" with females, and some parents refused to allow their daughters to live in the same building as male students. Charlotte Mayes (Sanders) and her sister, Pearl Mayes (Langston), for example, had been students at the Female Seminary. For the fall 1909 semester they attended school in Pryor, almost ten miles from their home, but after they had endured four months of hard traveling, their parents relented and allowed them to enroll at the Male Seminary for the spring semester. Some of the local students lived with their families and commuted daily. Although fifty-two children dropped out after the fall semester, almost as many new students enrolled for the spring term.[61]

After the girls arrived, all boys were assigned to the second floor along with Principal F. A. Chapman, Second Assistant J. Grover Scales, and Third Assistant A. Jack Brown. The girls lived on the third floor with the female assistant teachers, Cassie Iliff, Maud Woolford, and Janana Ballard. The female primary students were housed in the larger third-floor rooms, which were divided by low, thin-walled partitions that enabled the instructors to hear the children when they misbehaved.[62]

Reminiscent of her former principal, Florence Wilson, Janana Ballard was a stickler for punctuality and cleanliness. One student, Annie Chair (Thompson), later recalled that once a week Ballard lined up the primary-grade students and made them remove their shoes and socks. Any girls with "stinkey feet" had to perform chores in the kitchen or classrooms. But despite the occasional punishments they prescribed, most of the teachers, especially the men, were remembered as being "like another student."[63]

The daily schedule and course requirements remained the same during the 1909–10 school year. All students studied diligently, attended chapel services before the first class, and were required to keep their rooms spotless. The boys performed their morning military drills and cared for the seminary's mules and buggy teams, and the girls continued to exercise twice a day.[64]

Unfortunately for the students, the coeducational seminary didn't last long. On the Sunday prior to the 1910 Easter weekend, the seminary students made their way to church in Tahlequah or Park Hill (they still attended the church of their choice) and during services the school burned to the ground. Rumors circulated that the fire was started accidentally by boys who were smoking in the cupola. Regardless of the cause of the blaze, the destruction of the Male Seminary left everyone involved with the school frustrated. Because the Cherokee Nation now had little control over its schools, no plans were made to rebuild the institution. Although the school term had to be terminated eight weeks early, the seven members of the graduating class still received their diplomas at Northeastern State Normal School. The underclassmen were obliged to attend other Oklahoma schools.[65]

The Northeastern State Normal School program accepted any student, male or female, Indian or white, who had completed the eighth grade. The course of study included four years of high school as well as two years of teacher training. Those who completed the two-year program were then qualified to teach in the Oklahoma public school system. By 1919, the curriculum of the school had expanded to provide students with opportunities to earn bachelor's degrees. Although no official name change was approved by the Oklahoma state legislature, by 1925 the school was commonly referred to as Northeastern State Teachers College, and on 21 March 1939, the state legislature changed the name to Northeastern State College. In 1941 the Oklahoma State System of Higher Education was created, with authority over Northeastern State College and other state institutions of higher education.[66]

The curriculum as well as the size of the campus continued to expand, and after 1950 Northeastern State College offered graduate programs in the fields of education, liberal arts, business, and optometry. On 4 May 1974, the Board of Regents for Oklahoma Colleges changed the institution's name to Northeastern Oklahoma State University. During the administration of university president Roger Webb (beginning 2 April 1978), the school became known as Northeastern State University, but this change was not made official until the next decade.[67]

Years after she graduated from the Female Seminary in 1880, Nannie Catherine Daniel (Fite) expressed her hope that the thorough education she had received at the seminary would continue to be available for others, and that the school's "volume of usefullness be increased and enriched as it flows down the remote future." Although she reminded her fellow tribespeople that "the sun has set forever"[68] on her alma mater, the quality of education offered at the seminary did indeed set a precedent for the future Northeastern State University.

The course of study at the Cherokee Female Seminary was stringent, but as the next chapter illustrates, the students' lives were not filled only with work. Their seminary experiences gave pupils the opportunity to interact with classmates and townspeople outside of their own socioeconomic class.

5

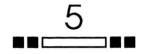

Life at the Seminary:
1876 – 1909

What was life like at the seminary? Did all the students enjoy their boarding-school experience? It is clear that the young seminarians were not denied their creativity nor were they isolated from the outside communities. Numerous events such as concerts, May anniversary celebrations, weddings, church services — even the public examinations — highlighted each academic year, giving students opportunities to meet new people and to expand their cultural horizons.

Students looked forward to spring and to the special May and June events — particularly the celebration that commemorated the first opening of the Female Seminary and the weeklong festivities that closed each year. The girls who could afford new dresses were eager to wear them, and all girls were anxious to visit with boys from the Male Seminary and to miss classes when possible. Concerts and other programs were held at this time to raise money for various projects, for example, to buy an organ, a piano, or other instruments for the school's music classes. A benefit tea party in 1883 raised enough money for the salary of an elocution teacher for the next school year.[1]

Since the roads near the school were not paved, a boardwalk was constructed that led from the seminary into town. Once every two weeks, teachers accompanied the high-school girls to Tahlequah to visit the ice cream "saloon," the opera house, or the art galleries. Students shopped at the mercantile stores, such as Sharp's Dry Goods, Winder's Store, or Richards and McSpadden's, but they were steered clear of the race track, the pool hall, and the Cherokee National Prison, where the gallows stood in plain view. In addition to shopping at the various stores and attending cultural events such as the popular Male Seminary orchestra concerts, they could roller skate at a rink for fifteen cents an hour or have their photographs taken in the town's portrait studio. The teachers also took time from their work to dine in Tahlequah and to socialize with the instructors from the Male Seminary.[2]

Students spent much of their time strolling around the grounds and nearby woods, playing tennis and basketball, and reading at Big Spring near the edge of the campus. Each evening, except Sunday, they received their mail, and on Saturdays they walked to the Illinois River or to nearby Natural Chimney Rock to collect flowers for their rooms. Eva Dameron (Uhle), an alumna, recalled that one afternoon the girls decided to play football, but because so many of them were bruised in the game they never played it again. Once a semester, the senior girls were allowed to invite their girlfriends from town to the seminary for an elegant dinner and to visit past the regular bedtime. Several students who attended the seminary in 1906 fondly remember dancing to the music of Nancy Woodall's mandolin in the Cookson sisters' room until the 9:00 P.M. curfew on Saturday nights and then continuing their conversations in the quiet of their lamp-lit closets. But despite the love for the school and the teachers that many students felt, a month before Christmas and summer vacations they started packing, and they talked incessantly about going home.[3]

The end of each school week was known as Sweet Friday because of the weekly spelling matches, events that were eagerly anticipated by the girls. Teams were chosen by student leaders and the girls assembled in the chapel, where the sides lined up facing each other. The competition was keen, for the students prided themselves on their ability to spell. At the end of each semester, the names of all students with at least a 90 percent average in all classes, including "domestic work" such as sewing, were listed on the honor roll in the *Cherokee Advocate*. The newspaper also printed short essays by students, and pupils such as Tennessee "Tinnie" Steele, who had an essay published in the *Baltimore Herald*, were also mentioned in the *Advocate*.[4]

The girls looked forward to the seminary's annual plays, since they took place at Tahlequah's Opera House—also the site of the Male Seminary's "oratory contests" (debates). The 1907 spring production was *A Midsummer Night's Dream*, and students designed and made the costumes, props, and scenery. The teachers traveled to Dallas, Texas, and Kansas City, Missouri, to get ideas for the presentation, and during the school year the girls and teachers "lived, ate, and absolutely memorized Shakespeare." The audience consisted of a thousand Indians from the Choctaw Nation's Wheelock Academy and from the Cherokee Nation.[5] Girls from more traditional families were able to show their talents, but in doing so they represented all the Cherokee girls. In the fall of 1903, representatives from the World's Fair in St. Louis requested "handicrafts" from the seminary girls for its American Indian display. The Board of Education paid for the materials, but only the few girls who were skilled in beadwork, pointlace, or basketry (usually the fullbloods) were able to spend all their time working on the project in the third-floor playroom ("Sleepy Holler"). Although they did not have to attend regular classes that year, they still had to pass their examinations to graduate. Those who failed had to take summer course work to receive credit.[6]

Cherokee dignitaries visited the seminary regularly. In 1899 the National Council members ate Thanksgiving dinner with the students (evidently the seminarians had no objection to the holiday) and periodically the council brought prominent individuals from outside the Cherokee Nation to see the school. In 1907, when Charles M. Haskell visited Tahlequah during his campaign for the governorship of the new state of Oklahoma, he accepted a dinner invitation at the seminary. Always accommodating, the girls wore their finest dresses and greeted him with the rousing jingle, "Haskell, Haskell, he's our man; If I can't vote, my sweetheart can!"[7]

The graduation activities for both seminaries were quite elaborate. Weeks prior to the celebration, the *Advocate* advertised the event so that everyone interested in attending could make plans. The activities usually lasted a week, with different events scheduled each evening. The final night of the 1877 festivities was typical. A large group of visitors gathered to hear some "well-delivered" compositions by students Mattie Bell, Belle Nicholson, and Nancy Robertson. The Park Hill Seminary (Female Seminary) Glee Club sang songs such as "Over There," "Cantilena," and "Reuben and Rachel." Another student, Margaret "Maggie" Hicks (Stapler), recited "The New Church Organ," and prominent Cherokee dignitaries gave speeches. An abundance of foods— meats, pies, cakes, and lemonade—was available for everyone, courtesy of the seminaries and townspeople. Steamboats, such as the *Ada*

Archer (named after a seminary student), took guests for short rides on the Illinois River. Those attending also had the option of promenading or playing sports. At other commencements, visitors attended church services, recitals, plays, and programs consisting of vocal solos, dances, instrumentals, and dramatic soliloquies.[8]

Hannah Worcester Hicks, one of Samuel Worcester's daughters, years later recalled one of the anniversary celebrations that took place at a 7 May observance:

> On one anniversary which I particularly remember, the large hall and parlor were beautifully decorated, and fragrant with perfume from great bunches of lovely wild pink azalea or bush honeysuckle. The military band from Fort Gibson was on hand that day, through the courtesy of General Belknap, Post Commander at that time. The exercises of the day included a most entertaining performance, the crowning of a May Queen. . . . It was a beautiful ceremony; distant music was heard, and as the sounds came near, a troop of young ladies appeared, all in lovely light dresses, escorting their Queen, singing as they marched and gathered around the throne (a bower of vines and flowers) and the Maid of Honor placed the crown (of lovely roses) on her head. In the afternoon when the exercises in the house were over, the band stationed themselves out in the blackjack woods back of the building, and the company, gentlemen and ladies in pairs, promenaded round and round to the music of the band, to their hearts' content. . . .[9]

The 1885 May party took place on Friday, 15 May. Both seminaries and the other schools of Tahlequah participated in the celebration. Attended by over seven hundred people, the party included music and singing as well as the crowning of May Queen Annie Trainer and Seminary Queen Olive Heath. This was followed by a Maypole dance and dinner with a "bountiful supply of delicacies." In 1892, the *Fort Smith Elevator* reported that after a concert at the Male Seminary, the festivity was so lively that many celebrants did not get back to Tahlequah until after midnight, "and we know of some, by Georgia, who had to walk back."[10]

The administrators made certain that the Female Seminary's final graduation festivities in spring 1909 were memorable. The elaborate weeklong activities began with a baccalaureate service at the Lyric Theatre featuring scripture reading as well as choral music by Beethoven and Gounod. The next evening was highlighted by the joint session of the Minervian Society and Germane Sodales in the seminary chapel, followed by the junior class performing the German play *A Treasure for the House.* Students also presented instrumental recitals of works by Chopin, Schumann, and von Suppe. The evening prior to commencement, students recited Tennyson's poem "The Princess."[11]

On graduation night, 27 May, after music and an address given by the superintendent of Indian schools, John Downing Benedict, the ten graduates received their diplomas from the Representative of Cherokee Schools, Albert Sydney Wyly (an 1890 graduate of the Male Seminary).[12] Always pragmatic, the teachers made certain their students left the seminary with a useful message. The last words on the commencement calendar read:

A sacred burden is this life ye bear,
Look on it, lift it, bear it solemnly,
Stand up and walk beneath it steadfastly,
Fail not for sorrow, falter not for sin,
But onward, upward, till the goal ye win.[13]

The beginning of each school year was a time of happy reunion for teachers and students, who had not seen one another all summer. If the girls' parents arrived with them, their fathers camped in the nearby grove of trees. During the school year, the students' female relatives were permitted to stay in the seminary for short visits, but no one else was allowed to spend the night in the building.[14]

While there were many opportunities for the students to enjoy themselves, they still had to obey rules first set forth by Florence Wilson. As at Mount Holyoke, discipline was administered through a demerit system that punished offenders by denying them certain privileges. Wilson was unquestionably a strict disciplinarian. Even one demerit a week could prevent a student from visiting her parents on the weekend or from participating in ball games, receptions, or shopping trips to Tahlequah. An offender might also be excluded from attending political rallies, church activities, or picnics. These punishments were doubly painful because students from the Male Seminary usually attended such functions.[15]

The 2 March 1881 edition of the *Advocate* published the seminary's "Rules of Student Conduct," which featured the demerit system. Most of the "crimes" were typical juvenile offenses such as tardiness, whispering during study hour, writing on the walls, exchanging notes during class, keeping dormitory lights on after 9:00 P.M., or leaving dormitory rooms during "still hour each Sunday." Students complained most frequently about being forbidden to "congregate or loiter" in the kitchen or the halls, or to laugh and play in the building. In an effort to teach the girls the importance of responsibility, they were not allowed to borrow money, jewelry, or clothing from others. This was deemed so important that a visiting minister delivered an entire sermon on the evils of "borrowing plumage." Students were punished for gossiping or speaking poorly of their families, but those who apologized for lying were usually forgiven and received no demerits.[16]

If a student received too many demerits, she could be suspended or expelled. Except for one fullblood student who was permanently excused for trying to set fire to the school in protest of the "white atmosphere"[17] and another who was caught kissing the cook (a black man),[18] mandatory expulsion was rare. In 1907, a few girls were each given seventy-five demerits and were temporarily suspended for secretly meeting with Male Seminary students in the nearby field known as Seven-Acre Pasture.[19]

Principal Wilson was adamant about keeping "her girls" away from seminary boys, and older students particularly resented the rules limiting contacts with the male students. Alumna Josephine Alice Crutchfield (Dale) later recalled that while attending football and baseball games at the Male Seminary, Wilson even ordered the girls to "Stay in the wagon! If every hairpin falls out of your hair, let it go! Stay in the wagon!"[20]

Obviously, contacts between male and female students were closely supervised. If a girl wrote a letter to a student at the Male Seminary, it was intercepted before it left the building, never to reach its destination. No "dates" were allowed, but if a boy wanted to spend time with a Female Seminary student after the monthly literary or musical recitals, the couple could sit in the parlor for an hour, provided a chaperone was in the room. Male seminarians often serenaded the girls at night and all girls were allowed to listen at their windows, providing that they did not converse with the singers. Boys often sent girls long-stemmed roses, and at graduation time there were so many flowers they had to be kept in bathtubs. Several students eloped with male seminarians, but because security was so strict at the Female Seminary, their peers speculated that the nuptial plans must have been made during Christmas or summer vacations.[21]

One afternoon a month, boys were allowed to visit their sisters and cousins, but new "blood relationships" could not be invented because of Principal Wilson's knowledge of Cherokee genealogy. The male seminarians were so eager to socialize with the females that they even put an advertisement in the *Advocate* saying that "we would accept an invitation [to visit the Female Seminary] at almost any date . . . provided we do not receive any demerits during the week" (the Male Seminary also had a demerit system).[22]

Not surprisingly, the girls believed that Principal Wilson disliked the seminary boys. On those nights that the boys serenaded the girls, Wilson often walked quietly past the girls' rooms in her stocking feet and lay down on a hall table and listened to their conversations. Wilson was indeed careful when it came to the seminary boys, but she never told the girls exactly why. Lola Garrett (Bowers), a former student, recalled that "nobody talked much about morals—until 'something' happened." Those "somethings" remain a mystery, but no cases of pregnancy, at least, have been located in any of the files of the principals or the medical superintendents.[23]

After the two seminaries combined in the fall of 1909, both male and female students lived in the same building, so all activities were closely monitored. Female instructors made certain their girls never strayed onto the second floor. Because boys and girls were in the same classes, older students were able to interact more, but they were not allowed to date—or according to one student, they were allowed to date as long as they did not get caught. Younger students had an opportunity to mingle during the daily two-hour recreational period.[24]

Wilson disliked smoking and would have expelled any student caught with tobacco. But her niece, Dora Wilson Hearon, discovered four offenders in their rooms one Sunday night in 1896. The girls had begged cigars from a worker at the seminary, but because all four were too ill from smoking even to sit up, Hearon decided that they had learned their lesson and did not report them to her aunt.[25]

Although the girls were allowed a limited variety of clothes for classes, they took pride in their appearance, and every evening before lights-out they selected an outfit for the next day. Styles ranged from "Mother Hubbard" dresses of red-and-white or blue-and-white calico, worn with plain white aprons, to navy, black, or cream skirts with white long-sleeved, high-collared blouses. During the colder months the girls wore dresses and petticoats of wool, and laced brogan shoes. On their daily walks, they wore hats or carried parasols, and while in town they wore sweaters emblazoned with the monogrammed letters

CNFS (Cherokee National Female Seminary). For church services, students were required to wear blue serge jacket suits, white middy blouses with blue ties, and black mortar-board caps. In contrast to the changing uniforms of the students, the attire of Principal Wilson remained basically the same for twenty-five years: black or gray chambray or gingham dresses with white collars and cuffs and matching hats.[26]

The students primped and fussed with their hair for hours. Many wore fashionable buns or pompadours, and in 1892 the *Advocate* reported that the latest fad at the school was "shingled hair." Some girls favored bangs, which they curled with slate pencils heated over lamp chimneys. One student, Fannie Blythe (Marks), later recalled that the hot pencils often left the girls' foreheads "branded," a telltale sign to their teachers that they had been preening, not studying.[27]

Although the rules and regulations did not say so, students were not allowed to attend class unless their hair was neatly combed. On one rare occasion, Principal Wilson sent Florence Williams (Edmondson) to her room to repair her "rag-tag and bob-ends." The girl returned with her hair parted in the middle and slicked back into a tight bun — an exact replica of Principal Wilson's severe hairstyle ("so tight and slick you could see yourself in it") — and for once Wilson let her pupils see her laugh.[28]

For special events and photographs, students were allowed to wear evening gowns of their choice, but Wilson disapproved of the girls wearing attention-getting corsets and hoop skirts. Affluent parents bought or made party dresses for their daughters, but some girls preferred to create their own "dream dresses" in sewing class with materials they bought. The poorer girls and orphans had to settle for wearing their regular school uniforms.[29]

The destruction of the seminary in 1887 disrupted the girls' lives. Although many of them left to attend other schools and did not enroll in the new school when it reopened in 1889, a number of them were on hand to participate in the ground-breaking ceremonies for the new structure. The laying of the new seminary cornerstone was accompanied by a series of "imposing ceremonies." Witnessed by almost two thousand residents of the Cherokee Nation, a procession marched through Tahlequah led by the town's brass band. It was followed by representatives of the Masonic Lodge of Indian Territory and by the students of the Male Seminary, the Tahlequah public schools, and the mission schools. Principal Chief Joel B. Mayes, Colonel William Potter Ross, and Assistant Chief Samuel Smith gave speeches, and "Russian Prince" Edwin V. Dolozorouki, the Female Seminary's music instructor and a veteran of the Crimean War, directed the seminary chorus.[30]

Not all the students enjoyed their tenures at the seminary. While many of the indigent girls were initially grateful to be able to work to attend the seminary, it did not take long for them to develop feelings of resentment, inferiority, and alienation. In the late 1880s, for example, the National Council allowed English-speaking mixed-bloods to enroll in the primary grades, which were formally reserved for those children from the "Cherokee-speaking class." As a result of this new enrollment, many children of one-half or more Cherokee blood were from four to as many as ten years older than their more progressive peers in the same grades. Since most fullbloods and some poor mixed-bloods worked for their room and board, they were exiled to the third floor with the primary students. Because they were often behind academically, many were also placed in classes with the younger girls, and some were no doubt embarrassed when they were required to read aloud. The older indigent girls who lived on the third floor were left behind on social excursions because only those in the high-school grades were allowed to attend events in Tahlequah and such activities as the male seminarians' ballgames. Unlike the pupils whose parents sent them spending money, the indigents were unable to afford party clothes, nor could they buy after-dinner snacks from local vendors—also a social occasion. Not surprisingly, many of these students only stayed at the seminary for a short time.[31]

The attitudes of some of the teachers also led to resentment among many fullbloods. The National Council employed many qualified white and mixed-blood instructors. A number of the latter were seminary alumnae and none were traditional Cherokee teachers.[32] Despite the instructors' sympathies for the traditional girls, they rarely understood the problems the fullbloods faced. In 1908, for example, Albert Sydney Wyly, a mixed-blood who was then seminary superintendent, expressed his impatience with the fullblood girls by referring to the mixed-bloods as "whiter" and therefore "more intellectual." He criticized the fullbloods for their "pathetic attachment to home," and remarked patronizingly that at least they possessed "a great deal of artistic ability."[33]

Other teachers were also insensitive to the problems of the traditional pupils. In 1895, Dora Wilson Hearon noted that she took the third-floor inspection duty because the other teachers were repelled by the students' head lice.[34] In 1907, prior to the school's first rehearsal of the annual Shakespeare production (*A Midsummer Night's Dream*), a mixed-blood senior responded to the administration's observation, "Fullblood girls to do Shakespeare? Impossible!" by saying, "You don't know [teachers] Miss Allen and Miss Minta Foreman!" implying that these instructors were indeed miracle workers.[35] It is likely that during preparations of these productions, the fullbloods and darker mixed-bloods felt stress because of their appearance. For example, Florence Waters (1/16 Cherokee blood) was told by a lighter-skinned classmate that she could not participate in the elocution class's production of *The Peri* because, as the girl explained, "Angels are fair-haired and you are too dark for an angel."[36]

The teachers also relentlessly reinforced the importance of learning and retaining the values of white society. At the same time, they repressed Cherokee values, thereby causing confusion among the more traditional students. Instructor Kate O'Donald Ringland later recalled that according to seminary philosophy, "anything 'white' was ideal,"[37] and an alumna remembered learning in the primary grades that the "white way was the only acceptable way."[38] DeWitt Clinton Duncan, an alumnus of the Male Seminary, spoke for his fellow National Council members in a lengthy *Cherokee Advocate* diatribe by asking, "Can the mental wants of an Indian youth be satisfied . . . by resources less fruitful than that which caters to the Anglo-Saxon mind? The Cherokee language, at the present advanced period of their [Cherokee] civilization, cannot meet the exigencies of our people."[39]

Students and teachers also took every opportunity to flaunt their white ancestry at the expense of the fullbloods. For example, in 1889 Spencer Seago Stephens, superintendent of the Female Seminary, proclaimed that "it is the white blood that has made us what we are. . . . if missionaries wish to lift up Indian tribes let them encourage inter-marriage with whites." Not confident that the Cherokees could obtain a high level of civilization by themselves, he asserted that along with education, "intermarriage will accomplish the purpose quickly."[40]

Commentary from Cherokee citizens who shared Stephens's belief in the positive influence of associating with whites appeared in the *Advocate*. A writer who signed himself "Cherokee" observed that "the gloom that pervades the red man's mind is fast disappearing: instead of darkness and doubt, his countenance is being lit up with intelligence." And to imply that the traditionalists of the tribe were perhaps heathenistic compared to their progressive peers, he further asserted that "those who cling with death-like tenacity to our old rites and ceremonies do not consider that a moral change is taking place in the [Cherokee] world."[41]

Interestingly, many of the acculturated alumnae would later embellish their seminary stories by claiming that they did not have any duties because the fullbloods did all the work for them, including cooking and cleaning. These assertions are false, for all seminarians were required to perform daily chores. While many girls did indeed have to work for tuition, there is a big difference between a wage-earning job and laboring for classmates. Even though these tales were not always true, the stories correctly imply that there were class distinctions at the school and that there was not much difference between the way a white woman might look at a woman of color and the way elitist seminarians viewed their "unenlightened" classmates.

With the National Council advocating white education, and many of the teachers and students commenting that perhaps traditional Cherokee culture was backward, the traditionalists were continually pressured to adopt a different culture if they wanted to attend the seminary. One mixed-blood student commented in her memoirs that life at the seminary was "quite normal." But normal for whom? The acculturated seminarians, like those in the 1850s, never acknowledged that perhaps the "backward" traditionalists valued their culture and did not want to lose it.[42]

In this respect, the Cherokee Female Seminary was similar to the federal boarding schools and some mission schools, and the negative impact of the seminary upon some of its students was much the same as the impact of the federal schools on children of other tribes. The major problems for the Indians who were forced to attend federal schools (and the traditional Cherokees who opted to attend the seminary) included their inability to communicate with teachers because of language differences, a lack of parental involvement and support, and the loss of contact with their culture. They missed the tribal stories, religion, and dances, and the ties with the elders of the tribe who taught its myths and legends. Insecurity was compounded by teachers and administrators who assumed they knew the students' needs and capabilities. Whereas the federal boarding schools were controlled by white Americans, the Female Seminary was controlled by Cherokees who subscribed to the values of white Americans.[43]

The seminary differed from the federal schools, however, in that children from many different tribes attended federal and mission schools at the same time, often resulting in pan-Indian identities. Also, at the seminary many students did not feel the loss of certain tribal customs— if they ever adhered to them in the first place. For many students, life at the seminary was not a great contrast to their home life. Unlike students at some federal and mission schools, Cherokee girls were not forced to attend the seminary; it was an option for the citizens of the Cherokee Nation (as long as they could afford it). Those students who did not like the curriculum or philosophy were not punished for it. They did not have to enroll, nor did they have to stay.

The fullblood and traditional girls were not simply passive recipients of whatever education they could get. Some of the more acculturated fullblood girls enrolled at the seminary were from families who could afford the tuition and were thus able to live with the mixed-bloods on the second floor, thereby elevating their status. Over the years, at least 160 fullbloods were enrolled in the seminary—about 9.6 percent of the seminary population—and they stayed an average of four semesters per girl, two semesters longer than the mixed-bloods, but five semesters less than all graduates.[44] This was probably because girls of the same family attended school together, which helped to alleviate homesickness. Many of them did not speak Cherokee nor did they have any interest in traditional Cherokee customs. As one alumna recalled, the "fullbloods went to Tahlequah to become like the white folk,"[45] and many of their families had succeeded in achieving this goal. These children came to the seminary armed with the knowledge of white society that was necessary to enable them to function among their acculturated peers, and many were even adopted into the "big happy seminary family," a phrase used by a mixed-blood (1/32 Cherokee blood) to refer to the upper echelons of the student hierarchy.[46]

Even the darker-skinned students participated in the seminary's productions in blackface, productions that poked fun at blacks. Although blacks were given property and citizenship within the Cherokee Nation by the 1866 treaty, separation of the Cherokee and black races remained in effect, as did the separation of whites and blacks in other parts of the country. Children of the freedmen could attend only the "Negro High School" (also known as the "Colored High School") or the few primary schools established for blacks, and the only blacks allowed at the seminaries were the workers, such as the cooks, laborers, and dishwashers. Indeed one male seminarian later referred to a black man as a "nigger." Prior to the Civil War, highly acculturated mixed-bloods strived to imitate whites (often with all their prejudices), and traditionalists associated slavery with the progressive Cherokees. But the subjugation of the blacks within the Cherokee society gave even some of the poor, darker-skinned students (whose parents often were anti-slavery and frequently were themselves subjugated by other Cherokees) an opportunity to feel superior to another race, to feel equal to the dominant white race, and to identify with the progressive culture within their own tribe. The separation of the red and black races at the behest of the Cherokees demonstrated that many Cherokees—traditionalists and progressives alike—needed to prove their superiority over blacks in order to keep from being lumped into the category of "people of color" along with the former slaves.

At the same time that whites deemed Indian peoples to be inferior beings who stood in the way of the expanding industrial, "civilized" society, many progressive Cherokees viewed their fellow Cherokees as their inferiors and as impediments to achieving their goal of a new, "enlightened" Cherokee Nation that would be comprised of the best elements of white society. The Cherokee Female Seminary, attended by students with varying cultural attitudes and appearances but dominated by progressives, mirrored the goals, aspirations, and world view of many members of the tribe's progressive leadership.

6

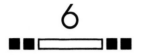

Medicine for the Rosebuds:
Health Care at the Seminary

The seminarians and other Cherokees were in better mental and physical condition than most tribes in the United States in the second half of the nineteenth century. They were certainly much healthier than their contemporaries among many of the less acculturated tribes of western Indian Territory and Oklahoma, such as the Cheyennes, Arapahos, Kiowas, and Comanches. Cherokees suffered from diseases such as malaria, measles, and smallpox, the latter two acquired through contact with whites. Yet because they had been subjected to more contact with whites than most other tribes, they also had probably developed more immunities to viral illness, which did not have the same devastating impact upon them as upon other tribes.

The seminary's teachers and students were aware of the need for healthful living and were dedicated to exercise and hygiene. Each day, students fastidiously cleaned the areas most often open to inspection — the kitchen, parlor, and classrooms — and teachers wearing white gloves examined the private rooms of the students. The scrubbed floors, polished banisters, manicured lawns, and formal flower beds all reflected the institution's devotion to order and cleanliness, primary virtues of late-nineteenth-century American life. But despite the tidy conditions, students suffered from a number of recurring health problems. The seminary was filled to capacity almost every school year from 1876 to 1909, and the crowded living conditions, combined with a flood-prone basement and an unreliable heating system, threatened to undermine the health of both students and teachers.

Little is known about the students' health care until 1876 because of lack of documentation. After that time, however, physicians left behind detailed reports of their patients. Medical records indicate that after 1876, most of the pupils and school personnel at the female and male seminaries were afflicted with virtually the same ailments, such as "intermitting and remitting fevers" and digestive disorders. Also prevalent each school year were headaches, catarrh, tonsillitis, rheumatism, neuralgia, scrofula, jaundice, earache, colic, bronchitis, ulcers, "sore eyes," "skin eruptions," and what was delicately described as the "class of ailments peculiar to the sex in attendance." Cases of head lice were widespread among the fullblood primary pupils, who often brought the problem with them from home. Despite the large numbers of students who suffered from homesickness and who were the victims of prejudice, only a few cases of "hysteria" were reported, and no students were listed as depressed.[1]

Diseases that erupted in the Cherokee Nation at large often spread to the seminary. School workers who did not live at the school, such as cooks, laundresses, repairmen, and woodcutters, often exposed students to infections brought from the outside. Students also became infected by their families during vacations, or by visitors to the seminary.

Between 1876 and 1909, more than twenty students and teachers died at the seminary from measles, pneumonia, typhoid fever, or smallpox, while hundreds of other students experienced less serious health problems. Many ill students had to leave school to recover at home, and others suffered injuries severe enough to cause them to withdraw from the institution. In stark contrast to the usual daily banter at the seminary, quiet descended on the school whenever a student or teacher died, as black horses pulling a wagon draped in black came to take the body into Tahlequah.[2]

In 1882 and again in 1901, smallpox spread across the Cherokee Nation; although students had been vaccinated, many still contracted the disease.[3] Typhoid was prevalent at the seminary in 1884 and 1889. During the spring of 1884, a severe outbreak of scabies, known as "The Itch," almost caused administrators to close the school. To prevent a recurrence of this highly contagious parasitic skin infection, officials placed a renewed emphasis on cleanliness, and no cases were reported during the next school year.[4]

The impressive Female Seminary building was a source of pride to the Cherokee people, but its construction probably contributed to the students' health problems. When the seminary reopened in 1872, after the damage sustained during the Civil War had been repaired, the hospital rooms proved inadequate. Sick-rooms were small, and two or more ill students often had to share a single bed. When epidemics erupted, the infirmaries became overcrowded, noisy, and unsanitary. The insufficient space meant that some ill students were confined to their dorm rooms, thereby spreading infections to their healthy room-mates.[5]

Heeding the suggestions of the seminary superintendent, the Reverend T. M. Rights, in 1876 the Cherokee Board of Trustees of High Schools added an infirmary to the second floor of the seminary building. This alleviated the crowded conditions somewhat, but only for students in grades one through eight. No accommodations were available for the high-school students, who continued to be cared for in their living quarters. During the spring months of 1877, a measles epidemic forced the seminary staff to transform classrooms into makeshift infirmaries.[6]

Traditional Cherokee doctors were never invited to attend to the students, and there are no reports indicating that pupils left school to participate in ceremonies for health reasons. Instead, during the seminary's early years, the National Council hired university-trained physicians from Tahlequah on a case-by-case basis. A permanent physician was not appointed to serve the seminary until 1876, after improvements had been made on the building and enough funds were available to secure an additional staff member. In December 1876, the council and the principal chief, Charles Thompson, appointed Walter Thompson Adair, a mixed-blood physician, as medical superintendent of the male and female seminaries.[7] As required by law, Adair was both a citizen of the Cherokee Nation and a "regular graduate of some reputable medical institution"—in this case the St. Louis Medical College. Adair was, in fact, the first Cherokee to graduate from medical school.[8] During the Civil War he had served as staff surgeon in Stand Watie's Cherokee Confederate command and later as chief surgeon of the First Indian Division.[9]

Adair's work at the Female Seminary was particularly demanding. The young women needed "special attentions," and despite aid from a robust nurse known as "Aunt Cynthia," their modesty sometimes limited Adair's ability to perform examinations. Also, Cherokee law stipulated that the cost of any therapeutics used to treat his patients must come out of his salary. His varied responsibilities also included a multitude of nonmedical duties, such as repairing doors and locks.[10]

Although Adair already had a busy schedule, on 18 November 1880 the Cherokee National Council augmented his duties by appointing him supervisor of medical care at the Cherokee National Prison in Tahlequah and at the Cherokee Asylum for the Deaf, Dumb, Blind, and Insane in Grand Saline, six miles to the south. His peers also elected him president of the Board of Medical Examiners in the Cherokee Nation. Adair's salary was $1,500 per year, but he was still required to pay for any medicines he used. The relentless pace left him exhausted and "financially embarrassed." He supported his family from the same salary, and since he was not supplied with lodging, he had to pay for his own accommodations. By contrast, the principals of the seminaries received only $700 per annum (down $100 from their 1850s salary), but they were provided with room, board, and medical care.[11]

Because of his busy schedule, Adair was not always immediately on hand for emergencies, and accidents were common among students and teachers. One year, for example, a heated chafing dish exploded in the face of a visiting music teacher who was dyeing her hair, and occasionally the students' coal-oil lamps blew up. Until Adair arrived to take care of any emergency, seminary personnel provided first aid as best they could. Deep cuts were sutured with needle and thread by the home economics teachers. One spring night in 1881, a student at the Female Seminary dislocated her shoulder and hip in a fall from a second-story window while sleepwalking. The music instructor, Narcissa Owen, reduced the luxated shoulder, but neither she nor Adair, who came the next day, realized the full extent of the girl's injuries. The student was left permanently crippled because of her untreated hip.[12]

Traditional Cherokee medicines were not used at the seminary, but home remedies occasionally proved successful when the physician was not available. In the winter of 1880, when a student developed pneumonia and became delirious with fever, Owen and her niece, Lelia Breedlove, who was also a teacher, prepared a concoction consisting of mashed raw potatoes mixed with hot water and (because the ground outside was frozen) dirt from a potted plant. This "potato poultice" was applied to the girl's chest for several hours, and by morning her fever was gone.[13]

A dedicated physician, Adair attempted to discover and eliminate the causes of diseases afflicting his patients. He attributed the various fevers to "blood poisoning," caused by either septic matter or "poisonous effluvia" in the atmosphere that "entered through the epidermis and mucous membranes" of the students and into the blood, "giving rise to typhoid fever." He concluded that the culprit was a hidden cesspool around or beneath the seminary building. Determined to find and eradicate the source of what he termed "the gentleman" (noxious effluence), Adair located and repaired a broken water pipe under the first-floor parlor. The council provided funds for improved drainage and ordered the medical superintendent to submit a monthly report regarding sanitary conditions at the school.[14]

Doctor Adair was especially concerned about malarial outbreaks. Like most physicians of the era, he believed malaria was carried by musty, foul-smelling air associated with standing water. He declared the flood-prone basement the prime suspect in the "accumulation of dampness" and the consequent "circulation of malaria." In particular he pointed to the overworked laundry. He thought that the dampness caused by "soap-sud evaporation" leaking through the small spaces in the first floor must be the source of the disease. As a safeguard, he requested that the laundry be moved to a separate site. While he defended his "soap-sud" theory, Adair finally acknowledged that students from homes located near "large water course areas, low lands and prairie lands" could have brought the malarial infection with them.[15]

Adair also believed that a possible cause of the students' problems was lack of exercise. He asserted that studying more than six hours a day was "ruinous [because] the powers of the mind are sufficient to break down the energies of the body." He recommended more "flower-bed work" for the girls, but the principal of the seminary from 1875 to 1901, Ann Florence Wilson, took his advice a step farther. She required the students to take morning and afternoon walks, and on occasional evenings she held mandatory "physical culture drills" in the chapel, exercises that included toe touches and "waist twists." At noon, when the girls were dismissed from their morning classes, they were required to walk a certain distance and were penalized five demerits if they did not comply. In the spring, pupils regularly walked three and a half miles a day to collect wildflowers for their botany class. Students also played tennis and basketball. Since ministers from neighboring congregations frowned upon dancing, Wilson would not permit such activity, but she did encourage singing games and "rhythmic exercises" accompanied by music, which, the approving local preachers said, "made the girls look like angels." She sometimes added dance steps but prudently called such activities "exercise," not dancing.[16]

Although Adair was ever diligent in his work, he occasionally faced criticism from the families of his patients. In 1884, after eleven-year-old Susan Parris died of typhoid fever, her family accused Adair of "Malpractice, Insobriety and Culpable Negligence and Inattention." Adair responded that the charges came from those who were "conspiring my overthrow" or who wanted to "acquire my official place."[17] Supported by witnesses, he refuted the charge of insobriety, and he successfully defended himself and his prescribed treatments, which included mercurial purgation, turpentine emulsion, quinine, liniment massage, Dover's powder, spiced poultices, febrifuges, and hot whiskey toddies.[18] After his first experience, in an effort to protect himself from further charges of malpractice, Adair promptly notified a student's parents when their child became ill and gave them the opportunity to select a physician of their choice.[19]

Following the Parris incident, Adair defended the seminary's health conditions against some adverse public comment. He assured Principal Chief Dennis Bushyhead that the school was indeed a healthful facility and that both students and teachers were physically fit. The seminary was not, he asserted, a "clandestine, unsavory place blighting the vital spark" of those who lived there, and he elaborated upon the improvements in sanitation made during his tenure. The basements were clean and dry; repairs were promptly made; debris was removed daily by convicts of the Cherokee National Prison; and soap, water, and "elbow grease" were applied to every part of the building.[20]

Adair believed that the extreme mid-winter cold in the building caused almost all the pneumonia and other lung or throat ailments. He requested that the council provide dry wood for the dorm-room stoves and that a competent person be made available for the maintenance of the temperamental furnaces. With these measures in effect Adair predicted that the health of the students would continually improve. Despite his efforts and optimism, however, the incidence of illness remained basically unchanged.[21]

The completion of the new seminary building in 1889 was followed by changes in medical personnel. Adair resigned his position at the seminaries, the insane asylum, and the national prison to become superintendent of the Cherokee National Orphan Asylum in Grand Saline. He was replaced by another mixed-blood Cherokee, Dr. Joseph M. Thompson. The new medical superintendent had attended the Male Seminary, and had graduated from the Missouri Medical College (now Washington University) in St. Louis in 1889, the year he came to the seminary.[22]

Thompson found no serious illness during the first year after the Female Seminary reopened in 1889. He enthusiastically reported on the clean and well-ventilated rooms and the healthful combination of good food, clean water, and comfortable building temperature. He did note that the fruit and vegetable storerooms outside the Female Seminary subjected the foodstuffs to decay, but that at least the pantry was safely separated from the main building.[23]

Thompson departed three years later to study children's diseases in New York City. Isabel "Belle" Cobb, an 1879 seminary graduate who received her medical degree from the Women's Medical College of Pennsylvania in 1892, requested that she be considered for the position as either the new medical superintendent or the superintendent of the Female Seminary. She was correct, however, when she commented in her letter to Chief C. J. Harris that she doubted if any "of our [Cherokee] men were quite ready to propose a step like this [having a female medical superintendent]."[24]

Instead, the National Council hired Dr. Richard L. Fite, a graduate of the Southern Medical School in Atlanta. After his graduation in 1882, Fite had moved to Tahlequah to begin his practice. Two years later Fite married Nannie Catherine Daniel (an 1880 seminary graduate), which made him a citizen of the Cherokee Nation. In addition to his duties at the two seminaries, Fite attended to patients at the insane asylum and the national prison, and he also served one year as superintendent of the Cherokee Colored High School, six miles northwest of Tahlequah.[25]

Fite had to deal with numerous structural problems of the Female Seminary building. After only four years, parts of the new structure had begun to deteriorate. It was necessary to replace broken windows, repair holes in the iron roof, and purchase a new furnace after heavy rains flooded the basement. Since the fence surrounding the property had fallen into disrepair, hog and cattle droppings often littered the school grounds. The seminary sewage lines were cracked and could not carry the effluvia a sufficient distance from the school. Rainy weather proved disastrous, for the refuse overflowed into a small ditch that adjoined Tahlequah's water source. Not surprisingly, Fite treated numerous cases of chills, fever, diarrhea, and "La Grippe."[26]

Fite resigned in November 1897 and was succeeded by another Missouri Medical College graduate, Dr. Charles McClelland Ross. This twenty-three-year-old great-grandson of the former principal chief John Ross had graduated from the Male Seminary in 1887. Prior to his tenure as medical superintendent, Ross had shared a practice with Dr. Jesse Crary Bushyhead, son of Dennis Bushyhead, another former chief, until his office was destroyed during the Great Tahlequah Fire of 1895. Assisting Ross at the Female Seminary was Jennie Martin, a graduate of Howard-Payne College in Fayette, Missouri. Ross remained superintendent until 1908, when at age forty, he was electrocuted while crossing over a barbed-wire fence that touched a downed electrical line.[27]

Despite building maintenance and efforts by students, teachers, and "reservoir and tank cleaners" to keep their "modern house conveniences" in good repair, by 1900 the bathroom plumbing had deteriorated so badly that the washrooms were nailed shut. Everyone had to use the outhouses that were located beyond the domestic science department. Because the toilets were situated over running water, Ross reported the same potential hazardous cesspool problem that had concerned Dr. Adair fifteen years earlier.[28]

Although daily exercise had always been considered important, Ross's tenure as medical superintendent coincided with a renewed emphasis upon physical fitness. In addition to the daily walks and team sports, other activities were initiated. Visiting instructors from Chicago and St. Louis began teaching the "Del Mar System" of calisthenics, and Dora Wilson, a graduate of Drury College, introduced Grecian dances. Upon completion of morning constitutionals, students marched throughout the seminary halls accompanied by loud, uplifting music.[29]

The seminarians' diet also became more varied. Grocery receipts from stores in Tahlequah, St. Louis, Kansas City, Fayetteville, and Chicago indicate that students were served a variety of fruits, vegetables, grains, and meats, as well as eggs, butter, oil, sugar, and salt.[30] Parents of some of the students who lived near the seminary brought buttermilk, desserts, produce from their gardens, and fresh fish from the Illinois River to help pay the tuition for their daughters. By 1900, the administration was even concerned that some girls were overweight and began emphasizing a healthier diet.[31]

As a preventive measure, Principal Wilson administered a spoonful of sulphur and molasses to each student before she entered the dining hall every evening. Some students added to their caloric intake (and demerit tally) by cooking fudge or chicken over lanterns in their dorm-room closets in the middle of the night. Limited only by the amount of spending money their relatives sent them, many students bought hot bread, sugar cookies, salted nuts, suckers, chewing gum, and tamales from vendors who visited the seminary each evening after dinner, or from Winder's Store located near Hendrick's Spring at the base of the hill.[32]

Except for their consumption of excess fat, salt, and sugar, students were provided with what appears to be the best possible diet at the time, which helped them to avoid most ailments caused by vitamin or mineral deficiencies. However, "bowel complaint," constipation, and hemorrhoids were daily occurrences,[33] possibly because the food was cooked improperly, over-fried, or served in the wrong combinations or amounts. Perishables were stored in a cool cellar, but despite the pasteurization of milk, a lack of refrigeration in the early years of the seminary caused a form of "summer complaint" among students during the warm months.

Health problems were prevalent at the seminary, but most students were relatively healthy in comparison to other young Americans of those decades. Americans living in rural areas, especially in the South, often lived in poverty. They were not educated about basic sanitation practices and had no health-care programs available. Rural whites— and blacks—often depended upon inadequate home remedies. Many lived too far from medical help or could not afford a physician's services. In contrast to rural white children who were plagued by common health problems, students at the seminaries during the same time period were reportedly free of parasites, pellegra, diphtheria, and whooping cough. The concentrated student population at the school, however, contributed to the spread of such childhood diseases as measles and mumps as well as influenza and other respiratory ailments.

Cherokee seminary pupils enjoyed a wholesome diet, a regular exercise program, warm and dry housing, and "modern medical care." Reservation Indians, however, depended upon rations from the federal government that were often inadequate, had no exercise, lived in their own battered tipis or army barracks with leaking roofs, and received medical attention from physicians whose medicines were in short supply. The seminarians also were spared the emotional grief that reservation life engendered in tribes who were forced to give up their healthy way of life as hunters and who had to cope with the mental stress that came with a rapidly changing lifestyle. The seminarians had comparatively little sense of being confined, but if they did they could return to their familiar home environment, unlike reservation Indians who had nowhere else to go.[34]

7

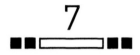

Farewell to the Seminary:
Graduates and Former Students

Over a period of thirty academic years, 212 students graduated from the Cherokee Female Seminary. Approximately forty graduates and nongraduates (young women who left the Female Seminary to attend other high schools) went on to attend colleges or universities, and half of those received degrees. But more than 2,770 girls did not graduate from the Female Seminary or from any other high school. Many left the seminary before they had completed their first semester, and some left after only one week. Why did they not stay to complete their tenure at the Cherokee school?

Many dropouts did have problems with the course of study, but not all of them were unable to master the difficult subjects. According to the student grade lists from 1876 to 1903 (none are available from the 1850s or the early 1870s), most students were able to cope with the Mount Holyoke–style curriculum. Prior to their enrollment in the Female Seminary, many had attended the Cherokee common schools, the Cherokee Orphan Asylum, one of the missionary schools, or high schools outside the Cherokee Nation, and they had reasonably good educational backgrounds.[1] In addition, many mixed-blood parents hired private tutors if their daughters had difficulty with their studies, or if the common-school teachers were incompetent.

The seminary graduates, of course, had made high grades (eighties to nineties) throughout their years at the school. Most of them were from the comparatively affluent areas of the Nation, near Tahlequah, which enabled them to visit their families more often than students from remote areas.[2] Many of the graduates were related to one another and, like the fullbloods, had attended the school at the same time as their relatives, which helped to combat homesickness.[3] And, like successful students today, the girls who performed best had received encouragement from their literate parents. Of the parents whose records could be examined, graduates' fathers had a 98 percent literacy rate, and their mothers, 100 percent, compared to the 82 percent and 86 percent literacy rates of the nongraduates' fathers and mothers, respectively. Most of the fullbloods' parents could not write in English, and just 50 percent of their fathers and 51 percent of their mothers could read. It is noteworthy that not all the white fathers who married Cherokee women could read, yet often their fullblood wives could.[4]

Most seminary students who dropped out after one semester, however, still made medium to high grades (seventies to nineties). These dropouts usually left because of personal illness, the illness of a family member, their impending marriage, or homesickness. Other disruptions, such as the seminary's closure in 1856, the destructive fire in 1887, the departure of Principal Wilson in 1901, and the creation of Northeastern State Normal School in 1909, caused students to enroll in other schools. In 1893, several girls voluntarily went home because of the crowded living conditions. In 1902, because of the increased prosperity of the Nation's farmers, a "large force" was necessary to harvest crops, so many students returned to the farm to do the "home work."[5] As previously stated, a large number of these dropouts (except for those who married immediately) enrolled in and graduated from other institutions. Although some academic careers were interrupted by such things as the Civil War, the destruction of the school by fire, smallpox epidemics, and the availability of other educational opportunities, no student—not even any of the graduates (many of whom enrolled for more than ten semesters)—remained at the seminary from first grade through graduation.[6]

Dropouts who made low grades (fifty or below) were in the minority. They often left soon after enrolling (sometimes within the first day or month). These girls were usually (but not always) traditional fullbloods or mixed-bloods of one-half to three-quarters Cherokee blood who had attended distant Cherokee-speaking common schools and were not prepared for the difficult curriculum or the oppressive "white atmosphere" of the school. Some of the girls who withdrew from school were put off by the factionalism they found there. Political discussions at the school had the potential to become quite volatile since female relatives of members of the Treaty Party, the Ross faction, and the traditional Keetoowah Society were in attendance at the same time.[7]

Many students left the school to become agriculturists, but others had a profound interest in the whites' more lucrative businesses. Because many of their parents and siblings owned and operated stores in Tahlequah or other parts of the Cherokee Nation, the girls had already developed the confidence to pursue careers in the business world and were not afraid to interact with whites. In addition, many of the more progressive girls came from families who had hired help to perform domestic chores, which allowed the daughters to set their sights on other kinds of work. Unlike the agricultural training that Indian students received at schools such as the Chilocco Indian Agricultural School in north-central Oklahoma, the seminary curriculum did not cater to girls whose families were farmers (although most of the girls' parents *were* in fact farmers).[8]

Many Cherokee men were trained at the Male Seminary and other prominent schools across the country, and at least two hundred alumni became physicians, dentists, lawyers, politicians (including three principal chiefs), real estate agents, and bankers, to name but a few professions. The female seminarians, however, were denied most of these jobs (including serving their tribe politically) even though their seminary training was essentially the same as the males'. The main difference between the two curricula was that the males performed military drills and spent more time discussing tribal politics, since it was hoped that the alumni would become Cherokee political leaders.[9]

Males did indeed dominate the Cherokee Nation. Student rolls and government records show that from the 1870s to 1907 the initial enrollment at the Male Seminary each year was often higher than at the Female Seminary, but the average attendance was always lower. In other words, the female school had fewer dropouts each academic year than did the male school. In fact, throughout the Cherokee Nation, there were almost always more females enrolled in school regardless of the male/female population ratio. Despite the similar classes offered at both schools, the higher attendance rate at the Female Seminary (resulting, one would assume, in a more stable education), and the excellent grades the female pupils earned, men were still able to secure more professional jobs. It can be said, however, that while Cherokee men may have desired to remain the dominant sex in Cherokee society, at least they did not want the women to receive an inferior education and thus develop a poor self-image.[10]

During the 1850s, the Female Seminary had been designed to educate affluent girls to become homemakers and teachers. The early alumnae did not, in fact, venture far from their home spheres except to teach or to participate in social organizations. All of the early alumnae were pressured by the ideal of the "true woman," which was constantly hammered into them by their teachers, parents, and preachers, and by the literature they read. The girls were aware that men were attracted to educated women but only if those women made marriage the central goal in their lives. Editorials in the *Rose Buds* and other commentaries suggest that the only avenues open to the girls were marriage or teaching. Attempting to predict her peers' futures, an 1856 graduate commented that "perhaps some may go to other parts of the world to impart instruction to the ignorant. Some will preside in the home circle. . . . But though disunited here [they will] be gathered once more to form an unbroken chain around our Father's throne in heaven!"[11] Many alumnae were perfectly happy with the goal of becoming homemakers, and according to Indian Agent Phillips, who toured Indian Territory during the Civil War, they succeeded: "During the war, whenever I entered the house of a woman educated at the Cherokee Female Seminary, I found refinement and culture. I also found flowers on the mantelpiece, books and other evidences of taste and thought in the house, and could see in the dress and in the faces of the children the fruits of the mothers' civilization."[12]

Some seminarians were not satisfied with the prospect of being limited to the home and answering to husbands. A question posed in an 1855 editorial in the *Rose Buds* (taken from the *Lesbian Wreath*) hints at the uncertainty of marriage: "The State of Matrimony: Is it a free State or a slave State?"[13]

Of the 74 known alumnae from the 1850s, only 8 taught school and at least 62 married.[14] Eliza Missouri Bushyhead (Alberty) is the only known early alumna who had a career other than teaching. She and her husband worked as co-stewards of the Male Seminary and together operated the Tahlequah Hotel. After his death, Eliza made the hotel into the most famous in Indian Territory. Also active in Cherokee politics (as much as she was allowed to be), Alberty was an influential spokesperson for the plan to have the state of Oklahoma purchase the Female Seminary and the move to create the Northeastern State Normal School.[15]

Early seminarians as well as students after the Civil War were influenced by many individuals, groups, and ideas. But the later students were unique in being exposed to the philosophies of Florence Wilson and other quasi-feminist teachers. They also were profoundly affected by the example of many of their female relatives who were widowed during the Civil War and consequently forced into self-sufficiency. During this era, seminary administrators and the girls' parents became more open-minded regarding the expansion of the woman's sphere. More jobs were available for women, especially in the late nineteenth century, and with the advent of birth control, women were not as tied to the home by children as they once were. These later alumnae were more adventurous. Many students were brazen enough to smoke, to play football, to make fun of the feared Principal Wilson in front of her, and to sneak out in the middle of the night to meet with boys. Why should they not explore their potential after leaving school?

Many students and alumnae were disenchanted with the rules set forth by men and women who supported the ideal of the "true woman," and they aspired to broaden their spheres. But since few Cherokees (or white Americans) in the nineteenth and early twentieth centuries advocated that women be outspoken and individualistic, most alumnae never worked outside the home. Some were no doubt confused by the mixed messages they were receiving concerning what they should do with their lives. For example, Cherokee leaders such as Chief Dennis Bushyhead would gently remind the girls of what the men expected of them ("the Nation is unanimous in its high estimate of woman's influence upon a nation's destiny"),[16] yet Florence Wilson and the rigorous seminary curriculum led them to believe they could accomplish more than just successfully organize their homes.

Anne Firor Scott explained in her study of the Troy Female Seminary in New York State that its alumnae differed widely in their adherence to the idea of the woman's sphere being limited to the home. Some females were content with their roles as submissive wives and wise mothers, while others had no desire to live solely for their families.[17] Alumnae of the Cherokee Female Seminary fit into both categories, as well as into others that fell somewhere between the two extremes. Even though they were given the educational background to succeed in college and to pursue careers, many alumnae had no goal other than being a wife and mother; they willingly replaced their own identity with that of their husbands. Others decided to work but cut short their careers after marrying. Some women decided not to marry at all. Others limited their career choice to social work, for they were reluctant to abandon the female sphere completely, even though they were not entirely comfortable in it.

One later alumna who believed in a limited woman's sphere was Beulah Benton Edmondson. In a 1902 speech interpreting Cherokee history, she revealed that she was quite proud of the "advancements" the females of her tribe had made (although her version of the older Cherokee woman is somewhat stereotypical even for her own time):

> The Cherokee maiden of today, it is true, still wears paint and feathers, the decorations of her grandmothers, but the paint she has learned to apply to her cheek with the delicate touch of an artist, and the feathers, worn on a chapeau of Parisian pattern, lends additional grace to her refined features. Instead of the woman's ungraceful part of the war dance formerly in vogue among the Cherokees . . . the two-step, and other fashionable dances are surreptitiously practiced by the seminary girls of today. . . . The young women our alma mater has trained and who have gone out among our people as wives, mothers and teachers have done far more toward educating and elevating their race than the powerful "Uncle Sam" by dins of arms and his compulsory system has been able to force upon the tribes of the west.[18]

Although the seminary was a finishing school for most alumnae, the seminary's founders also inadvertently created a "prep school" for numerous career women. Because of the male and female seminaries' stringent courses of study, their graduates were given sixty-two hours of college credit at Northeastern State Normal School.[19] Many seminary graduates (approximately thirty from each school) took advantage of the two-year headstart and enrolled in the Tahlequah institution. But almost forty women transferred to colleges and universities elsewhere, although only a dozen graduated from them. Other schools of choice in Oklahoma were the University of Oklahoma; Henry Kendall College in Muskogee; Hill's Business College in Oklahoma City; St. Louis Convent in Pawhuska; and Willie Halsell College and Bacone College in Muskogee. Some girls opted to travel farther away, to the University of Arkansas; Haskell Institute in Kansas; Northfield Seminary in Massachusetts; Buena Vista Female Seminary in Virginia; Oswego Female College and Kansas Agricultural College in Kansas; St. Teresa Academy in Kansas City; Drury College, Kirkwood Seminary, Spaulding's Commercial College, Hardin College, Howard Payne College, and Forest Park University in Missouri; Monticello Seminary in Illinois; Ward Belmont College in Tennessee; and the University of Chicago. One alumna studied voice in Paris. Considering that the Cherokees modeled their school after Mount Holyoke and hired five of its alumnae as teachers, it is curious that no Cherokee Female Seminary alumnae attended that Massachusetts school. None of the 1850s alumnae attended a school other than their seminary.[20]

Eldee Starr was typical of those graduates from the post–Civil War period who were eager to pursue careers in the state of Oklahoma after attending other schools. She taught at the Female Seminary, then worked for the United States Indian Division's Restricted Division Main Office in Muskogee and for the Tahlequah and Field Office from 1918 to 1928. Starr later became United States file clerk in the Muskogee District. Others who followed careers included Eliza Covel Keys, who took over as postal clerk of the Pryor Post Office after her father died, and Eliza Ballard (Sanders), who was hired to copy the Cherokee Dawes Roll. Charlotte Mayes (Sanders) worked in the post exchange at Camp Gruber and at the Douglas Bomber Plant in Tulsa during World War II. Callie Starr (Wyly), the sister of Eldee and Maymee, served as a Works Project Administration supervisor and during World War II was civilian placement officer at Camp Gruber. Afterward, she served as a social worker for the Osage Agency. Before their marriages, Rosanna Cunningham (Reed) worked as a dental assistant and Letitia Florence Skidmore (Haynes) was a telephone operator and stenographer. Lulu May Tittle (Hefner) opened and operated the first millinery store in Nowata, Oklahoma, and later invested in numerous oil wells drilled on her property, which helped her garner the distinction of owning the most land in Nowata.[21]

Perhaps the Female Seminary alumnae to achieve the greatest success, professionally, were Rachel Caroline "Callie" Eaton and Isabel "Belle" Cobb, both of whom were 1/32 Cherokee, and who both remained single (although Eaton was married for a short time, she later divorced). Eaton graduated from the seminary in 1888 and enrolled in Drury College, where she received her bachelor of science degree, graduating cum laude. Afterward, she studied at the University of Chicago, where she earned her master and doctor of philosophy degrees in history. Rachel's sister, Martha Pauline Eaton (York), and brother, John Merrit, also graduated from the seminaries.[22]

Eaton had a long and productive career. She was hired as head of the history department at the State College for Women in Columbia, Missouri. Later she served as professor of history at Lake Erie College in Painesville, Ohio, and was dean of women and head of the history department at Trinity University in Texas. In addition to achieving high academic positions, Eaton produced numerous written works, including *John Ross and the Cherokee Indians, Oklahoma Pioneer Life, Domestic Science Among the Primitive Cherokees,* and *History of the Pioneer Churches in Oklahoma.* In 1936, she was inducted into the Oklahoma Memorial Association's Hall of Fame.[23]

Belle Cobb came to Indian Territory from Tennessee in 1870 at the age of eleven. Her father, Joseph Benson Cobb, was an affluent rancher. She graduated from the Female Seminary in 1879, attended the Glendale Female Seminary in Ohio for two years, then returned to the Female Seminary, where she taught until the school burned in 1887. In 1888, Cobb enrolled in the Women's Medical College of Pennsylvania, and four years later received her medical degree. She returned to Indian Territory to practice medicine at Wagoner—usually performing surgery in her patients' homes, since there was no hospital available at the time. Cobb also joined various literary societies, was an active Republican, and was supervisor of the rural Sunday schools. Even though the Cherokee Nation took great pride in Cobb's status as a physician, she was denied employment as medical superintendent of her alma mater.[24]

Other than teaching, many women of the middle and upper classes who had attended the seminary did not choose professions, usually because their husbands could support them. Instead, they followed the Progressive spirit, as did white women in the rest of the country, and joined social clubs. Many of the Cherokee women were dedicated to social reform, and some became active leaders within the Cherokee Nation and other communities. Alumnae joined organizations such as the Order of the Eastern Star (OES), the White Shrine of Jerusalem (based in Bartlesville, Oklahoma), the Society of Oklahoma Indians, various Federations of Woman's Clubs, the Hyechka Music Club, the Pocahontas Club of Blue Mound, the Fortnightly Club, the Tahlequah Music Study Club, and a number of literary and music societies.[25]

Aneliza Eulalia Sevier was elected worthy grand matron of the Indian Territory's Grand Chapter of the OES. Bluie Adair (Lawrence) was a member of the Ele-sunt Club and a charter member and organizer of the William Penn Adair Chapter, and she was appointed to the board of trustees of the Carnegie Library. She worked for the Red Cross during World War II and was the women's chairman of Cherokee County's Council of National Defense. While president of the Civic League of Tahlequah, Lawrence was instrumental in having over three thousand trees planted throughout Tahlequah.[26]

Although many alumnae belonged to Indian clubs and often supported Indian causes, Jennie Fields Ross (Cobb) was one of the few to devote all of her time to Indian organizations. She also possessed more Cherokee blood (seven-eighths) than the socially active alumnae. She was a member of the Society of Oklahoma Indians, the OES in Grove, Oklahoma, and was an honorary member of the Six Nations Confederacy based in Ontario. She and her husband, Jessie Clifton Cobb, raised seven orphaned Indian children as their own.[27]

Ellen Howard Miller actively served her community and state. During World War I she chaired the War Savings Service. She became a life member of the advisory board of the Boy Scouts of America, and in 1921 was elected state chairman of birds and natural life of Oklahoma, probably because she had majored in ornithology at the University of Oklahoma. In 1925, Miller served as state parliamentarian for the Oklahoma Federation of Women's Clubs and as president of the Pioneer Club of Oklahoma. She was instrumental in planning the veterans' memorial bridge over the Caney River in Bartlesville, Oklahoma, and that city's Johnson Park. She was a member of the American Legion, the OES, and the Delphian Society, and was an honorary member of the Izaak Walton League of Oklahoma.[28]

Although women were not given the vote until 1921, alumnae were politically active before the turn of the century, probably because of Florence Wilson's influence and because the fathers of many of the girls were politicians. The majority of the women were Democrats. Jennie Fields Ross Cobb organized the Ohoyohoma Indian Club in Oklahoma City in 1918 for the Indian men of the Oklahoma state legislature and their wives, and she served as the enrolling and engrossing clerk for the Oklahoma state senate. Nannie Katherine Daniels (Fite) served as a delegate to the National Democratic Convention in San Francisco in 1920, was chairman of Oklahoma's Educational Department of the Democratic National Committee, and was vice-chairman for Oklahoma's Woodrow Wilson Foundation. Beulah Benton Edmondson moved to New York to work for the suffrage movement. Her parents and friends called her "Indian Princess," and interestingly enough, after she married Tammany Hall leader Richard Coker, they moved to Ireland to live in his castle.[29]

Teaching was almost the only job available to the early alumnae, and most of them remained within the Cherokee Nation to teach at the common schools. But many of the later alumnae who worked also chose the teaching profession, either in the public schools,[30] the Cherokee Orphan Asylum, the Cherokee Male Seminary, or their alma mater.[31] One of the most devoted educators, Janana Ballard (Lamar), taught in the Cherokee public school system, at both seminaries, and at Northeastern State Normal School.[32]

A few graduates influenced entire school districts. Carlotta Archer was elected superintendent of instruction of Mayes County, where she served from 1908 to 1920, and was the only woman to serve on the Cherokee Nation's Board of Education. Minnie Benge was elected supervisor of public instruction for Cherokee County in 1920. Dr. Rachel Caroline Eaton was supervisor of schools in Rogers County in 1920. Amanda Payne Morgan (Bell) was elected superintendent of public instruction for Cherokee County in 1912. Sallie Pauline Parris (Foreman) was supervisor of public instruction of Cherokee County in 1912, and Ida Wetzel (Tinnin) served as supervisor of schools in Bentonville, Arkansas.[33]

The Northeastern State Normal School opened in 1909, but most seminary students opted to attend public schools near their homes or schools outside the Cherokee Nation. The Normal School was more popular among seminary alumnae who desired teaching degrees or who already had experience and returned for refresher courses. At least fifteen Female Seminary graduates and thirty nongraduates studied at the school. Some seminary alumnae had many years of teaching experience prior to enrolling. Elinor M. Meigs, after teaching twenty years, enrolled in 1916 at age fifty-four, and Florence "Florry" Ann Caleb (Smith), age forty-four, had taught for fourteen years.[34]

While the women described in this chapter were impressive representatives of their tribe, there was another group of alumnae who had little choice of roles that they could assume if they aspired to having jobs. While all the alumnae were limited by their gender, just as white women were, many of the Cherokee Female Seminary alumnae were limited by yet another factor: their appearance. The dark-skinned girls possessing more Cherokee blood usually were confined to work within the Cherokee Nation, often on the family farm, regardless of their academic qualifications. While at the seminary, they were seen as charming exceptions to the mixed-blood norm. However, outside their Nation they were placed in the generic category of "Indian" and were victims of prejudice, despite the fact that some were highly educated as a result of the seminary training. It was difficult for them to follow in the footsteps of Susan LaFlesche, one of the most acclaimed exceptions among Indian women in the late 1800s. LaFlesche was an Omaha woman who not only "looked Indian," but was a Christian and the first Indian woman to receive a medical degree (three years before Belle Cobb received hers). She became the darling of the Connecticut Indian Association, but she also was hailed as an oddity, a sterling example of a transformed primitive. Whether she would have been treated as such a curiosity if she looked white is unknown, but it is unlikely, considering that Belle Cobb was not treated as a rarity.[35]

Like numerous mixed-bloods today, many of the seminary alumnae who looked Caucasian found that their appearance, in combination with their educational backgrounds, was an advantage. They were able to slip back and forth between the white and Cherokee cultures (or at least the Cherokee culture they were used to), depending on their needs. Because of their—and their husbands'—non-Indian appearance, many alumnae fit easily into white society when they settled across the United States and as far away as Europe. These women were quite different from the aforementioned members of the "black bourgeoisie," in that the Cherokee women could indeed achieve status and respectability in white society.[36] They also were unlike many members of other tribes who went to school and returned home only to find that they needed parts of both the white and Indian worlds but could not cope in either one. The women who moved from the Cherokee Nation to attend college found that upon their return they were accepted among their peers and faced little, if any, cultural confusion, although uneducated and traditional Cherokees saw these women as elitist and did not especially respect their accomplishments.[37]

The seminary graduates were, on the whole, the most acculturated and affluent girls who attended the seminary, although some did hail from less affluent backgrounds. After the 1880s, they also were among the most Caucasian-looking alumnae. Of the 212 graduates, at least 189 eventually married.[38] Most of them married white men, or men who had a smaller amount of Cherokee blood than they had. In some cases the husbands had a greater degree of Indian blood, but in every such instance they were physicians, politicians, or members of prominent Cherokee families (usually wealthy ones). Clearly, the more a woman subscribed to the values of white society, and the more "white blood" she had, the more likely she was to marry a non-Cherokee, a tribal member with high social status, or a man who at least had the same degree of white blood that she possessed.[39] Indicative of the latter were the numerous Female Seminary alumnae who married alumni of the Male Seminary.[40] Obviously, among the white men, the Cherokee women educated at the Female Seminary were just as desirable as white women. Because of the reverence held for the Female Seminary within the Cherokee Nation, a man who married an alumna would garner distinction. In this respect, an educated Cherokee woman, especially a seminary-trained woman, definitely held power.

After one compares the blood quantums of the entire families of seminarians, it is apparent that the women who married white men, or men with a lesser degree of Cherokee blood than they had, tended to claim on the Dawes Roll a lesser degree of Cherokee blood than their siblings had claimed. Perhaps this was an attempt to appear "whiter" (in an American society that repressed minorities) while still retaining a Cherokee identity. In contrast to the efforts of many modern Americans to find their Cherokee roots, a number of the seminarians appeared more interested in their non-Indian backgrounds. Male Seminary graduates tended to follow the same pattern of selecting marriage partners of the same socioeconomic level, but not as many married white women. Whether or not white women found the male seminarians desirable, or if many white women were even available within the Cherokee Nation, requires further investigation.[41]

As seminary alumnae, many of the progressive women (graduates and nongraduates alike) gained a strong identity. The women were still subordinate in the male-dominated society, but the comradery among the progressive females helped shape one of the many subcultures within the seminary and within the larger Cherokee society. This particular subculture consisted of highly educated, mixed-blood, middle- to upper-class females who had adhered to the mores of white society even before enrolling in the seminary. They often looked Caucasian, believed the traditional Cherokee culture was antiquated, and were impatient with the uneducated Cherokees around them. They married white or mixed-blood men, aspired to careers (in or out of the Cherokee

Nation), and hailed from districts with large populations of mixed-bloods (Cooweescoowee, Tahlequah, and Delaware). Moreover, they were often socially prominent within their particular communities, were as progressive as white women in other parts of the country, and believed themselves the Cherokee "elite."[42]

The common threads among the members of the progressive sub-culture created a bond among them that lasted until death. These women actively participated in the Cherokee Seminaries' Students Association or the Pocahontas Club, and some alumnae (both graduate and nongraduates) are revered by many in Cherokee and Oklahoma society for simply having attended the seminary. Many Oklahomans even claim that their ancestors graduated from the seminary when in fact they had enrolled for only one semester or did not even enroll at all.[43]

Many alumnae based much of their identity on being students at the school, but others obviously did not. Nevertheless, all had one thing in common: ancestry. The National Council viewed those with even minute amounts of Cherokee blood as Cherokees, although some traditionalists believed strong cultural adherence should be a prerequisite for tribal membership. The nontraditionalists were also intensely proud of their Cherokee lineage, yet they had little desire to participate in the more traditional aspects of their Cherokee ancestors' culture (to learn the Cherokee language or attend religious tribal ceremonies, for example). But in contrast to other alumnae, the progressive women's Cherokee lineage was only one facet of their identity. Because of their education, appearance, religious adherences, jobs, and where they lived, they also had multiple loyalties: to their white and Cherokee family members, to the Cherokee Nation, to the state of Oklahoma, and to the United States of America. They do not appear to have been confused by their allegiances to more than one nation, and they were not culturally ambivalent. Those who moved outside the Cherokee Nation did not abandon the Cherokee component of their identity, since the portion of the tribe they hailed from adhered to the ways of white society. They were not ashamed of being part Cherokee. Others, however, had no need for any aspect of Cherokee society and became fully integrated into white society.

The women of this highly acculturated subculture were not bicultural. Their feet were firmly planted in the portion of Cherokee society that adopted the ways of the white world. Most of them were not multilingual, nor were they knowledgeable about Cherokee traditions. They often looked white, and they were Christians who had no interest in Cherokee religion.[44] But the influence of the seminary upon the progressive women did not make them reject their Cherokee heritage. These women saw themselves as Cherokees—as did the federal government—but they were a part of the Cherokee tribe that was adapting to the non-Indian world around them. These alumnae were not advocates of "de-Indianizing" their tribe, for despite their belief in the superiority of white culture, they were staunch advocates of keeping their Cherokee Nation distinct from—and superior to—all other Indian and non-Indian nations. Rather, they promoted a "new Indianness" among educated Cherokees who were good Christians and patriotic citizens of the Cherokee Nation and of the United States, people who could manage their own affairs according to the ways of white, not traditional Cherokee, society.

Another subculture consisted of marginal women, those females who "looked Indian" and were highly educated. They appeared to be of one race yet they adhered to the cultural mores of another. These women were usually accepted among the faction of acculturated Cherokees and often among the more traditional element because of their appearance. Yet their appearance limited them in white society, often resulting in confusion and frustration, for many of these women aspired to emulate the Caucasian-looking alumnae.

Yet another subculture was made up of alumnae who were more "Indian" in appearance and who had limited education. They were less likely to aspire to or to be accepted into Cherokee society's upper class (many of them, however, were highly respected among all Cherokees), and they often married men with the same amount of Cherokee blood (or sometimes more) that they possessed. Because they looked like Cherokees, they did not have the option of abandoning their racial identity. Like the "black bourgeoisie," some of these students may have felt inferior, since the seminary taught them to judge themselves by white society's standards. Little information is available about their positions within the more traditional family structures, but it is probable that besides assuming the roles of sister, daughter, wife, or mother, because of their tenure at the seminary (regardless of what they thought about the school) they were a tremendous influence—either positive or negative, depending on the family's values—upon the uneducated members of their families. Often they were the only ones in their families who could read and write in English and understand white politics.

The varied appearances and differing social and political aspirations of the students inevitably created disparities among them relating to race and culture. For example, at least 30 percent of the students were one-sixteenth Cherokee or less, yet they still considered themselves Cherokees. Many of these girls had never heard the Cherokee language spoken. One student admitted years later, "I did not realize what my Indian heritage meant to me when I attended the Cherokee Female Seminary."[45] She knew she was a Cherokee, but she had been taught nothing of the traditional culture and thus assumed that all tribespeople lived as the seminarians did. It is probable that this alumna, along with many others like her, did not pass to her children any Cherokee culture. But the fullbloods who were fluent in their native language and who participated in tribal ceremonies also saw themselves as Cherokees, and their tenure at what they saw as an oppressive school only strengthened their ties to their valuable tribal traditions. Certainly, not all the pupils were proud to be seminary alumnae.

Who was considered a Cherokee during the time the seminaries were open? The seminaries admitted only Cherokees (with a few exceptions), regardless of the students' degree of Cherokee blood or cultural adherence, so an individual who possessed even a modicum of Cherokee blood was apparently considered a member of the tribe. But the tribespeople who were progressive and those who were traditional each considered themselves "more Cherokee" than the other. The progressives believed that because of their enlightening educational and religious experiences, their intermarriage with whites, and their successful reestablishment in Indian Territory after removal from the East, they were the new and improved Cherokees. The traditionalists, on the other hand, often viewed the mixed-bloods as non-Indian "sell-outs," or "white Cherokees," who did not even know the clan to which they belonged.

While lineage was the fundamental parameter used for tribal membership, exact blood quantums were not an issue until the federal government began the allotment of Cherokee lands. As previously stated, many alumnae took advantage of the enrollment and began using their blood quantum as a source of identity. Prior to this time, proof of Cherokee lineage in combination with appearance, cultural adherence, and residency within the bounds of the Cherokee Nation were the identifying features among the Cherokees. Cherokees attending the seminaries were indeed separating race and culture, with at least two distinct definitions of Cherokee culture—progressive and traditional—compounded by appearance. If a person looked like a Cherokee then it was assumed he or she was traditional, and if an individual was obviously a mixed-blood, then he or she must be progressive, although this was not always the reality. While all Cherokees were of the same race (sometimes with other races mixed in), they did not adhere to the same cultural values.[46]

How influential were the seminarians? In the realm of Cherokee society, the seminarians were in the minority. For instance, in 1852, 1,100 children attended Cherokee schools and approximately 50 of them were enrolled in the seminaries (.045 percent); in 1880, of the 5,413 children of school age (between six and twenty), 1,308 females and 1,740 males attended the Cherokee schools, but only 184 attended the seminaries (.06 percent); in 1899, 4,258 attended the public schools, and 215 enrolled at the seminaries (.05 percent); and in 1903, 5,505 children enrolled in public schools, while 724 studied at the seminaries (.13 percent). It is clear that the ratios of seminary population to public school population were very uneven. However, the male and female seminary alumni had received a rigorous education; they held important jobs in education, industry, the health professions, law, social work, and other fields; and they had a high degree of visibility. All of these factors meant that the almost 6,000 alumni of both schools would directly influence not only their families but anyone else living in Indian Territory or the state of Oklahoma. The alumni of the Male Seminary were especially powerful within the tribe; hundreds of them controlled the Cherokee Nation by becoming district sheriffs, counselors, judges, and solicitors, as well as Cherokee Supreme Court justices, executive secretaries, National Council members, and principal chiefs. The wives of many of them were Female Seminary alumnae.[47]

Despite the Female Seminary's class system and the differences of opinion among students concerning Cherokee identity, the value of education, and the role of women, the seminary survived as a tribal institution for over five decades. It is remembered by alumnae as a bastion of acculturation, assimilation, enlightenment, or tribal survival, depending on their own needs, value systems, and perceptions. The hundreds of Cherokee girls who passed through its halls were profoundly influenced, both positively and negatively, by their experiences at the school.

The school was not suitable for every female Cherokee, for its atmosphere and attitude were white and it contributed to a demeaning class system. Just as other Indians resented the federal boarding schools, traditional Cherokees resented the Female Seminary, not only because of its philosophy but also because the National Council spent large sums of money on it and not all Cherokee females could afford to enroll. One modern-day Keetoowah member has said (anonymously), "The closing of the Female Seminary was the best thing that ever happened."[48] Clearly, not all tribe members subscribed to the school's philosophy, but a large portion of them did. Perhaps even some full-bloods who did not care for the school's philosophy viewed it as a symbol of tribal unity. Ultimately, the girls who benefited the most from what the seminary had to offer were those who already subscribed to the values the school espoused. Obviously, the five white girls and members of other tribes who attended the school did not enroll in order to learn about Cherokee culture.

Even though the Female Seminary was sold to the state of Oklahoma over eighty years ago, the memory of the seminary still has an impact on the tribe and on Oklahoma. Many of the alumnae joined the Pocahontas Club, an organization dedicated to preserving Indian history and aiding Indian people. This club and the Cherokee Seminaries' Students Association have provided former students with an opportunity to reminisce about their seminary experiences as they gather for the anniversary observance each spring. Only a few of the alumnae remain, but an organization called the Descendants of Cherokee Seminaries' Students Association continues to honor the school and its alumnae by sponsoring the annual May celebration. The fond memories the seminarians had of their school were quite similar to the feelings of pride many other Indian students had for the federal boarding schools they attended. For some Indians, boarding schools were places of refuge and safety where they were able to make lasting friendships, despite the oppressive atmosphere.

The Cherokee Female Seminary was an effective agent of acculturation within the tribe, and it also trained young women to fit into their "proper sphere" as defined by men and women. It made the women attractive marriage partners, was a source of identity and pride for many alumnae, and contributed to the development of comparatively healthy individuals (both mentally and physically). Although the school was the bane of many traditional tribespeople because it imposed the "white ideal" upon pupils, the education the Female Seminary offered gave a strong educational background to those who went on to colleges and universities. The training offered by the school was invaluable to the acculturated girls' success in business and in social circles within and outside of the Cherokee Nation. It was unquestionably the catalyst for the prosperity of many Cherokee women and their families.

The building once called the Cherokee Female Seminary remains a focal point on the campus of Northeastern State University, where it is known today as Seminary Hall. To many Cherokees, this old Female Seminary building and the pillars of the first seminary, which stand in front of the tribal museum complex at TSA-LA-GI, remain symbols of adaptation and progress in a changing and often inhospitable world.

Epilogue

In the last two decades, the history of American Indian women has emerged as an important field of study.[1] Historians, both women and men, are helping to broaden our understanding of American Indian women by chronicling the contributions of Indian females to their cultures and by eradicating the pervasive stereotypes of either the subservient and haggard "squaw" who liked to torture captured white men, or the royal and beautiful (and Caucasian-looking) "Indian Princess" who preferred to marry a white man. Among the general public, however, Indian women—and all Indians for that matter—are still lumped into one group with the same characteristics.[2]

Gerda Lerner has stated quite accurately that "no single framework, no single-factor, four-factor, or eight-factor explanation can serve to contain all that history of women is."[3] The study of Indian women can be quite complicated indeed. This examination of the Cherokee Female Seminary and its sometimes enigmatic alumnae has touched on numerous intriguing issues that require further investigation. It would be fascinating to learn what the traditional girls thought as they strived to adapt to the seminary's curriculum and atmosphere and what they thought about the tribe's changing culture. What were their conversations like with the progressive women? If they could not look like the white ideal woman, what type of woman was their ideal?

The women of the Female Seminary were oppressed because of their gender, just as black, white, Asian, Hispanic, and other American Indian women were oppressed. It is probable that the alumnae who were "Indian" in appearance faced double discrimination amidst white society on the basis of their appearance (and race), despite their education. It is doubtful that the more Caucasian-looking alumnae faced discrimination on the basis of their Cherokee lineage, despite their appearance. I suspect that those alumnae who attended the school in the 1890s and early 1900s found that because of the accomplishments of the Cherokee tribe—achievements that were so similar to the admired aspects of white society—their Cherokee blood was a novelty and they were accepted into most white groups.

Related areas of interest that require further investigation are the relationships between the progressive seminarians and black women and women of other cultural groups (was it the same as between white women and black women?), and the relationship between Cherokee women and white women. Were the seminary graduates respected because they were educated women or because they were educated *Indian* women? Were educated black women respected as much as educated Indian women were, or less so because of their skin color? Were the educated, politically prominent Cherokee mixed-blood men oppressed because of their race? Another aspect that requires extended analysis is the role change of all Cherokee women over time, including the Cherokee women who remained in the Southeast.

Cultural ambiguity and the meaning of "Cherokee" in the nineteenth and early twentieth centuries require more study, but such an investigation might not yield a definitive answer to these questions. Most of the individuals connected with the school were not traditional, conservative Cherokees. They had long before accepted "white" mores and values, and that is how they chose to live their lives. What makes this group of people so interesting is that despite their appearance, acculturation, and the fact that many of them expressed themselves as whites with "white values," they identified themselves as Cherokees, just as many mixed-bloods who know nothing about their Cherokee culture do today.

It is especially difficult for non-Indians to accept the reality that some Cherokees appeared white and "thought white" but did not label themselves as white. The concept of "white Indians" does not sit well with many who want Indians to look and act like "Indians" and who feel that anything less than the image of braids, feathers, and beadwork is inadequate (even though many tribes never wore such things). While it is tempting to define "Indianness" by non-Indian standards—and that is indeed the norm—to do so is inappropriate. Tribes decide their identity for themselves.

Interpreting certain historical and cultural events can be troublesome. It is difficult to determine in a clear-cut way whether or not the Female Seminary was entirely beneficial or entirely detrimental to the Cherokees. It was perhaps a bit of both. Personally, as an acculturated mixed-blood with a Ph.D., I understand the value of education as a tool of survival. In this respect I can identify with the seminarians who graduated and went on to colleges and universities across the country. Because of their ancestry, appearance, and the fact that they were not bound by a reservation, many felt that they were almost forced to adopt the white lifestyle. But I also understand the profound effects that racism and the loss of culture has on a person. Therefore, I can also identify with the Cherokee girls who did not want to go to the school. It is apparent to me that the school was essential to the survival of some Cherokees, but for others, enrolling in the school would have been a useless endeavor.

The Cherokees are a multifaceted and dynamic tribe; they have adapted, changed, conformed, and ultimately survived. Contrary to the public's belief that American Indians had greatly diminished in numbers and that their influence had been neutralized in the late 1800s, the Cherokees are now one of the most populous tribes in the country, and thousands of them are descendants of the seminarians. These children, grandchildren, great-grandchildren, nieces, and nephews of seminary students have been profoundly influenced by their ancestors' educational experiences. Many have become physicians, lawyers, educators, tribal administrators, and businessmen and women. For many descendants, a connection with the seminary is a prominent aspect of their identity. Regardless of its nurturing or deleterious role within Cherokee society, the Female Seminary, along with the Male Seminary, played key roles in maintaining tribal continuity.

Appendix A

Lineages of Cherokee Female Seminary Students
by Blood Quantum[1]

Portion of Cherokee Blood	No. of Students	No. of Graduates
Fullblood	160	2
7/8	15	12
3/4	69	1
5/8	33	5
9/16	1	0
1/2	157	16
7/16	6	0
13/32	3	0
3/8	75	6
5/16	5	0
9/32	5	0
1/4	221	27
3/16	23	6
5/32	18	4
1/8	241	26
3/32	3	0
1/16	285	45
3/64	4	0
1/32	150	37
1/64	38	6
1/128	5	0
White	5	1
Seneca and Cherokee	3	1
Delaware and Cherokee	15	1
Creek and Cherokee	1	1
Total	1,541	197
Unknown Approx.	1,459	15

Appendix B

Female Seminary Alumnae, 1855–56, Who Taught in the
Cherokee Public Schools

Name	School System
Mary Buffington Adair (Adair)	Caney Creek School
Caroline Elizabeth Bushyhead (Quarles)	Muddy Springs School
Eliza Missouri Bushyhead (Alberty)	Vann's Valley
Victoria Susan Hicks (Lipe)	Gunter's Prairie
Nannie Holmes (Benge)	Lee's Creek School
Nancy Jane Rider (Hicks)	Mount Claremore School
Lucinda M. Ross (Hicks)	Oak Grove School
Emma Lowrey Williams (Gunter)	Green Leaf School

Appendix C

Female Seminary Alumnae, 1872–1909, Who Taught in the
Cherokee Public Schools

Name	School
Sadie K. Adair	Tom Devine
Lucile Archer	Arcadia
Annie Ballard (Conner)	Prairie City
Janana Ballard (Lamar)	Pryor Creek
Lucinda Ballard	Browning Springs
Golda Barker	Rogers
Jennie Barnes	Justice
Mabel Benge	Rowe
Maggie Bumgarner	Requa
Lena Carlile (Vowell)	Spaniard Creek
Eunice Marie Chamberlin (Nix)	Pleasant Hill
Ella Mae Covel (Keys)	Bryan's Chapel; Park Hill
Belle Cunningham (Graham)	Horn
Bessie/Betsy Cunningham (Wyly)	Oaks
Lillie Cunningham	White Oak; McKey
Mary Davis	Delonegah; Bethel
Ella Downing	Osceola
Nannie Drew	Ettawah
Nellie Duncan	Rogers
Mary Early	Public Schools
Martha Pauline Eaton (York)	Claremore
Beulah Benton Edmondson (Coker)	Cedar Bluff
Bettie Eiffert	Fort Gibson
Bertha "Byrdie" Lillian Faulkner (Gilbert)	Alkin
Lola Garrett (Bowers)	Pryor
Estella M. Ghormley (Kay)	Cleora

Ellen Gladney	Crittenden
Jennie Glass	Three Rivers
Senora Gray	Payne
Ollie Griffin	Starvilla
Mary Gulager	Eureka
Elba "Ebby" Gunter	Elm Grove
Birdie Harris	New Hope; West Point
Daisy Harris	Adair
Cora Hicks (Rogers)	Claremore
Josephine "Josie" Howard	Nowata
Mary Hubbard	Round Spring
Lulu James	Oolagah
Hattie Johnson	George's Fork
Clara Della Jones	Public Schools
Rosa Gazelle Lane	Claremore
Flora Lindsey	Browning Springs
Hattie Lindsey	Hanson
Elizabeth "Lizzie" Lynch (McEnery)	Delaware
Lizzie McLemore	Round Springs
Pixie Mayes	Utopia
Olivia Mitchell	Ballard Creek
Lelia Morgan	Arcadia
Mary Trimble Morris (Parlette)	Linder
Maggie Parks	Chelsea
Laura Patrick	Minnehaha
Grace Phillips (Majors)	Oologah
Susie Phillips (Schrimsher)	Nowata
Mary Edna Rider/Ryder	Fairfield; Bunch
Fannie Ross	Hart
Florence Ella Ross (Woodward)	Claremore; Osceola
Janie Ross	Texanna
Jennie Ross	Paw Paw
Janana Sanders (Willey)	Tyner's Valley
Sadie B. Sanders	Honey Creek
Juliette Schrimsher	Claremore
Maria L. Sequichy	Cooweescoowee and Delaware Districts
Aneliza "Annie" Eulalia Sevier	Advance
Callie O. Sevier	Juliett
Susie Ray Sevier	East Tahlequah
Nellie Silk	Clear Spring
Fannie Sixkiller	Cochran; Bald Hill
Juliette Smith	Unity
Daisy D. Starr	Fairfield
Eldee Starr	Crosslane
Lucy Starr (Hildebrand)	Muldrow

Clara E. Tyler	Tovey
Bessie Walker	Bark
Josie Wallis (Jackson)	Christy's
Genobia Ward (Douthitt)	Success
Lura Ward	Springs
Maud Ward	Fairland
Mineola Ward	Afton
Mabel Washborne (Anderson)	Vinita
Nannie Watts	Cochran
Ida Wetzel (Tinnin)	Bartlesville
Zoe Wyly	Duncan

Appendix D

Female Seminary Graduates Who Taught at the Female Seminary

Name	Class	Tenure
Cherokee "Cherrie" Adair (Moore)	1899	1901–2
Mary Jane "Bluie" Adair (Lawrence)	1892	1895–99
Carlotta "Carrie" Archer	1883	1894–1902
Janana Ballard	1896	1899
Mineola "Minnie" Benge	1901	1902–3
Caroline Blair (Smith)	1895	1898
Emily "Emma" Breedlove	1883	1885–87
Carrie Bushyhead (Quarles)	1855	1872
Florence "Florrie" Caleb (Smith)	1885	1894
Isabel "Belle" Cobb	1879	1882–87
Martha "Mattie" Cobb (Clarke)	1881	1883–84
Ella Mae Covel	1899	1900
Belle Cunningham (Graham)	1900	1909
Rachel Caroline "Callie" Eaton	1888	1896–97
Beula Benton Edmondson (Coker)	1902	1906
Lola Garrett (Bowers)	1905	1909
Rosanna Harnage (McDaniel)	1901	1903
Buena Vista Harris (Rasmus)	1897	1898
Flora Sabrina Lindsey	1895	1898–1902
Cora Archer McNair (Wyly)	1895	1897–1901
Elizabeth "Lizzie" Bushyhead McNair	1888	1894–95
Mary Llewellyn Lelia "Lillie" Morgan (Mayes)	1894	1897–1900
Susie Phillips (Schrimsher)	1895	1898
Adda "Addie" Roche Ross (Norrid)	1888	1893
Eldee Starr	1899	1902–4
Lula Mayfield Starr (Hastings)	1893	1896
Mayme Starr	1899	1901
Mineola "Minnie" Ward (Allen)	1899	1901–3

Appendix E

Nongraduates of the Female Seminary Who Taught
at the Female Seminary

Name	Tenure
Sally Alberty (Shell)	1892
Irene Alexander	1894
Ada Archer (Jones)	1883–85
Katherine Archibald	1906
Florence Breedlove	1892
Mary V. Brewer	1882
Eloise H. Bushyhead (Butler)	1877–79; 1900
Betsey Cunningham (Wyly)	1900
Mary Ann "May" Duncan (Shelton)	1889–93; 1896; 1900–1901
Arminta "Minta" Ross Foreman	1898–1902
Olive Heath	1899
Annie Rebecca Lindsey	1906
Patsy Mayes	1898–1900
Eliza Morgan	1900
Dannie Ross	1899–1901
Oklahoma Spradling	1895–98
Sue Thompson	1890–92

Appendix F

Male and Female Seminarians Who Married Each Other

Mary Jane Adair (non-grad) / William Percival Pettitt (non-grad)
Josephine Barker (1900) / Robert Lee Mitchell (1895)
Florence Ann Caleb (1885) / Henry Benton Smith (1886)
Martha Candy (1885)/ Joel Bryon Mayes (1856)
Sallie Pearl Cochran (n.g.) /Hall Mayes (n.g.)
Delila L. Jane Daniel (n.g.) / William Wallace Ross (n.g.)
Cherokee Vashti Edmondson (1897) /Robert Bruce Garrett (1901)
Eugenia Katherine Eubanks (1900) /Walter Marcenas Charlesworth (1901)
Jennie Glass Fields (n.g.) / George W. Fields (1902)
Sarah Lulu Foreman (1895) / John Gunter Lipe (n.g.)
Mary Hampton (1904)/ Eugene Willard Tiger (1903)
Josephine Landrum Howard (1901) / Andrew Lewis Rogers (n.g.)
Ida Lois Lindsey (1908) / Jarrette Bell Harlan (1905)
Nellie Katherine McLeod (n.g.) / George Starr Ross (n.g.)
Martha McNair (1856) / Joel Bryon Mayes (1856)
Elizabeth Clyde Morris (1890)/ William Presley Thompson (1884)
Julia Anna Phillips (1894) / James Turner Edmondson (1894)
Susie Phillips (1895) / Ernest Vivian Schrimsher (n.g.)
Anna Belle Price (1905) / John Casper Lipe (1889)
Margaret Lavinia Rogers (1856) / Allison Woodville Timberlake (1856)
Aneliza Eulalia Sevier (1900) / Edward Foreman Blackstone (1899)
Eva Lena Sloan (n.g.) / Isaac Day (n.g.)
Nannie E. Tyner (n.g.) / Franklin Clyde Glenn (n.g.)
Grace Roper Wallace (1903) / Rhoderick Dhu Richards (1903)
Cornelia Eliza West (n.g.) / Samuel Lee Trout (n.g.)
Kate Eugenia Yeargain (n.g.) / O. Lonzo Conner (n.g.)

Appendix G

Graduates of the Cherokee Female Seminary
(Husbands' Names in Parentheses)

February 1855

Mary Buffington Adair (Walter Thompson Adair)
Caroline Elizabeth Bushyhead (William Robert Quarles)
Charlotte Candy (William Fields)
Eliza Forester (Benjamin W. Trott)
Caroline Hastings (Jenkins Whitesides Maxfield)
Lucy Lowrey Hoyt (Monroe Calvin Keyes)
Amanda McCoy (Daniel Bushyhead)
Nannie Patrick (James R. Gourd)
Nannie Rider (Daniel Ross Hicks)
Sallie Rider (Samuel King Riley)
Martha Wilson (Rev. Walter Adair Duncan)

February 1856

Mary Ellen Adair (Rev. Joseph Franklin Thompson)
Eliza Missouri Bushyhead (David R. Vann; Bluford West Alberty)
Elizabeth Annie Duncan (Isaac Brown Hitchcock)
Victoria Susan Hicks (DeWitt Clinton Lipe)
Nannie Holmes (George Washington Benge)
Martha McNair (Joel Bryon Mayes)
Margaret Lavinia Rogers (Allison Woodville Timberlake)
Lucinda M. Ross (Charles Renatus Hicks)
Alabama Elizabeth Scrimsher/Schrimsher (John Lafayette Adair; Dennis Wolfe
    Bushyhead)
Martha Nannie Thompson (John Ticanooly Adair; Augustus Van Edmondson)
Mary Delilah Vann (George Drew; Joel Bryan Mayes)
Sallie Josephine Vaught (George Washington Nave)

Martha Whiting (_____ Fox)
Emma Lowrey Williams (Daniel McCoy Gunter)

27 January 1879
Isabel Cobb
Tennessee "Tinnie" Vann Steele (Robert Colburn Fuller)

27 June 1879
Anna Cora Archer (William Ross Shackelford)
Fannie Blythe (Lemuel Walker Marks)
Elizabeth Dougherty (Ellis Buffington Wright)

2 July 1880
Caroline V. Armstrong (Frank M. Overlees)
Nannie Catherine Daniel (Richard Lafayette Fite)
Lillie Maxfield (Claude Hanks McDaniel)
Sallie Clementine Rogers (John Thomas McSpadden)
Sarah Stapler Ross (Samuel Houston Adair)
Margaret Hicks Stapler
Jeanette Starr (Francis Alexander Billingslea)

30 June 1881
Ella Adair (DeWitt Clinton Wilson)
Eleanor Margaret Boudinot (John Henry Nave)
Martha Cobb (Clement George Clarke)
Joanna Coody Rogers (John Calhoun Duncan)

28 June 1883
Carlotta Archer
Emma Breedlove
Mae Washburn (John Carlton Anderson)

28 June 1884
Mary Ann Elizabeth Duncan (Harvey Wirt Courtland Shelton)

25 June 1885
Oregonia Bell (Spratt Scott)
Florence Anna Caleb (Henry Benton Smith)
Martha Fields (Phillip Donahoo)

13 May 1886
Mary Jett Norman (George Albert McBride)

28 June 1888

Rachel Caroline Eaton (James Alexander Burns)
Elizabeth Bushyhead McNair
Addie Roche Ross (William Henry Norrid)

28 June 1890

Charlotte Delilah Hastings (Samuel Grant Victor)
Elizabeth Clyde Morris (William Presley Thompson)
Gulielma Ross (James Sanford Davenport)

23 June 1892

Sarah Jane Adair (James Augustus Lawrence)
Florence Wilson McSpadden (Phillip Wharton Samuel)
Martha Adair Mayes (Edwin Mooring Pointer)

29 June 1893

Martha Eulalia Miller (Jackson H. Merchant)
Lulu Mayfield Starr (William Wirt Hastings)
Janana Thompson (William Penn Phillips)

28 June 1894

Lulu Dale Duckworth (Walter I. Jones)
Mary Llewellyn Morgan (William Lucullus Mayes)
Julia Anna Phillips (James Turner Edmondson)
Georgia Ella Prather (Lee S. Robinson)

27 June 1895

Caroline Blair (Richard Henry Smith)
Josephine Crittenden (William Robert Sartain)
Sarah Lulu Foreman (John Gunter Lipe)
Flora Sabrina Lindsey (Charles Golston Watts)
Cora Archer McNair (William Buffington Wyly)
Susie Phillips (Ernest Vivian Scrimsher)

26 June 1896

Janana Ballard (_____ Lamar)

25 June 1897

Anna Ballard (Crawford Conner)
Martha Pauline Eaton (James Mooring York)
Cherokee "Cherrie" Vashti Edmondson (Robert Bruce Garrett)
Beuna Vista Harris (Bascom Porum Rasmus)
Cora Archer Musgrove (James Herbert Moore)

Gertrude Whitman Rogers (George Shimon)
Dora Olive Ward (William Pugh Cunningham)

1 June 1898
Lena Carlile (C. W. Vowell)
Jennie McClellan Foreman (David Jesse Faulkner)
Pixie Alberty Mayes
Juliette Melvina Scrimsher/Schrimsher (Abraham Vandyke Robinson)
Lura Ward (Gilbert Thompson Loux)

29 June 1899
Cherokee "Cherrie" Cornelia Adair (Junius Brutus Moore)
Lucinda Ballard (William Lee Harlan)
Ella Mae Covel
Nellie Mae Duncan (Eugene Nixon Williamson)
Alice French
Lulu Belle James (Robert Lee Huggins)
Grace Phillips (Preston Majors)
Fannie Vann Ross (Walter Ellis Duncan)
Eldee Starr
Mamie Starr
Mineola Ward (Everett Virgil Allen)

25 May 1900
Josephine Baker (Dr. Robert Lee Mitchell)
Mollie Lipe Blackstone (Edward Knippenberger)
Belle Cunningham (Thomas Oscar Graham)
Eugenia Catherine Eubanks (Walter Maecenas Charlesworth)
Mary Elizabeth Gulager
Bettina Lucile McIntosh (George Houston)
Jennie Fields Ross (Jesse Clifton Cobb)
Aneliza Eulalia Sevier (Edward Foreman Blackstone)

30 May 1901
Mineola "Minnie" Benge
Mary Garrett (Sid Campbell)
Rosanna Harnage (Frederick McDaniel)
Josephine Landrum Howard (Andrew Jackson Rogers)
Mary Jane McSpadden (Thomas R. Crookshank)
Juliette Taylor Smith
Lelia Alice Laitland Thornton (G. S. MacKey)

29 May 1902
Sarah Eleanor Ballard (Roy Wood)
Golda Barker (Charles V. Knight)

Beulah Benton Edmondson (Richard Croker)
Bertha Lillian Faulkner (Charles Clarence Starr)
Mary Angeline Rider (Alfred A. Campbell)
Elizabeth Vann Ross (Carl Mills)
Susie Ray Sevier (Lawrence McAllister)
Dora Anna Starr (Ewing Markham)
Clara Estella Tyler (Frank Selman)
Genobia Anna Ward (Allen Douthitt)
Lola Llewellyn Ward (John Black Tinnin)

9 June 1903
Laura Effie Duckworth (Guy Boatwright)
Victoria Lipe Foreman (James Stephenson Kennedy)
Carolina Bertha Freeman (Garland Baird)
Allie Rhea Garrett (John Chisholm Breedlove)
Sallie Pauline Harris (William Everett Foreman)
Janie Stapler Hicks (John Griffith Harnage)
Rosa Gazelle Lane
Virginia Lee Lindsey
Caroline Quarles McNair (James Walker McSpadden)
Elizabeth Peach McSpadden (Jesse Bartley Milam)
Maude Hoyt McSpadden (Woodley Gail Phillips)
Elizabeth Adair Morgan
Llewellyn Hopewell Morgan (Samuel P. Matthews)
Susie Vivian Scott
Grace Raper Wallace (Rhoderick Dhu Richards)
Leola Fay Ward (William Newton)

3 June 1904
Lulu Elizabeth Alberty (John Woodson Conner)
Frances Bushyhead (James Knox Gibbon)
Eunice Marie Chamberlin (Frank Edward Nix)
Clara M. Couch
Joseph Alice Crutchfield (Joseph Oscar Dale)
Roxie Cunningham (Edward B. Reed)
Estella Marie Ghormley (Charles Kay)
Mary Hampton (Eugene Willard Tiger/Tyger)
Elizabeth Covel Keys
Nelle/Nellie Blackwell Meek (Emerson Elliott)
Amanda Payne Morgan (Frank Rolla Bell)
Phoeba Montana Rider (Jesse Albert Barbre)

1 June 1905
Lola Garrett (Ephriam Monroe Bowers)
Caroline Elizabeth Ghormley (Johnson Harris)

Mary Holand/Holland (Ernest Trenary)
Sallie Jennings (Marion Gibson)
Mamie Butler Johnson (Francis M. Adams)
Mary Anna Martin (Timothy Meigs Walker)
Ethel Martin (Henry Pierson)
Maude Rosamond Meigs (Eustace Adolphus Hill)
Sallie Mayo Morgan (Vail Kimsey)
Anna Belle Price (John Casper Lipe)
Janie Stapler Ross (William Penn Adair)
Ethel Corinne Scales (Charles Inglish)
Anna Elizabeth Skidmore (Andrew Johnson McDaniel)
Martha Wallace (Miles C. Chastain)

31 May 1906
Annie May Balentine (William Potter Ross)
Ruth Ballard (Hardy Frank Fleming)
Ella Jay Chandler (William Edmonds)
Mary Ada Condray (Emett Barker)
Mary Louis Crafton (Daniel Baker)
Birdie Adair Dameron (George Pierce Cantrell)
Fannie Adair Danenburg (Bancroft C. Kress)
Dora Early (Newell Tucker)
Penelope Adair Faulkner (Eugene Gilbert)
Bertha Elizabeth Frellick (Colonel E. Mayes)
Fannie Etta Holland (Ulyssus Grant Hall)
Clyde Horn (Edmond Brigham Arnold)
Josephine Meigs (James K. Blake)
Ara Ellen Ross (Franklin Gritts Milligan)
Charlotte Lucinda Starr (James Robert Wyly)
Edith Lyle Stover (Edwin Bentley Hunt)
Joy Lorraine Washburn (E.P. McCartney)

29 May 1907
Lelia Eaton
Olive Estelle Edmondson (Cicero Johnson Howard)
Allie Johnson
Vera Jones
May McSpadden (Charles Walton Poole)
Zoe McSpadden (Earl Preston Whitehill)
Nola Alice Monroe (Ward C. Crawford; Frederick Oyler)

27 May 1908
Catherine Crafton (Kline Jordan)
Lucile Freeman (Roy Bearman)
Addie Gravitt

Alice Lynd Gravitt
Frances Jane Lindsey (Joseph Daniel Hicks)
Ida Lois Lindsey (Jarrette Bell Harlan)
Ada Painter (E. B. Bell)
Bertha Reed (_____ Perkins)
Ida Whetzell/Wetzell (Grover Tinnin)

27 May 1909
Gladys Mildred Anderson
Sallie Martha Bledsoe (L. C. Freeman)
Narcissa Brown (James Edward Wells)
Electa Crittenden
Minnie Berkely Feland
Anna Victoria Hanes (E. Dickerson)
Clara Elizabeth Melton (Marcus Grover Cox)
Ella Quatie Richards (Frederick Albert Dedman)
Anna Laura Turner (Homer F. Gilliand)
Lena Norene Ward (Joseph Tryon Attenberry)

31 May 1910
Elizabeth Dee Bailey (Augustus Chouteau)
Lorena Allen Bean (William Francis Graham)
Susie Lowrey Martin (Robert Walker)
Grace Reid (Troy Arrington)

Notes

Introduction

1. Although the seminary opened in 1851 and closed in 1909, it offered classes for only forty academic years. I have estimated the total number of students enrolled, since class rolls for nine of those years are missing. My estimate of the enrollment is lower then the apparent totals on the surviving rolls because many of the girls attended the seminary for more than one year (although some stayed less than a week) but their names are recorded only once.

2. I categorized the students' socioeconomic backgrounds by referring to census records and tribal rolls, some of which were not indexed or were nearly impossible to read. Many students died before the rolls were opened (and their blood quantums were not given on the earlier census records), so I have pieced together their backgrounds by referring to records of siblings, parents, or children. My search for information was complicated by the fact that many girls married and used their husbands' names, and others used nicknames. The names of these former students had to be located through newspapers, alumnae catalogs, and Emmet Starr's *History of the Cherokee Indians and Their Legends and Folk Lore* (Oklahoma City: Warden, 1979), an invaluable resource. Many of the students were alive during enrollment, yet their names are not on the rolls, and many others had died prior to enrollment, leaving no family, and thus no clue as to their backgrounds. Of the 1,953 names I could locate, I found information on almost 70 percent of them. Also see Appendix A.

3. Personal interview with Judith Hughes, 7 June 1989, Grand City, Oklahoma.

4. In the process of learning about the values and lifestyles of the seminarians, I have discovered that the image of the seminary as home to a fun-loving group of Cherokee girls is not exactly accurate, despite what the alumnae claimed. What little has been written about the seminary has been based on the commentaries of highly acculturated, mixed-blood alumnae who attended the school only for a few semesters, usually in the period between the late 1880s and 1910, and when they were from six to twelve years old. Quite often, these women were in their eighties or nineties when interviewed. Comparing the stories of alumnae with records of the school that were compiled

when the seminary was in operation leads me to believe that while interviews and oral histories are indeed invaluable, they are often embellished and inaccurate; they are best approached with caution and certainly should not be used exclusively.

Chapter 1: Foundations

1. "Letter from Mr. Worcester to the Corresponding Secretary, July 4, 1827," *Missionary Herald* 23 (July 1827): 275–77, 379; Robert F. Berkhofer, Jr., *Salvation and the Savage: An Analysis of Protestant Missions and American Indian Response, 1787–1862* (Lexington: University of Kentucky Press, 1965), 21. For an account of Samuel Austin Worcester's tenure at Brainerd, see Althea Bass, *Cherokee Messenger* (Norman: University of Oklahoma Press, 1936).

2. Joseph Tracy, "History of the American Board of the Commissioners for Foreign Missions," in *History of American Missions to the Heathen, from Their Commencement to the Present Time* (Worcester, Mass.: Spooner and Howland, 1940), 62–63; Henry Thompson Malone, "The Early Nineteenth-Century Missionaries in the Cherokee Country," *Tennessee Historical Quarterly* 10 (June 1951): 131. For information regarding Brainerd Mission, see Robert Sparks Walker, *Torchlights to the Cherokees: The Brainerd Mission* (New York: Macmillan, 1931). The missions established by the ABCFM were Hightower, New Echota, Ahmohee, and Running Water in Georgia, and Creek Path, Willstown, Cowdy's Creek, and Red Clay in Tennessee.

3. George Gist, or Sequoyah (a name that was possibly the Cherokee version of Gist), isolated eighty-six Cherokee syllables that he then represented with eighty-six different characters. Perfected around 1821 and disseminated through newspapers and through translations of the Bible, Sequoyah's invention enabled virtually all Cherokees who memorized the characters to be able to read. The Cherokee was the only tribe in the United States to have its own written language. Information regarding Sequoyah's life and career can be found in John Benjamin Davis's article, "The Life and Work of Sequoyah," in *Chronicles of Oklahoma* (hereafter cited as *CO*) 8 (June 1930): 149–80, and in Grant Foreman's book *Sequoyah* (Norman: University of Oklahoma Press, 1938).

4. James Mooney, *Myths of the Cherokees and Sacred Formulas of the Cherokees* (Nashville: Charles and Randy Elder, 1982), 11. Excellent accounts of the missionary effort among the Cherokees and its effects on Cherokee culture are given in William G. McLoughlin, *Cherokees and Missionaries: 1789–1839* (New Haven: Yale University Press, 1984); idem, *Champions of the Cherokees: Evan and John B. Jones* (Princeton: Princeton University Press, 1990); idem, *Cherokee Renascence in the New Republic* (Princeton: Princeton University Press, 1986); and Henry Thompson Malone, "The Early Nineteenth-Century Missionaries in the Cherokee Country."

5. Other authoritative works on the early history of the Cherokees are Henry Thompson Malone, *Cherokees of the Old South: A People in Transition*

(Athens: University of Georgia Press, 1956), and Mooney, *Myths of the Cherokees*.

6. W. R. L. Smith, *The Story of the Cherokees* (Cleveland, Tenn.: Church of God Publishing House, 1928), 125–26; Treaty concluded 28 November 1785, as noted in Charles C. Royce, *The Cherokee Nation of Indians* (Chicago: Aldine, 1975), 5–6.

7. See Royce, *Cherokee Nation*, for provisions of the treaty of 2 July 1791, 30–31; treaty of 26 June 1794, 43; treaty of 24 October 1804, 55–56; treaty of 25 October 1805, 61–62; treaty of 27 October 1805, 62; treaty of 7 January 1806, 65–66; treaty of 14 September 1816, 81–82; treaty of 8 July 1817, 84–85; treaty of 14 February 1833, 121–23.

8. Mooney, *Myths of the Cherokees*, 61–62; William G. McLoughlin, *The Cherokee Ghost Dance: Essays on the Southeastern Indians, 1789–1861* (Macon, Ga.: Mercer University Press, 1984), 8–9.

9. Smith, *Story of the Cherokees*, 126; Malone, *Cherokees of the Old South*, 51; treaty of 2 July 1791, in Royce, *Cherokee Nation*, 30–31; McLoughlin, *Cherokee Ghost Dance*, 79; Dianna Everett, *The Texas Cherokees: A People between Two Fires, 1819–1840* (Norman: University of Oklahoma Press, 1990).

10. Mooney, *Myths of the Cherokees*, 69, 101–2; Malone, *Cherokees of the Old South*, 51; treaty of 2 July 1791, in Royce, *Cherokee Nation*, 30–31; McLoughlin, *Cherokee Ghost Dance*, 79; Douglas C. Wilms, "Cherokee Acculturation and Changing Land Use Practices," *CO* 56 (Fall 1978): 331–43.

11. Smith, *Story of the Cherokees*, 56–57; Mooney, *Myths of the Cherokees*, 29, 83; Malone, *Cherokees of the Old South*, 53; *Fifth Annual Report of the Bureau of Ethnology to the Secretary of the Smithsonian Institution, 1883–84* (Washington, D.C.: U.S. Government Printing Office, 1884), 158; J. H. Moore, *The Political Condition of the Indians and the Resources of the Indian Territory* (St. Louis: Southwestern Book and Publishing Company, 1874), 28–29, 31. For a compilation of the Cherokee "Old Families" and intermarried whites, see Starr, *History of the Cherokee Indians*, 303–672; William G. McLoughlin and Walter M. Conser, Jr., "The Cherokees in Transition: A Statistical Analysis of the Federal Cherokee Census of 1835," *Journal of American History* 64 (December 1977): 678–703; Social Science Research Council Summer Seminar on Acculturation, "Acculturation: An Exploratory Formulation," *American Anthropology* 56 (December 1954): 973–1002; Lawrence French, *Psychocultural Change and the American Indian: An Ethnohistorical Analysis* (New York: Garland, 1987).

12. Mooney, *Myths of the Cherokees*, 82–87; McLoughlin, *Cherokee Ghost Dance*, 3–4, 7, 10–11; idem, *Cherokees and Missionaries*, 25–30; Malone, *Cherokees of the Old South*, 137–38; Rev. Jedidiah Morse, *A Report to the Secretary of War of the United States on Indian Affairs, Comprising a Narrative of a Tour Performed in the Summer of 1820* (New Haven: South Converse, 1822), 155; Wilms, "Cherokee Acculturation"; Theda Perdue, "The Traditional Status of Cherokee Women," *Furman Studies* (1980): 19–25; idem, "Southern Indians and the Cult of True Womanhood," in Walter J. Fraser, Jr., R. Frank Saunders, Jr., and Jon L. Wakelyn, Jr., eds., *The Web of Southern Social Relations: Essays on Family Life, Education, and Women* (Athens: University of Georgia Press,

1985), 35–51; idem, "Cherokee Women and the Trail of Tears," *Journal of Women's History* 1 (Spring 1989): 14–30; Mary E. Young, "Women, Civilization, and the Indian Question," in Mabel E. Deutrich and Virginia C. Purdy, *Clio Was a Woman: Studies in the History of American Women* (Washington, D.C.: Howard University Press, 1980), 98–110; J. P. Reid, *A Law of Blood: Primitive Law of the Cherokee Nation* (New York: New York University Press, 1970). For an anthropological viewpoint of Cherokee village and family structure, war organization, clan revenge, and the changing political structure after contact with Europeans, see Fred Gearing, *Priests and Warriors: Social Structures of Cherokee Politics in the 18th Century* (Memoir 93, The American Anthropological Association, vol. 54, no. 5, pt. 2, October 1962); and Alexander Spoehr, "Changing Kinship Systems: A Study in the Acculturation of the Creeks, Cherokees, and Choctaws," Field Museum of Natural History, *Anthropological Series* 33 (January 1947): 153–235. For a comparative look at Indian females, see Sylvia Van Kirk, "The Role of Native Women in the Fur Trade Society of Western Canada, 1670–1830," *Frontiers* 7 (1984): 9–13; idem, *Many Tender Ties: Women in Fur Trade Societies in Western Canada, 1670–1830* (Norman: University of Oklahoma Press, 1983); Patricia Albers and Beatrice Medicine, *The Hidden Half: Studies of Plains Indian Women* (Washington, D.C.: University Press of America, 1983).

13. McLoughlin, *Cherokee Ghost Dance*, 18, 23. For discussions of ways the white prejudices were adopted by the Cherokees, see Sam G. Riley, "A Note of Caution—The Indian's Own Prejudice as Mirrored in the First Native American Newspaper," *Journalism History* 6 (Summer 1979): 44–47; Moore, *Political Condition*, 32.

14. For information regarding the life and political career of James Vann, see the essay by William G. McLoughlin, "James Vann: Intemperate Patriot, 1768–1809," in his *Cherokee Ghost Dance*, 39–72.

15. John Bartlett Meserve, "Chief John Ross," *CO* 6 (September 1935): 423; A. Bass, *Cherokee Messenger*, 102; Thomas Nutall, *Journal of Travels into the Arkansas Territory, etc.* (Philadelphia, 1821), 129; Malone, *Cherokees of the Old South*, 127.

16. For information about the history of the institution of slavery among the Cherokees, see Theda Perdue, *Slavery and the Evolution of Cherokee Society, 1540–1866* (Knoxville: University of Tennessee Press, 1979); R. Haliburton, Jr., *Red Over Black: Black Slavery among the Cherokee Indians* (Westport, Conn.: Greenwood, 1977); McLoughlin, *Champions of the Cherokees*, 337–76.

17. McLoughlin, *Cherokee Ghost Dance*, 117; idem, *Cherokees and Missionaries*, 25; Leslie Hewes, *Occupying the Cherokee Country of Oklahoma*, University of Nebraska Studies, New Series, No. 57 (Lincoln: University of Nebraska Press, 1978), 4; *Cherokee Phoenix*, 14 May 1828, 2; Abraham Eleazar Knepler, "Digest of the Education of the Cherokee Indians" (Ph.D. diss., Yale University, 1939), 287; *Columbian Star*, 11 March 1826; E. Raymond Evans, "Highways to Progress: Nineteenth-Century Cross Roads in the Cherokee Nation," *Journal of Cherokee Studies* (Fall 1977): 394–400.

18. Walker, *Torchlights to the Cherokees*, 155–57. See Theda Perdue, *Cherokee*

Editor: The Writings of Elias Boudinot (Knoxville: University of Tennessee Press, 1983), for insight into Boudinot's philosophies. Ralph Henry Gabriel's *Elias Boudinot, Cherokee, and His History* (Norman: University of Oklahoma Press, 1941) is a less objective account of Boudinot's life. For information regarding the Cornwall Foreign Mission School, see Edward C. Starr, *A History of Cornwall, Connecticut: A Typical New England Town* (New Haven: Tuttle, Morehouse, and Taylor, 1941); Elias Boudinot is discussed specifically on pages 276–78.

19. Elias Boudinot, *An Address to the Whites, Delivered in the First Presbyterian Church, May 26, 1826* (Philadelphia: W. F. Geddes, 1826), 15.

20. For details of the life and political career of John Ross, see Gary E. Moulton, *John Ross, Cherokee Chief* (Athens: University of Georgia Press, 1978); idem, "Chief John Ross" in R. David Edmunds's *American Indian Leaders: A Study in Diversity* (Lincoln: University of Nebraska Press, 1980), 88–106; Rachel Caroline Eaton, *John Ross and the Cherokee Indians* (Menasha, Wis.: George Banta, 1914); Gertrude McDaris Ruskin, *John Ross: Chief of an Eagle Race* (Tahlequah, Okla.: John Ross House Association, 1963). For information regarding the *Cherokee Phoenix*, see Robert G. Martin, Jr., "The *Cherokee Phoenix*: Pioneer of Indian Journalism," *CO* 6 (September 1947): 102–18.

21. McLoughlin, *Cherokee Ghost Dance*, 75–77; Malone, *Cherokees of the Old South*, 87; Berkhofer, *Salvation and the Savage*, 132–34, 137–39.

22. "Order of the Seven Clans," 10 April 1810, in *Laws of the Cherokee Nation Adopted by the Council at Various Periods* (Tahlequah, Okla.: Cherokee Advocate Office, 1852), reprinted in vol. 5 of *Constitution and Laws of the American Indian Tribes* (hereafter cited as *CLAIT*) (Wilmington, Del.: Scholarly Resources, 1973), 4.

23. Mooney, *Myths of the Cherokees*, 106–7; "Acts Resolved by the National Committee and Council," 25 October 1820, *CLAIT*, 5:11–12; 12 November 1825, ibid., 62–63; n.d., ibid., 15–18. For an account of the Cherokees' adoption of a republican form of government, see Rennard Strickland, *Fire and Spirits: Cherokee Law from Clan to Court* (Norman: University of Oklahoma Press, 1975).

24. Constitution of the Cherokee Nation, 6 September 1839, Art. 2, Sec. 1, in *The Constitutions and Laws of the Cherokee Nation Passed at TAH-LE-QUAH, Cherokee Nation* (Washington: Gales and Seaton, 1840), reprinted in *CLAIT*, 1:6; Art. 3, Secs. 1, 3, 7, 14, ibid., 7–8; Art. 4, Secs. 1, 14, ibid., 9, 11; Art. 5, Sec. 1, ibid., 12. The Constitution of 1839 is basically the same as the Constitution of 1827.

25. Janet Ethridge Jordan, "Politics and Religion in a Western Cherokee Community: A Century of Struggle in a White Man's World" (Ph.D. diss., University of Connecticut, 1975), 41; Gabriel, *Elias Boudinot*, 138; Moore, *Political Condition*, 28–29; Art. 1, Sec. 2 of the Cherokee Constitution, *CLAIT*, 1:5–6. For commentaries on Cherokee revitalization movements, see Russell Thornton, "Nineteenth-Century Cherokee History: Comment on Champagne," and Duane Champagne, "Cherokee Social Movements: A Response to Thornton," both in *American Sociological Review* 50 (February 1985): 124–30.

26. Berkhofer, *Salvation and the Savage*, 137–39; Mooney, *Myths of the Cherokees*, 113–14; Art. 2 of Principles Established by the National Committee and Council, June 1825, *CLAIT,* 5:45; Act Resolved by the National Committee and Council, 3 July 1828, ibid., 117. For an account of White Path's rebellion, see William G. McLoughlin's essay, "Cherokee Anti-Mission Sentiment, 1823–1824," in his *Cherokee Ghost Dance*, 117.

27. Francis Paul Prucha, *American Indian Policy in the Formative Years: The Indian Trade and Intercourse Acts, 1790–1834* (Lincoln: University of Nebraska Press, 1962), 231–32; Edward Everett Dale and Jessie L. Radar, *Readings in Oklahoma History* (Evanston, Ill.: Row, Peterson, 1930), 137–38; Mooney, *Myths of the Cherokees,* 117; Perdue, "The Conflict Within: The Cherokee Power Structure and Removal," *The Georgia Historical Quarterly* 73 (Fall 1989): 467–91.

28. Mooney, *Myths of the Cherokees,* 128–29; "Act Resolved by the Committee and Council," 26 October 1829, *CLAIT,* 5:136–37; Elias Boudinot, *Letters and Other Papers Relating to Cherokee Affairs; Being in Reply to Sundry Publications Authorized by John Ross* (Athens, Ga.: Office of the "Southern Banner," 1837), 3–4, reprinted in Perdue's *Cherokee Editor,* 26–30, 157–225.

29. For accounts of Cherokee removal, see Francis Paul Prucha, "Andrew Jackson's Indian Policy: A Reassessment," *Journal of American History* 56 (December 1969): 527–39; Grant Foreman, *Indian Removal: The Emigration of the Five Civilized Tribes of Indians* (Norman: University of Oklahoma Press, 1932); Angie Debo, *And Still the Waters Run: The Betrayal of the Five Civilized Tribes,* reprint (Norman: University of Oklahoma Press, 1989); Ronald Satz, *American Indian Policy in the Jacksonian Era* (Lincoln: University of Nebraska Press, 1975).

30. Carolyn Thomas Foreman, *Park Hill* (Muskogee, Okla.: Star Printery, 1948), 26; Russell Thornton, *American Indian Holocaust and Survival: A Population History since 1492* (Norman: University of Oklahoma Press, 1987), 114–18; idem, *The Cherokees: A Population History* (Lincoln: University of Nebraska Press, 1990), 47–80; William L. Anderson, ed., *Cherokee Removal: Before and After* (Athens: University of Georgia Press, 1991), 75–95.

31. Morris J. Wardell, *Political History of the Cherokee Nation: 1838–1907* (Norman: University of Oklahoma Press, 1938), 52–53; Grant Foreman, *Five Civilized Tribes* (Norman: University of Oklahoma Press, 1934), 292–95. Also see Gary E. Moulton, "Chief John Ross and the Internal Crisis of the Cherokee Nation," in H. Glenn Jordan and Thomas M. Holm, eds., *Indian Leaders: Oklahoma's First Statesmen* (Oklahoma City: Oklahoma Historical Society, 1979), 114–25.

32. "Act of Union Between the Eastern and Western Cherokees," 12 July 1839, *CLAIT,* 1:3–4; *Fort Smith Herald,* 18 July 1849, 2; G. Foreman, *Five Civilized Tribes,* 296–310, 321–37, 403.

33. *Annual Report of the Commissioner of Indian Affairs for 1837* (hereafter cited as *ARCIA*), 25th Congress, 2d session, Sen. Doc. 1 (serial 314), 540.

34. "An Act to organize the Nation into eight Districts and for holding elections," 4 November 1840, *CLAIT,* 1:37–40.

35. "An Act of Establishing the Seat of Government," 19 October 1841, *CLAIT,* 5:54; C. W. "Dub" West, *Tahlequah and the Cherokee Nation: 1841–1941* (Muskogee, Okla.: Muskogee Publishing Company, 1978), 2, 14; Henry C. Benson, *Life among the Choctaw Indians and Sketches of the Southwest* (Cincinnati: L. Swormstedt and A. Poe, 1860), 245; Hannah Worcester Hicks, "The Diary of Hannah Worcester Hicks," *American Scene* 13 (1972): 5–21.

36. "An Act to establish a Printing Press and to regulate the National Newspaper," 25 October 1843, *CLAIT,* 1:76–77; "An Act providing for the building of a printing office," 23 December 1843, ibid., 5:102.

37. "Granting lots therein named for the use of the Cherokee Lodge of Masons, and Cherokee Division of the Sons of Temperance," 30 October 1852, in *Laws of the Cherokee Nation Passed during the Years 1839–1867* (St. Louis: Missouri Democrat Press, 1868), reprinted in *CLAIT,* 6:92; C. T. Foreman, *Park Hill,* 24; Butler to Drennan, 30 September 1852, *ARCIA for 1852,* 32d Congress, 2d session, H. Doc. 1, 401.

38. See "Cherokee Affairs West of the Mississippi," in Royce, *Cherokee Nation,* 114–19.

39. Benson, *Life among the Choctaw Indians,* 227–28; Grant Foreman, ed., *A Traveler in Indian Territory: The Journal of Ethan Allen Hitchcock, Late Major-General in the U.S. Army* (Cedar Rapids: Torch Press, 1930), 36–37, 48–49.

40. Samuel C. Williams, "Christian Missions to the Overhill Cherokees," *CO* 12 (March 1934): 67–68; A. Knepler, "18th-Century Cherokee Educational Efforts," *CO* 20 (March 1942): 55; Walker, *Torchlights to the Cherokees,* 114; Eaton, *John Ross,* 4; Malone, *Cherokees of the Old South,* 55.

41. Mooney, *Myths of the Cherokees,* 84; *Fifth Annual Report of the Bureau of Ethnology,* 241; E. C. Routh, "Early Missionaries to the Cherokees," *CO* 15 (December 1937): 449; Morse, *A Report to the Secretary of War,* 158; C. T. Foreman, "An Early Account of the Cherokees," *CO* 34 (Summer 1956): 149; McLoughlin, *Cherokees and Missionaries,* 46–48.

42. Michael C. Coleman, *Presbyterian Missionary Attitudes toward American Indians, 1837–1893* (Jackson: University of Mississippi Press, 1985), 13; Knepler, "Education of the Cherokee Indians," 128–29; Dorothy C. Bass, "Gideon Blackburn's Mission to the Cherokees: Christianization and Civilization," *Journal of Presbyterian History* 52 (Fall 1974): 203–26. For an account of Gideon Blackburn's whiskey meddlings, see William G. McLoughlin, "The Mystery Behind Parson Blackburn's Whiskey, 1809–1810," in his *Cherokee Ghost Dance,* 365–84.

43. McLoughlin, *Cherokees and Missionaries,* 319; Sydney Henry Babcock and John Y. Bryce, *History of Methodism in Oklahoma: Story of the Indian Mission Annual Conference of the Methodist Episcopal Church, South* (Oklahoma City: Times Journal Publishing Company, 1937), 13; Edmund Schwarze, *History of the Moravian Missions among the Southern Indian Tribes of the United States* (Bethlehem, Pa.: Times Publishing Company, 1923), 136; *Cherokee Phoenix,* 28 May 1828, 2; ibid., 3 December 1828, 3; ibid., 21 January 1829, 2.

44. Mooney, *Myths of the Cherokees,* 136–37; Robert H. Skelton, "A History of the Educational System of the Cherokee Nation, 1801–1910" (Ph.D. diss.,

University of Arkansas, 1970), 74–124; Benson, *Life among the Choctaw Indians*, 255; "Extracts from the Journal at Dwight," *Missionary Herald* 21 (August 1825): 244; "Report of the Prudential Committee," ibid., 19 (July 1823): 205. For a history of Dwight Mission, see Betty Payne and Oscar Payne, *A Brief History of Old Dwight Cherokee Mission: 1820–1953* (Tulsa: Dwight Presbyterian Mission, 1954); C. T. Foreman, "The Cherokee Gospel Tidings of Dwight Mission," *CO* 12 (December 1934): 454–69.

45. Muriel Hazel Wright, *Springplace: Moravian Mission and the Ward Family of the Cherokee Nation* (Guthrie, Okla.: Cooperative Publishing Company, 1940), 51; C. T. Foreman, ed., "Journal of a Tour in the Indian Territory," *CO* 10 (June 1932): 242, 256. Also see the Orr Papers at the Gilcrease Museum in Tulsa, Oklahoma, for letters pertaining to Dwight Mission before and after removal.

46. *ARCIA for 1835*, 12; Charles R. Freeman, "Reverend Thomas Bertholf, 1810–1817," *CO* 11 (December 1933): 1019.

47. C. T. Foreman, "Journal of a Tour," 256.

48. "Extracts from a Letter of Dr. Palmer Dated at Fairfield, February 15, 1831," *Missionary Herald* 27 (July 1831): 212–13; Benson, *Life among the Choctaw Indians*, 230–31.

49. *Cherokee Advocate*, 4 October 1844; John W. Morris, Charles R. Goins, and Edwin C. McReynolds, *Historical Atlas of Oklahoma*, 3d ed. (Norman: University of Oklahoma Press, 1986), map 25; Schwarze, *History of the Moravian Missions*, 238–39; G. Foreman, *Five Civilized Tribes*, 359.

50. McLoughlin, *Cherokee Ghost Dance*, 229, 246; *Cherokee Phoenix*, 8 May 1830, 1.

Chapter 2: Establishing the Seminary

1. "An Act relative to Schools," 26 September 1839, *CLAIT*, 1:28; G. Foreman, *Five Civilized Tribes*, 359.

2. Art. 6, Secs. 1 and 9, of the Cherokee Constitution, *CLAIT*, 1:14–5; "An Act prohibiting the Teaching of Negroes to Read and Write," 22 October 1841, ibid., 5:55–56.

3. Sec. 3 of "An Act relative to Schools," 26 September 1839, ibid., 1:28.

4. Letter appointing Stephen Foreman Superintendent of Education, 8 January 1842, in File X, "Cherokee Female Seminary," Oklahoma Historical Society (hereafter OHS), Oklahoma City, Oklahoma. For more information on Stephen Foreman, see "Stephen Foreman," in Daniel F. Littlefield, Jr., and James W. Parins, *A Bibliography of Native American Writers, 1772–1924* (Metuchen, N.J.: Scarecrow Press, 1981), 240; C. T. Foreman, *Park Hill*, 41–42.

5. "An Act relating to Public Schools," 16 December 1841, *CLAIT*, 5:56–57; "An Act to further amend an Act relative to Public Schools," 23 December 1843, ibid., 5:95; *Cherokee Advocate*, 5 October 1844, 3; ibid., 16 January 1845, 4; ibid., 30 January 1845, 3; ibid., 20 February 1845, 3; ibid., 25 September 1845, 3; Foreman to P. M. Butler, 5 July 1843, *ARCIA for 1843*, 28th Cong., 1st sess., H. Exec. Doc. 2 (serial 439), 353–54; Wardell, *Political History*, 155.

6. James M. Payne to G. Butler, 23 August 1852, *ARCIA for 1852*, 32d Cong., 2d sess., H. Exec. Doc. 1 (serial 673), 407.

7. Ibid.; G. Foreman, *Five Civilized Tribes*, 410.

8. "Act resolved by the National Committee and Council," 15 October 1825, *CLAIT*, 5:47; Art. 10 of the 29 December 1835 treaty, in Royce, *Cherokee Nation*, 127.

9. G. Butler to Wm. Armstrong, *ARCIA for 1845*, 29th Cong., 1st sess., Sen. Exec. Doc. 1 (serial 470), 510. In his book *American Feminists* (Greenwood, Mo.: Greenwood Press, 1980), Robert Riegal asserts that "education was a method of transmitting traditional social patterns and not of reforming society." Comments of the council and the seminarians, however, suggest that the purpose of education *was* to reform Cherokee society. For further discussion of the valued character of early-nineteenth-century women, see Phillida Bunkle, "Sentimental Womanhood and Domestic Education, 1830–1870," *History of Education Quarterly* 14 (Spring 1974): 13–31; Barbara Welter, "The Cult of True Womanhood: 1820–1860," in Esther Katz and Anita Rapone, eds., *Woman's Experience in America: An Historical Analogy* (New Brunswick, N.J.: Transaction Books, 1980), 193–218, which first appeared in *American Quarterly* 18 (Summer 1966): 151–74; Gilda Lerner, "The Lady and the Mill Girl: Changes in the Status of Women in the Age of Jackson, 1800–1840," *Midcontinent American Studies Journal* 10 (Spring 1969): 5–14; D. Harland Hagler, "The Ideal Woman in the Antebellum South: Lady or Farmwife?" *Journal of Southern History* 46 (August 1980): 405–18; Glenda Riley, "Origins of the Argument for Improved Female Education," *History of Education Quarterly* 9 (Winter 1969): 455–70; idem, *Inventing the American Woman: A Perspective on Women's History* (Arlington Heights, Ill.: Harlan Davidson, 1986), 89–110; Barbara J. Berg, *The Remembered Gate: Origins of American Feminism, The Woman and the City, 1800–1860* (New York: Oxford University Press, 1978), 60–110; Anne Firor Scott, *The Southern Lady: From Pedestal to Politics, 1830–1930* (Chicago: University of Chicago Press, 1970).

10. *Cherokee Advocate*, 1 May 1845, 3; Mrs. A. James Marshall, *The Autobiography of Mrs. A. J. Marshall* (Pine Bluff, Ark.: Adams-Wilson Printing Company, 1897), 20–21; C. T. Foreman, "Miss Sophia Sawyer and Her School," *CO* 32 (Winter 1954–55): 395–413; Emily Penton, "Typical Women's Schools in Arkansas before the War of 1861–1865," *Arkansas Quarterly* 4 (Winter 1945): 325–28; Mary L. East, "Before the Days of Co-eds," *Little Rock Gazette*, 8 July 1945; *Arkansas Democrat*, 26 February 1847, 3; *Arkansas Gazette*, 16 November 1852, 3F; Perdue, "Southern Indians," 42; James W. Parins, *John Rollin Ridge: His Life and Works* (Lincoln: University of Nebraska Press, 1991), 14–16, 36.

11. *Cherokee Advocate*, 14 August 1845, 3; ibid., 21 August 1845, 3; Sarah Hibbard to Moses Downing, 3 July 1845, *ARCIA for 1845*, 29th Cong., 1st sess., Sen. Exec. Doc. 1 (serial 470), 592; McLoughlin, *Champions of the Cherokees*, 222–23.

12. *The 100th Anniversary of the Opening of the Cherokee National Seminaries: 1851–1951* (Tahlequah, Okla.: Northeastern State College, 1951), n.p.; "An Act for the Establishment of two Seminaries or High Schools: one for the education

of Males, and the other for Females, and for the erection of buildings for their accommodation," 26 November 1846, *CLAIT,* 5:146–47 (part 2 of volume).

13. For information on other boarding schools in Indian Territory, see Muriel H. Wright, "Wapanucka Academy, Chickasaw Nation," *CO* 12 (December 1934): 402–31; W. David Baird, "Spencer Academy, Choctaw Nation, 1842–1900," *CO* 45 (Spring 1967): 25–43; Angie Debo, *The Rise and Fall of the Choctaw Republic* (Norman: University of Oklahoma Press, 1986), 60–61; idem, *The Road to Disappearance: A History of the Creek Indians* (Norman: University of Oklahoma Press, 1941), 119–21; G. Foreman, *Five Civilized Tribes,* 58–63, 125–26, 194–95; C. T. Foreman, "Education among the Chickasaw Indians," *CO* 16 (March 1938): 139–65.

14. "An Act relative to Schools," 26 September 1839, *CLAIT* 5:31 (part 2 of volume); "An Act making provisions for carrying into effect the Act of the last annual session of the National Council, for the establishment of one Male and one Female seminary or High School," 12 November 1847, secs. 1, 15, and 19, ibid., 157, 160–61; *Cherokee Advocate,* 8 October 1849, 2.

15. Starr, *History of the Cherokee Indians,* 229, 280.

16. Ibid., 118, 122, 295; C. T. Foreman, "The Coodey Family of Indian Territory," *CO* 25 (Winter/Spring 1947/48), 339; *Cherokee Advocate,* 8 October 1849, 2.

17. Starr, *History of the Cherokee Indians,* 229, 474.

18. For information about William Potter Ross, see Mrs. William Potter Ross, *The Life and Times of William Potter Ross* (Fort Smith, Ark.: Weldon and Williams, Printers, 1893). For short biographical sketches of the Ross family members, see the William Potter Ross Papers at the Cherokee National Historical Society (hereafter CNHS), Tahlequah, Oklahoma.

19. Starr, *History of the Cherokee Indians,* 292; Ida Wetzel Tinnin, "Educational and Cultural Influences of the Cherokee Seminaries," *CO* 37 (Spring 1959): 65.

20. Starr, *History of the Cherokee Indians,* 229, 285, 289.

21. Ibid., 79.

22. Ibid., 130, 133.

23. Ibid., 232–43; Rolls and Grades of Cherokee Female Seminary Students from 1876–1904, otherwise known as Florence Wilson's "Great Leather-Bound Record Book," in the vault of the Office of Records and Admissions, Administration Office, Northeastern State University, Tahlequah, Oklahoma.

24. "Act for the Establishment of two Seminaries or High Schools," 26 November 1846, *CLAIT,* 5:147.

25. C. T. Foreman, *Park Hill,* 5–7, 78, 157; Starr, *History of the Cherokee Indians,* 231.

26. Grace Steele Woodward, *The Cherokees* (Norman: University of Oklahoma Press, 1963), 239, 248; G. Foreman, ed., *Indian and Pioneer Histories,* vol. 82, 153; *Cherokee Advocate,* 15 January 1849.

27. C. T. Foreman, *Park Hill,* 51–52. The state of Oklahoma purchased the Murrell Home in 1948. It is open to the public and is located alongside a nature trail and picnic area. Inside the home are many of the original pieces

of furniture, paintings, and clothing owned by Murrell. A videotape chronicles the history of the mansion.

28. C. T. Foreman, *Park Hill*, 35, 47–49; *Cherokee Advocate*, 19 February 1849.

29. *Worcester v. Georgia*, 5 Pet. 1 (1831); William G. McLoughlin, "The American Board and the Removal Crisis, 1829–1853," in *Cherokees and Missionaries*, 239–65.

30. For information on the life and career of Samuel Austin Worcester, see A. Bass, *Cherokee Messenger*; Muriel H. Wright, "Samuel Austin Worcester: A Dedication," *CO* 37 (1959): 2–21; and Sarah Alice Worcester, *The Descendants of Reverend William Worcester, with a Brief Notice of the Connecticut Wooster Family*, 2d ed. (Boston: E. P. Worcester, Publisher, Hudson Printing Company, 1914), 115–16.

31. Benson, *Life among the Choctaw Indians*, 231–32; G. Foreman, ed., "Notes of a Missionary Among the Cherokees," *CO* 16 (June 1938): 184. Also see "Letter of approval regarding Samuel Austin Worcester's application to erect a printing establishment near the Fork of the Illinois for publication of books in the Cherokee language, under the direction, and at the expense of the A.B.C.F.M.," in folder 38 of the Samuel Worcester Papers, Thomas Gilcrease Institute of American History and Art Library, Tulsa, Oklahoma.

32. C. T. Foreman, *Park Hill*, 11–13, 60; idem, *Oklahoma Imprints* (Norman: University of Oklahoma Press, 1936), 10–12.

33. For information on Ann Eliza Worcester, see Nettie Terry Brown, "The Missionary World of Ann Eliza Worcester Robertson" (Ph.D. diss., North Texas State University, 1978); Hope Holway, "Ann Eliza Worcester Robertson as a Linguist," *CO* 37 (Spring 1959): 35–44; G. Foreman, "The Honorable Alice M. Robertson," *CO* 10 (1932): 11–17; Virginia E. Lauderdale, "Tullahassee Mission," *CO* 26 (1948): 285–300; Althea Bass, "William Schenk Robertson," *CO* 37 (1959): 28–34; and Emma E. Evarest, "Famous Women: Mrs. A. E. W. Robertson, Ph.D." *Chaperone Magazine* 9 (August 1894): 445–48, the latter available in box 1, folder 4, Alice Robertson Collection, at the McFarlin Library, Special Collections, University of Tulsa. An original manuscript regarding the life of Ann Eliza Worcester Robertson is contained in the same folder.

34. Ruble to McKissick, 22 August 1846, *ARCIA for 1846*, 29th Cong., 2d sess., H. Exec. Doc. 4 (serial 497), 359–60; McLoughlin, *Cherokee Ghost Dance*, 482.

35. C. T. Foreman, "Gustavus Loomis, Commandant of Fort Gibson and Fort Towson," *CO* 18 (March-December 1940): 222–23; idem, *Park Hill*, 13, 71–72; "An Act to prevent the introduction and Vending of Ardent Spirits," 28 September 1839, *CLAIT*, 1:29; Worcester to Duval, 17 July 1844, *ARCIA for 1844*, 28th Cong., 2d sess., H. Exec. Doc. 23 (serial 463), 394–95, 401.

36. See inventory list of items placed inside the capsule, Northeastern State University archives. The capsule was opened during the Cherokee seminaries' annual homecoming, 7 May 1989.

37. West, *Tahlequah*, 121; Thomas Lee Ballenger, *Around Tahlequah Council Fires* (Muskogee, Okla.: Motter Bookbinding Company, 1935), 32; G. Foreman,

ed., *Indian and Pioneer Histories*, 59:15; *Cherokee Advocate*, 18 December 1848; C. T. Foreman, *Park Hill*, 78–79.

38. *Cherokee Advocate*, 1 April 1847; Woodward, *The Cherokees*, 242; A. Bass, *A Cherokee Daughter of Mount Holyoke* (Muscatine, Iowa: Prairie Press, 1937), 13; Augustus W. Loomis, *Scenes in the Indian Country* (Philadelphia, 1859). Although Loomis claims to have seen the Male Seminary from the balcony of the Female Seminary, this is highly unlikely because of topography—Stick Ross Mountain stands between the sites of the schools.

39. Ballenger, *Around Tahlequah Council Fires*, 119; *Cherokee Advocate*, 30 January 1845, 3; ibid., 2 April 1846; C. T. Foreman, *Park Hill*, 40–41, 160; Walker, *Torchlights to the Cherokees*, 35; Stephen Foreman to Butler, 5 July 1843, *ARCIA for 1843*, 28th Cong., 1st sess., Sen. Exec. Doc. 1 (serial 431), 347; ibid., Worcester to Butler, 3 July 1843, 348–49; ibid., Report of Butler, 30 September 1843, 414; Butler to William Armstrong, *ARCIA for 1845*, 510.

40. Sec. 2 of "An Act making further provision . . . for the establishment of one Male and one Female Seminary," 12 November 1847, *CLAIT*, 5:158.

41. For the history of Mount Holyoke College, see Arthur C. Cole, *A Hundred Years of Mount Holyoke College* (New Haven: Yale University Press, 1940), and Sarah D. Locke Stow, *History of Mount Holyoke Seminary, South Hadley, Massachusetts, during Its First Half Century, 1837–1887*, 2d ed. (South Hadley, Mass.: Mount Holyoke Seminary, 1887).

42. See Beth Bradford Gilchrist, *The Life of Mary Lyon* (Boston: Houghton Mifflin, 1910).

43. East, "Before the Days of Co-eds"; C. T. Foreman, *Park Hill*, 95; A. Bass, *Cherokee Daughter*, 11; Virginia McLoughlin, ed., "Letters and Reports of Oswald Langdon Woodford, 1827–1870," 32, unpublished typescript, Williston Memorial Library/Archives, Mount Holyoke College; *Fort Smith Herald*, 31 October 1849; file entitled "Missions/Missionaries: U.S. (Native Americans), Lists, Notes, etc. and Home Missions, and Freedom," LD 7093.8 M5, Williston Memorial Library/Archives, Mount Holyoke College.

44. A. Bass, *Cherokee Messenger*, 277; *Cherokee Advocate*, 21 August 1845, 3; file entitled "Mount Holyoke Seminary and the Cherokee Indians," LD 7093.8 M5, Williston Memorial Library/Archives, Mount Holyoke College.

45. Cole, *Mount Holyoke*, 26, 120, 353, 391–95.

46. "Mount Holyoke Alumnae who were Missionaries with American Indians by Tribal Group," in "Missions/Missionaries" file, LD 7093.8 M5, Williston Memorial Library/Archives, Mount Holyoke College.

47. Neile Whitney, "The Death and Rebirth of Mount Holyoke," unpublished paper, 7 May 1979, in Student Papers File, Cherokee Collection, Williston Memorial Library/Archives, Mount Holyoke College.

48. Cole, *Mount Holyoke*, 123–24.

49. W. McLoughlin, *Cherokee Ghost Dance*, 478; V. McLoughlin, "Letters and Reports," 1, 8.

50. David Vann and William Potter Ross, Washington, D.C., to Mary Chapin, Mount Holyoke, 19 June 1850, letter in Cherokee Collection, Williston Memorial Library/Archives, Mount Holyoke College. Also see the letter from

Ellen Whitmore to the Goodales in Marlborough, Massachusetts, telling of the visit of the Cherokee delegation to Mount Holyoke Seminary in search of a teacher for the Park Hill Seminary (Cherokee Female Seminary), in the Ellen Whitmore Collection, CNHS, Tahlequah, Oklahoma.

51. Secs. 2 and 3 of "An Act making further provisions for carrying into effect . . . the establishment of one Male and one Female Seminary or High School," 12 November 1847, *CLAIT*, 5:158; "Act of the National Council," 23 December 1842, ibid., 1:73; G. Foreman, *Five Civilized Tribes*, 410.

Chapter 3: The Early Years

1. G. Foreman, *Five Civilized Tribes*, 408; V. McLoughlin, "Letters and Reports," 4; G. Woodward, *The Cherokees*, 249; Lola Garrett Bowers and Kathleen Garrett, *A. Florence Wilson: Friend and Teacher* (Tahlequah, Okla.: Rockett's Printers and Publishers, 1951), 3–4; C. T. Foreman, *Park Hill*, 97.

2. Sec. 6, "An Act making further provisions for carrying into effect . . . the establishment of one Male and one Female Seminary or High School," 12 November 1847, *CLAIT*, 5:159; Palmer to Butler, 5 August 1852, *ARCIA for 1852*, 32d Cong., 2d sess., H. Exec. Doc. 1 (serial 673), 403; Payne to Butler, 23 August 1852, ibid., 407–8; Avery et al. to Butler, 8 September 1854, *ARCIA for 1854*, 33d Cong., 2d sess., S. Exec. Doc. 1 (serial 746), 331; "An Act making further provisions for carrying into effect . . . the establishment of one Male and one Female Seminary or High School," 12 November 1847, *CLAIT*, 5:159; letter from Ellen Whitmore to Mary Chapin, 16 March 1852, Cherokee Collection, Williston Memorial Library/Archives, Mount Holyoke College.

3. Secs. 5 and 6, "An Act making further provisions for carrying into effect . . . the establishment of one Male and one Female Seminary or High School," 12 November 1847, *CLAIT*, 5:158–9; Avery et al. to Butler, 8 September 1854, *ARCIA for 1854*, 33d Cong., 2d sess., S. Exec. Doc. 1 (serial 746), 331; entry for Wednesday, 1 May 1852, in Lola Garrett Bowers and Kathleen Garrett, *The Journal of Ellen Whitmore* (Tahlequah, Okla.: Northeastern State College, 1953), 20.

4. V. McLoughlin, "Letters and Reports," 27. Names of early alumnae were compiled from Jack F. Kilpatrick, ed., "The Wahnenauhi (Lucy Lowrey Keys) Manuscript: Historical Sketches of the Cherokees Together with Some of Their Customs, Traditions, and Superstitions," Anthropological Papers No. 77, Bulletin 196 (Washington, D.C.: Smithsonian Institution, Bureau of American Ethnology, 1966), 179–213; Starr, *History of the Cherokee Indians*, 491–680; Thomas Lee Ballenger, "Names of Students of the Cherokee Male and Female Seminaries, Tahlequah, Oklahoma, from 1876 to 1904," 72–73, bound manuscript in Special Collections, Northeastern State University; various issues of the *Cherokee Advocate*; and interviews in G. Foreman, ed., *Indian and Pioneer Histories*.

5. G. Foreman, *Civilized Tribes*, 408–9; C. T. Foreman, *Park Hill*, 97; Reid

A. Holland, "Life in the Cherokee Nation, 1855–1860," *CO* 49 (Autumn 1971): 294; Mrs. W. P. Ross, *William Potter Ross*, preface.

6. C. T. Foreman, *Park Hill*, 80; Whitmore to Chapin, 16 March 1852, letter in Cherokee Collection, Williston Memorial Library/Archives, Mount Holyoke College; "An Act making further provisions for carrying into effect . . . the establishment of one Male and One Female Seminary or High School," 12 November 1847, *CLAIT*, 5:158; Avery et al. to Butler, 8 September 1854, *ARCIA for 1854*, 331.

7. C. T. Foreman, *Park Hill*, 79–80; Sarah M. Everett to Nancy S. Everett, 31 March 1838, cited in Cole, *Mount Holyoke*, 39.

8. Entry for Wednesday, 13 November 1851, Bowers and Garrett, *Journal of Ellen Whitmore*, 17–19; C. W. Goodale, "Notes on the Life of Ellen Rebecca Whitmore," *Cherokee Homecoming Brochure*, 7 May 1938, 2, in John Vaughan Library Archives, Northeastern State University; A. Bass, *Cherokee Messenger*, 68; C. T. Foreman, *Park Hill*, 80, 84.

9. Stephen T. Autry and R. Palmer Howard, M.D., "Health Care in the Cherokee Seminaries, Asylums and Prisons: 1851–1906," *Oklahoma State Medical Association Journal* 65 (December 1972): 495–96; C. T. Foreman, *Park Hill*, 78; G. Foreman, ed., "Notes of a Missionary Among the Cherokees," *CO* 16 (June 1938): 171–89; Starr, *History of the Cherokee Indians*, 252; Walker, *Torchlights to the Cherokees*, 45–46.

10. Cherokee Collection, Uncatalogued Letter File, Williston Memorial Library/Archives, Mount Holyoke College; C. T. Foreman, *Park Hill*, 85; Ross, *William Potter Ross*, 196; Brown, "Life of Ann Eliza Worcester Robertson," 92; Wright, "S. A. Worcester," 4. Daniel Hitchcock and his daughter, Sarah Daisy, died of cholera in 1867.

11. Whitmore to Chapin, 16 March 1852, and O. L. Woodford to his parents, 26 May 1852, in V. McLoughlin, "Letters and Reports," 25, both in Cherokee Collection, Williston Memorial Library/Archives, Mount Holyoke College.

12. Whitmore to Chapin, 16 March 1852, and letter from Ellen Whitmore, Tahlequah, to Mrs. David Goodale, Marlborough, Massachusetts, 11 March 1851, in Alumnae Files, Missions/Missionaries: U.S. (Native Americans), Lists, notes, etc., and Home Missions and Freedmen box, both at Mount Holyoke Williston Memorial Library/Archives; G. Foreman, *Five Civilized Tribes*, 410; Butler to Dean, 10 September 1856, *ARCIA for 1856*, 34th Cong., 3d sess., S. Exec. Doc. 5 (serial 875), 688; Butler to Rector, 8 September 1857, *ARCIA for 1858*, 35th Cong., 1st sess., S. Exec. Doc. 11 (serial 919), 499; Butler to Rector, 18 September 1857, ibid., 505; *Cherokee Rose Buds*, 2 August 1854, 3; *Wreath of Cherokee Rose Buds*, 14 February 1855. There is no information regarding the source of the students' morphine. A regular exercise program was not instituted until the 1870s.

13. C. T. Foreman, *Park Hill*, 84–85; Ross, *William Potter Ross*, 196.

14. Sarah Worcester to her brother Leonard, 20 December 1853, document 27, box 8, Alice Robertson Collection, McFarlin Library, Department of Special Collections, University of Tulsa; C. T. Foreman, *Park Hill*, 94–95; A. Bass, *Cherokee Daughter*, 20; Elizabeth Alden Green, *Mary Lyon and Mount Holyoke*,

Opening at the Gates (Hanover, N. H.: University Press of New England, 1979), 385 n.35; Flora B. Ludington to Mrs. John H. Bass, 16 November 1936, and Pauline Avery File, LD7092.8, in Alumnae Files, both in Williston Memorial Library/Archives, Mount Holyoke College; Mrs. W. P. Ross, *William Potter Ross,* 196; C. T. Foreman, *Park Hill,* 95; G. Foreman, ed., *Indian and Pioneer Histories,* vol. 2, 34; Pauline Avery File, Alumnae Files, Williston Memorial Library/Archives, Mount Holyoke College.

15. G. Foreman, *Five Civilized Tribes,* 410; William Potter Ross, "Public Education among the Cherokee Indians," *American Journal of Education* 1 (August 1855): 121.

16. *Cherokee Advocate,* 14 October 1851, 1; Gary Moulton, ed., *The Papers of Chief John Ross, Vol. II: 1840–1866* (Norman: University of Oklahoma Press, 1985), 358; George Butler to Col. John Drennen, 30 September 1852, *ARCIA for 1852,* 32d Cong., 2d sess., H. Exec. Doc. 1 (serial 673), 401; Payne to Butler, 23 August 1852, ibid., 407; Butler to Drew, 13 September 1853, *ARCIA for 1853,* 33d Cong., 1st sess., H. Exec. Doc. 1 (serial 710), 382; C. T. Foreman, *Park Hill,* 81.

17. Avery to Butler, 2 August 1855, *ARCIA for 1855,* 34th Cong., 1st sess., S. Exec. Doc. 1 (serial 810), 451; Duncan to Butler, 25 September 1856, *ARCIA for 1856,* 34th Cong., 3d sess., S. Exec. Doc. 5 (serial 875), 691; "Examination Day" schedule, box 1, folder 48, Alice Robertson Collection, McFarlin Library, Department of Special Collections, University of Tulsa. The author of the schedule is not given, but it was probably Avery.

18. C. T. Foreman, *Park Hill,* 98; Whitmore to Chapin, 16 March 1852, and O. L. Woodford to his sister, 27 June 1855, in V. McLoughlin, "Letters and Reports," 25; *Wreath of Cherokee Rose Buds,* 14 February 1855, 2.

19. C. T. Foreman, *Park Hill,* 97.

20. Woodward, *The Cherokees,* 248; Ruskin, *John Ross,* 38, 40.

21. C. T. Foreman, *Park Hill,* 88, 99–100; *Missionary Herald,* 5 February 1852; *Baptist Missionary Magazine* 32 (July 1852): 296.

22. C. T. Foreman, *Park Hill,* 102.

23. Ibid.; V. McLoughlin, "Letters and Reports," 30; Wardell, *Political History,* 120–21.

24. Reese to Butler, 12 October 1854, *ARCIA for 1854,* 33d Cong., 2d sess., S. Exec. Doc. 1 (serial 746), 327; C. T. Foreman, *Park Hill,* 99.

25. The two "Co-Editresses" were Catharine Gunter and Nancy E. Hicks; in 1855, the girls referred to themselves as "Editors": Elizabeth A. Duncan, Lucinda M. Ross, Caroline E. Bushyhead, and Mary B. Adair.

26. The 2 August 1854 *Cherokee Rose Buds* and the 4 August 1855 *Wreath of Cherokee Rose Buds* can be found in Archives, NSU; the 14 February 1855 *Wreath of Cherokee Rose Buds* is located in Anthropological Archives, Smithsonian Institution.

27. *Wreath of Cherokee Rose Buds,* 4 August 1855, 5.

28. Ibid., 1 August 1855, 2.

29. Ibid., 5, 7; *Wreath of Cherokee Rose Buds,* 4 August 1855, 2–3, 6; ibid., 14 February 1855, 1, 6.

30. *Sequoyah Memorial*, 2 August 1855, 3.

31. *Wreath of Cherokee Rose Buds*, 2 August 1854, 5; *Wreath of Cherokee Rose Buds*, 4 August 1855, 3.

32. See Rufus Anderson, *Memoir of Catherine Brown, A Christian Indian of the Cherokee Nation* (New York: J. P. Haven, 1825).

33. This is the first of six verses of "Lines on the Grave of Catharine [*sic*] Brown," in *Wreath of Cherokee Rose Buds*, 14 February 1855, 1.

34. *Cherokee Rose Buds*, 2 August 1854, 5. Also see Barbara M. Welter, "The Feminization of American Religion, 1800–1860," in Mary Hartman and Lois Banner, ed., *Clio's Consciousness Raised* (New York, 1974), 137–57.

35. See Herbert Aptheker, ed., *The Correspondence of W. E. B. Du Bois* (Amherst: University of Massachusetts Press, 1973–78).

36. *Twin Territories*, June 1899.

37. *Cherokee Rose Buds*, 2 August 1854, 2, 7.

38. *Godey's Lady's Book*, January 1857, 82.

39. *Cherokee Rose Buds*, 2 August 1854, 2.

40. Ibid.

41. *Wreath of Cherokee Rose Buds*, 14 February 1855, 2, 5, Anthropological Archives, Smithsonian Institution; *Cherokee Rose Buds* 2 August 1854, 6.

42. *Wreath of Cherokee Rose Buds*, 14 February 1855, 2.

43. *Cherokee Rose Buds*, 2 August 1854, 1–2.

44. *Wreath of Cherokee Rose Buds*, 1 August 1855, 1–2.

45. Ibid.

46. *Sequoyah Memorial*, 31 July 1856, 2.

47. *Wreath of Cherokee Rose Buds*, 14 February 1855, 3.

48. Ibid., 5.

49. Ibid., 4, 6.

50. For information on John B. Jones, see McLoughlin, *Champions of the Cherokees*; for information on the Keetoowah Society, see Howard Q. Tyner, "The Keetoowah Society in Cherokee History" (Master's thesis, University of Tulsa, 1949); James Duncan, "The Keetoowah Society," *CO* 4 (1926): 251–55. The Knights of the Golden Circle also were known as the Southern Rights Party.

51. *Cherokee Rose Buds*, 2 August 1854, 3; *Wreath of Cherokee Rose Buds*, 1 August 1855, 4; E. Franklin Frazier, *Black Bourgeoisie* (Glencoe, Ill.: Free Press, 1957).

52. For more information on scientific racism, see Charles Caldwell, *Thoughts on the Original Unity of the Human Race* (New York: E. Bliss, 1830); Samuel George Morton, *Crania Americana; or, A Comparative View of the Skulls of Various Aboriginal Nations of North and South America to Which Is Prefixed an Essay on the Varieties of the Human Species* (Philadelphia: J. Dobson, 1839); Robert E. Bieder, *Science Encounters the Indian, 1820–1880* (Norman: University of Oklahoma Press, 1986); Thomas F. Gossett, *Race: The History of an Idea in America* (Dallas: Southern Methodist University Press, 1963); Curtis Hinsley, *Savages and Scientists: The Smithsonian Institution and the Development of American Anthropology, 1846–1910* (Washington D.C.: Smithsonian Institution Press, 1981);

Reginald Horsman, "Scientific Racism and the American Indian in the Mid-Nineteenth Century," *American Quarterly* 27 (May 1975): 152–68.

53. Starr, *History of the Cherokee Indians*, 232–33, 678; Avery to Butler, 2 August 1855, *ARCIA for 1855*, 451. See Appendix G for a list of the seminary graduates.

54. Royce, *Cherokee Nation*, 198; Ballenger, *Around Tahlequah Council Fires*, 56; McLoughlin, *Champions of the Cherokees*, 335–36; Sarah Worcester to her brother, John Orr Worcester, 3 March 1856, box 8, document 34, in Alice Robertson Collection, McFarlin Library, Department of Special Collections, University of Tulsa.

55. Duncan to Butler, 25 September 1856, *ARCIA for 1856*, 34th Cong., 3d sess., S. Exec. Doc. 5 (serial 875), 691.

56. Cherokee Council to Luke Lea, Commissioner of Indian Affairs, 17 February 1853, in *Letters Received, 1824–1881* (microfilm 234), DP Roll 96 1853–54; Holland, *Life in the Cherokee Nation*, 297–99; Butler to Rector, 8 September 1857, *ARCIA for 1857*, 35th Cong., 2d sess., S. Exec. Doc. 42 (serial 919), 499–500; E. Rector to Charles E. Mix, 12 October 1858, *ARCIA for 1858*, 35th Cong., 2d sess., S. Exec. Doc. 39 (serial 974), 531; Elias Rector to Greenwood, 23 September 1859, *ARCIA for 1859*, 36th Cong., 1st sess., S. Exec. Doc. 46 (serial 1023), 521.

57. G. Butler to Dean, 10 September 1856, *ARCIA for 1856*, 689; George Butler to E. Rector, 8 September 1857, *ARCIA for 1857* (serial 919), 499; Moulton, *John Ross*, 157.

58. Annual Message of the Principal Chief of the Cherokee Nation to the National Committee and Council in General Council Convened, 5 October 1857, *ARCIA for 1857*, 35th Cong., 1st sess., S. Exec. Doc. 11 (serial 919), 507; Annual Message of the Principal Chief of the Cherokee Nation, 3 October 1859, in G. Moulton, *John Ross*, 160.

59. Duncan to G. Butler, 18 September 1857, *ARCIA for 1857*, 505; G. Butler to E. Rector, 10 September 1858, *ARCIA for 1858*, 35th Cong., 2d sess., S. Exec. Doc. 1 (serial 974), 492; E. Rector to C. Mix, 26 October 1858, *ARCIA for 1858*, 480; Reese to Butler, 30 August 1859, *ARCIA for 1860*, 36th Cong., 1st sess., S. Exec. Doc. 2 (serial 1023), 546.

60. "An Act Relative to Public Schools," 16 December 1841, in *Laws of the Cherokee Nation Passed During the Years 1839–1867* (St. Louis: Missouri Democrat Printer, 1868) reprinted in *CLAIT*, 6:62–63; Reese to Butler, 2 October 1854, *ARCIA for 1854*, 33d Cong., 2d sess., S. Exec. Doc. 1 (serial 746), 330.

61. Ballenger, *Around Tahlequah Council Fires*, 121; "An Act Authorizing the Printing of Books in the Cherokee Language," 27 November 1866, in *Laws of the Cherokee Nation Passed During the Years 1839–1867*, reprinted in *CLAIT*, 6:64.

62. Dr. Dwight Hitchcock to his sister-in-law, Mrs. Robertson, 7 February 1861, in Letters from Dr. Daniel Hitchcock to Robertson family, in the Grant Foreman Collection, OHS; C. T. Foreman, *Park Hill*, 130–31; idem, "Sophia Sawyer," 408.

63. See W. Craig Gaines, *The Confederate Cherokees: John Drew's Regiment of Mounted Rifles* (Baton Rouge: Louisiana State University Press, 1989).

64. See Grant Foreman, *Fort Gibson: A Brief History* (Norman: University of Oklahoma Press, 1936), and Brad Agnew, *Fort Gibson: Terminal on the Trail of Tears* (Norman: University of Oklahoma Press, 1980). Fort Gibson was occupied by Confederate troops at the start of the Civil War but later was taken by Union forces. By April 1863, the fort was used by Cherokee regiments, part of the Kansas cavalry, and at least three thousand members of Hopkin's Battery of Volunteers.

65. Proctor to Coffin, 28 November 1863, *ARCIA for 1863*, 38th Cong., 1st sess., Exec. Doc. 1 (serial 1182), 340; Harlin to Coffin, 2 September 1863, *ARCIA for 1865*, 39th Cong., 1st sess. (serial 1248), 471; Peter Collier, *When Shall They Rest?: The Cherokees' Long Struggle with America* (New York: Holt, Rinehart, and Winston, 1973), 103; Moulton, *Papers of Chief John Ross*, vol. 2, 560–63.

66. Jones to the Commissioner of Indian Affairs, September 1871, *ARCIA for 1871–72*, 42d Cong., 2d sess., H. Exec. Doc. 1 (serial 1505), pt. 5, 979. For more information regarding the life and politics in the Cherokee Nation during and after the Civil War, see H. Craig Miner, *The Corporation and the American Indian: Tribal Sovereignty and Industrial Civilization in Indian Territory, 1865–1907* (Columbia: University of Missouri Press, 1976); V. A. Travis, "Life in the Cherokee Nation a Decade After the Civil War," *CO* 4 (March 1926): 16–30; Joseph B. Thoburn, ed., "The Cherokee Question," *CO* 2 (June 1924): 141–141v (reprint of the pamphlet of the same name published by the Office of the Commissioner of Indian Affairs, Washington, D.C., in June 1866); personal accounts of Ann Eliza Worcester Robertson, box 1, folder 39, Alice Robertson Collection, McFarlin Library, University of Tulsa; Alice Robertson Papers, "Incidents of the Civil War," box 1, OHS; William Potter Ross to his son Willie, in the William Potter Ross Papers, CNHS, Tahlequah, and the James Greene Walker diary, 1861–63 in James Green Walker Collection, Gilcrease Institute, Tulsa.

67. See Treaty of 19 July 1866, in Royce, *Cherokee Nation*, 212–18; Collier, *When Shall They Rest?*, 103; Moulton, *John Ross*, 194–95.

68. Collier, *When Shall They Rest?*, 103; Joe Jackson, "History of Education in Eastern Oklahoma from 1898 to 1915," (Ed.D. thesis, University of Oklahoma, 1950), 9; Schwarze, *History of the Moravian Missions*, 294; McLoughlin, *Champions of the Cherokees*, 429.

69. J. Harlan to E. Sells, 1 October 1865, *ARCIA for 1865*, 39th Cong., 1st sess., H. Exec. Doc. 1 (serial 1248), pt. 5, 471; Jones to Walker, 1 September 1872, *ARCIA for 1872–73*, 42d Cong., 3d sess., H. Exec. Doc. 1 (serial 1560), pt. 5, 620; Schwarze, *History of the Moravian Missions*, 294; C. T. Foreman, *Park Hill*, 148; *Cherokee Advocate*, 1 June 1872, 3.

70. *Cherokee Advocate*, 22 March 1873, 4; ibid., 23 August 1873, 3; ibid., 20 December 1873, 3; ibid., 7 January 1874, 3; ibid., 28 March 1874, 3.

71. Jones to Walker, 1 September 1872, *ARCIA for 1872–73*, 42d Cong., 3d sess., H. Exec. Doc. 1 (serial 1560), pt. 5, 620; Ross, *Life and Times*, 197;

C. T. Foreman, *Park Hill*, 149; *Cherokee Advocate*, 11 October 1873, 3; ibid., 2 May 1872, 1; ibid., 23 August 1873, 3. See file on Ellen Eblin, Missions/ Missionaries File, LD 7093.8 M5, Williston Memorial Library/Archives, Mount Holyoke College.

72. C. T. Foreman, *Park Hill*, 150; Edward P. Smith to Secretary of the Interior, 1 November 1874, *ARCIA for 1874–75*, 43d Cong., 2d sess., H. Exec. Doc. 1, pt. 5 (serial 1639), 379.

73. *Cherokee Advocate*, 22 March 1873, 4; ibid., 20 December 1873, 3; ibid., 7 January 1874, 3; ibid., 28 March 1874, 3.

74. Ibid., 10 October 1873, 3; ibid., 18 October 1873, 3.

75. Ibid., 22 March 1873, 4.

76. "An Act in Relation to the Male and Female Seminaries, and Establishing Primary Departments Therein for the Education of Indigent Children," 28 November 1873, in *Constitutions and Laws of the Cherokee Nation* (St. Louis: R. and T. A. Ennis Stationers, Printers and Book Binders, 1875), reprinted in *CLAIT*, 7:267–69

77. *Cherokee Advocate*, 4 April 1874, 2; Mrs. W. P. Ross, *William Potter Ross*, 197; E. P. Smith to the Secretary of the Interior, 1 November 1874, *ARCIA for 1874–75*, 379; W. McLoughlin, *Champions of the Cherokees*, 470; *Catalogue of the Cherokee Nation Female Seminary: 1886–1887* (St. Louis: Levison and Blythe Stationery Company, 1887), 5; Florence Wilson's "Great Leather-Bound Record Book," NSU.

Chapter 4: Teachers, Curriculum, and Administration

1. See the Female Seminary Grade Book—Ann Florence Wilson's "Great Leather-Bound Record Book," NSU, and Mary L. Stapler's "Class Book" containing grades for English, Grammar, Arithmetic, History, and Dictation, in the box labeled "Female Seminary—Miscellaneous—Programs, Recitals, Commencements, and Invitations," in Archives, NSU; Sec. 31 of "An Act Relating to Education," 7 December 1877, *CLAIT*, 10:239; CHN 99, Cherokee-*Schools: Female Seminary*, Docs. 2865–2870, 1 July 1905–May 1909; Cherokee (Tahlequah)-*Schools: Female Seminary*, Undated and 5 December 1874–16 January 1909.

2. Ann Florence Wilson's "Great Leather-Bound Record Book," or "Cherokee Female Seminary Records of Grades, 1876–1909," in NSU Office of Admissions and Records, Administration Building.

3. Letter dated 10 September 1889, in Cherokee Female Seminary Miscellaneous Box, Archives, NSU.

4. Compiled from Index to the Five Civilized Tribes, the Final Dawes Roll, M1186, roll 1, and the Enrollment Cards for the Five Civilized Tribes, 1898–1914, rolls 2–15, cards 1–11132, at Federal Archives in Fort Worth, in combination with Starr, *History of the Cherokee Indians*, 489–680.

5. G. Foreman, ed., *Indian and Pioneer Histories*, vol. 12, 426.

6. See Devon I. Abbott, "Ann Florence Wilson: Matriarch of the Cherokee Female Seminary," *CO* 67 (Winter 1989–90): 426–37. It was incorrectly stated by Althea Bass (*Cherokee Daughter,* 23) that Ann Florence Wilson attended Mount Holyoke. Bass later corrected her error, in a letter of 27 March 1947 to Lola Garrett Bowers (Cherokee Female Seminary class of 1905 and Fourth Assistant Teacher in 1909), Tahlequah, Oklahoma, now in the Lola Garrett Bowers Collection, John Vaughan Library, NSU (hereafter, letters in this collection will be cited as from LGB Coll.). Also see letter from Harriet J. Eustis, Registrar, Mount Holyoke, to Lola Garrett Bowers, 27 March 1947, LGB Coll., NSU. Much of the correspondence in the LGB Collection was obviously used in Bowers and Garrett, *A. Florence Wilson, Friend and Teacher.* Since the book is not footnoted, I have opted to use the primary correspondence concerning A. Florence Wilson when possible. See also Ned Harland Dearborn, *The Oswego Movement in American Education* (New York: Arno Press, 1969), 144–56; D. W. Hearon to L. G. Bowers, 10 April 1947, LGB Coll., NSU; Section 542 of "An Act Relating to Education," *CLAIT,* 10:276.

7. Dora Wilson Hearon (a niece of Ann Florence Wilson who was a seminary physical education instructor, 1895–96), Denver, Colorado, to L. G. Bowers, 10 April 1947, in LGB Coll., NSU; Mary Gaither (granddaughter of Harrison White and Sarah Jane McClellan) to L. G. Bowers, 11 April 1947, in LGB Coll., NSU; Superintendent of Schools, Van Buren, Arkansas, to L. G. Bowers, February 1947, in LGB Coll., NSU. See also "Cane Hill and Its Memories," *Arkansas Gazette,* 15 June 1947, 1; T. L. Ballenger, "The Cultural Relations between Two Pioneer Communities," *CO* 34 (Autumn 1956): 286–95.

8. Dr. Joseph C. Park (Principal of the Cherokee Baptist Academy from 1896 to 1901), Wellsville, N.Y., to L. G. Bowers, 25 March 1947, in LGB Coll., NSU; Mrs. Isabelle K. Hart, Oswego State Teachers College Alumni Association to L. G. Bowers, 20 February 1947, in LGB Coll., NSU; Shorey W. Ross, Park Hill, Oklahoma, to L. G. Bowers, 19 October 1949, in LGB Coll., NSU; Lucy Pulliam Williamson (former resident of La Grange, Favette County, Tennessee), Miami Beach, Florida, to L. G. Bowers, 17 February 1947, in LGB Coll., NSU. See also Dearborn, *Oswego Movement.*

9. D. W. Hearon to L. G. Bowers, 10 April 1947, and D. W. Hearon to L. G. Bowers, 31 March 1947, LGB Coll., NSU.

10. D. W. Hearon to L. G. Bowers, 10 April 1947, in LGB Coll., NSU.

11. "In relation to schools and orphans," 16 December 1870, in *Laws and Joint Resolutions of the National Council Passed and Adopted at the Regular and Extra Sessions of 1870–1872* (Tahlequah: National Printing Office, 1871), reprinted in *CLAIT,* 4:47–50; *Cherokee Advocate,* 26 March 1876, 3.

12. Teachers at the seminary between 1876 and 1887 included the Cherokee women Eliza Jane Ross, Lelia Breedlove, Carrie Bushyhead, Martha Black Fox, Mary Jane "Bluie" Adair (Lawrence), Cherokee "Cherrie" Adair (Moore), Belle Cobb, Eloise Butler, Carlotta "Cora" Archer ("charming and spirited"), and Mary Stapler (an "earnest Christian character," who died at the seminary in the 1870s of tuberculosis). Non-Indian instructors included Anna E. Putman, a native of Arkansas who was remembered for her "quiet, sweet and gentle

disposition"; music teachers Kate McDonald and Nel Taylor ("charming, poised, and dignified") from Missouri; Fannie Cummins ("particularly friendly and encouraging"); Florence "Florrie" Caleb (Smith), one of the few white girls to be educated in Cherokee schools (an "admirable person," an excellent piano coach and part-time sick-nurse); Rosalie Bell; Professor J. A. McKirahan, who also taught music and art. Eliza Jane Ross taught intermittently from 1877 to 1887. Eloise H. Butler taught from 1877 to 1879, when she became the second wife of Chief Dennis Bushyhead. Belle Cobb is profiled extensively in Chapter 7. See Kathleen Garrett, "Music on the Indian Territory Frontier," *CO* 33 (Autumn 1955): 344–45; *An Illustrated Souvenir Catalog of the Cherokee National Female Seminary, Tahlequah, Indian Territory: 1850–1906* (Chilocco, Okla.: Indian Print Shop, 1906), original copy at Western History Collection (hereafter WHC), University of Oklahoma, Norman; handwritten and typed notes of Lola Garrett Bowers, box 776, LGB Coll., NSU; "In Relation to the High Schools and Orphan Asylum," 12 December 1885, *CLAIT,* 7:30–31. Florence "Florrie" Lazalier Caleb married Walter A. Duncan. Carlotta Archer taught music from 1896 to 1902. Mary Jane "Bluie" Adair Lawrence taught music from 1895 to 1899; she was second assistant teacher in 1897 and first assistant in 1898–99. Cherokee "Cherrie" Adair Moore taught in 1901 and 1902.

13. Employees of the seminary and store receipts are listed in numerous places, such as Minutes of the Board of Education, 2 February 1876, in Cherokee Archives, vol. 512, 26; CHN 097, Cherokee-*Schools: Female Seminary,* Docs. 2735–2777, 11 May 1887–Dec. 1902; CHN 098, Cherokee-*Schools: Female Seminary,* Docs., 2778–2864, 31 December 1902–29 June 1905; CHN 099, Cherokee *Schools: Female Seminary,* Docs. 2865–2870, 1 July 1905–May 1909; Cherokee (Tahlequah)-*Schools: Female Seminary,* Undated, and 5 December 1874–16 January 1909, all at OHS; "Minutes, Board of Education, February 9, 1876," manuscript in Cherokee Archives, OHS, vol. 512, 26; *Cherokee Nation Papers: Education:* box 25, file 460, M943–1–10; box 25, file 466, M943–1–10; box 25, file 454, M943–1–10; box 1, file 11, M943–1–10, WHC.

14. *The Journal,* 17 May 1877, 1.

15. Cited in V. A. Travis, "Life in the Cherokee Nation a Decade after the Civil War," *CO* 4 (March 1926): 30.

16. Owen to Riley, 1877, *ARCIA for 1887,* 49th Cong., 2d sess., H. Exec. Doc. 1 (serial 2467), pt. 5, 147; Marston to Hayt, 11 September 1877, *ARCIA for 1877–78,* 45th Cong., 2d sess., H. Exec. Doc. 1 (serial 1800), pt. 5, 505; C. T. Foreman, *Park Hill,* 173; Mrs. W. P. Ross, *William Potter Ross,* 237; *Cherokee Advocate,* 20 June 1884, 2.

17. *An Illustrated Souvenir Catalog: 1850–1906,* n.p. For examples of the students' poetic abilities and superlative handwriting, see Sallie Rogers McSpadden's autograph book dated 4 June 1880, Cherokee Female Seminary Miscellaneous Items Box, Archives, NSU.

18. See schedules in the *Cherokee National Female Seminary Catalogue for 1886–87* (St. Louis: Levison and Blythe Stationery Company, 1887), 11; *Cherokee National Female Seminary Catalogue for 1896 and Announcement for 1896 and 1898* (n.p.), 9.

19. John Strange, ed., excerpt from *TSA-LA-GI Columns*, 6–7 (August 1982–January 1983): 7; Junetta Davis, "The Belles of Tahlequah," *Oklahoma Today* 35 (March-April 1935): 36–37; personal interview with Ellen Powers, 20 October 1988, Capital, Oklahoma. (Ellen Powers attended the Cherokee Female Seminary and Northeastern State Normal School. She died on 30 October 1988.)

20. Reminiscences of Charlotte Mayes Sanders, typed manuscript at CNHS, Tahlequah, Oklahoma.

21. Mrs. W. P. Ross, *William Potter Ross*, 138; C. T. Foreman, *Park Hill*, 173; Etta Jane Scraper, excerpt from *TSA-LA-GI Columns* 8 (Spring 1984): 2; G. Foreman, ed., *Indian and Pioneer Histories*, vol. 4, 88–9; statement of Dr. Isabel Cobb, ibid., vol. 65, 184–85; statement of Rose Gazelle Lane, in "Interviews with Pocahontas Club Members/Seminary Graduates," #cLL 598.1, Living Legends Collection (hereafter L. L. Coll.), Oklahoma Historical Society.

22. "An Act Relating to the Male and Female Seminaries," 22 November 1884, in *Laws and Joint Resolutions of the Cherokee Nation enacted by the National Council During the Regular and Extra Sessions of 1884-5-6, CLAIT*, 7:15–16; *Cherokee Advocate*, 20 June 1883.

23. Petition to the Board of Education, n.d., M 943–1–10, box 9, file 183, in *Cherokee Nation Papers: Education*, WHC; Report of the Joint Committee to investigate the burning of the Female Seminary, 16 May 1887, M 943–1–10, box 9, file 184, in *Cherokee Nation Papers: Education*, WHC; J. A. McKinahan to the Board of Education, 26 April 1887, M 943–1–10, box 10, file 185, in *Cherokee Nation Papers: Education*, W.H.C.; CHN 99 (microfilm), Cherokee (Tahlequah)-*Schools: Female Seminary*, Undated, and 5 December 1874–16 January 1909. The letter from Dennis W. Bushyhead to the Senate and Council, dated 9 May 1887, requested and advised "speedy resumption and permanent continuance" of the Female Seminary. The council approved his recommendation 21 May 1887.

24. Starr, *History of the Cherokee Indians*, 235, 240.

25. "Specifications of materials and labor for the construction of a Female Seminary for the Cherokee Nation at Tahlequah, Indian Territory, per plans, elevations, sections, and detail drawings by C. E. Illsley, Architect," 55, CHN 086, Microfilm roll 16, OHS; J. Strange, ed. "Cherokee Education" in Seminary file, CNHS, Tahlequah, Oklahoma.

26. "Survey of the Female Seminary Reservation, Cherokee Nation, April 28, 1890, by R. W. Walker, Surveyor," CHN 97 (microfilm), Cherokee *Schools: Female Seminary*, Documents 2735–2777, 11 May 1887–December 1902: Senate Bill Number Four, 6 July 1888, provided funds for additional work on the seminary, CHN 99. Benedict to Coppock, 9 November 1904, vol. 26, box 49, 632–33, Grant Foreman Collection, Gilcrease Institute, Tulsa, Oklahoma. For information regarding the structure, see *Historic American Buildings Survey, Report on the Cherokee Female Seminary* ("Seminary Hall"), (Washington: Department of the Interior, 1975), Archives, NSU; "Early Day Brickyards," in *Indian and Pioneer Histories*, ed. G. Foreman, vol. 59, 15–17; J. Strange, ed., "Seminaries" file, CNHS; Benedict to Morgan, *ARCIA for 1889–90*, 51st Cong.,

1st sess., H. Exec. Doc. 1 (serial 2725), pt. 5, 205; Bennett to Morgan, 10 September 1890, in *ARCIA for 1890–91*, 51st Cong., 2d sess., H. Exec. Doc. 1 (serial 2841), pt. 5, 93.

27. C. M. Sanders, Reminiscences; J. Strange, "Seminaries," 4–5; Ausley Welch interview, #cLL 216, L. L. Coll., OHS.

28. Statement of Rosa Gazelle Lane, interview, #cLL 598.1, L. L. Coll., OHS; *Kansas City Times*, 29 July 1889, 2; *Illustrated Souvenir Catalog: 1850–1906*, n.p.; Statement of May McSpadden Poole, student at the Female Seminary, 1906–7, in "Interviews of Pocahontas Club Members/Seminary Graduates," #cLL 598.1, L. L. Coll., OHS; Albert Sydney Wyly to John D. Benedict [1908], letter in Miscellaneous Female Seminary Box, Archives, NSU.

29. *Souvenir Catalog: 1850–1906*; interview with Mrs. Rod Richards, 9 November 1937, in *Indian and Pioneer Histories*, ed. G. Foreman, vol. 41, 437.

30. *Cherokee Advocate*, 22 April 1893, 2.

31. *Souvenir Catalog: 1850–1906*.

32. Coppock to Benedict, 15 July 1902, *ARCIA for 1902*, 57th Cong., 2d sess., H. Exec. Doc. 5 (serial 4459), 261; I. W. Tinnin, "Educational Influences," 60; receipt of Robert D. Patterson and Company, M943-1-10, Cherokee Nation Papers, WHC; see receipts in CHN 97, *Cherokee Schools: Female Seminary*, docs. 2735–2777, 11 May 1887 to December 1902; CHN 98, ibid., docs. 2775–2864, 31 December 1902 to 29 June 1905; and CHN 99, ibid., docs. 2865–2870, 1 July 1905 to May 1909.

33. *Souvenir Catalog: 1850–1906*; J. D. Benedict, 1 August 1906, *Report of the Supervisor of Cherokee Nation Schools*, in *ARCIA for 1906*, 59th Cong., 2d sess., H. Exec. Doc. 5 (serial 5118), 769.

34. *Souvenir Catalog: 1850–1906*; Zoe McSpadden Whitehill to L. G. B., 26 April 1957, in LGB Coll., NSU; A. S. Wyly to John Benedict [Spring 1909], in Female Seminary Miscellaneous Box, Archives, NSU, *Cherokee Schools: Female Seminary*, Doc. 2775–2864, 31 December 1902–29 June 1905, CHN 98, OHS; "Statement of Mrs. Edith Hicks Smith-Walker of Ft. Gibson, March 24, 1933, at Grant Foreman's, Muskogee," vol. 11, box 16, Grant Foreman Collection, Gilcrease Institute, Tulsa.

35. *Souvenir Catalog: 1850–1906*; G. Foreman, ed., *Indian and Pioneer Histories*, vol. 42, 27.

36. Mary Stapler's 1876 Grade Book, and C. M. Sanders, Tape I, Brad Agnew Collection, both in Archives, NSU.

37. For information on Booker T. Washington, see Samuel R. Spencer, Jr., *Booker T. Washington and the Negro's Place in American Life* (Boston: Little, Brown and Company, 1955); Hugh Hawkins, ed. *Booker T. Washington and His Critics: The Problem of Negro Leadership* (Boston: D. C. Heath and Company, 1962); Louis R. Harlan, *Booker T. Washington: The Wizard of Tuskegee, 1901–1915* (New York: Oxford University Press, 1983); idem, *Booker T. Washington: The Making of a Black Leader, 1856–1901* (New York: Oxford University Press, 1972).

38. *Cherokee Advocate*, 31 August 1881, 1.

39. Hewes, *Occupying the Cherokee Country*, 39.

40. Sec. 20 of "An Act Relating to Education," in *Compiled Laws of the Cherokee Nation* (Tahlequah, Indian Territory: National Advocate Print, 1881), reprinted in *CLAIT,* 9:236.

41. "Fourth Annual Message of Chief Dennis W. Bushyhead," in *Annual Messages of Hon. Chief D. W. Bushyhead,* 33, Special Collections, NSU; *Cherokee Advocate,* 17 November 1889, 1; Message of Chief Joel B. Mayes to National Council, 17 November 1889, in *Cherokee Letter Book,* vol. 14, 4; J. B. Mayes to T. J. Morgan, 18 October 1890, in *Cherokee Letter Book,* vol. 3, 11, Phillips Collection, Western History Collections, University of Oklahoma, Norman.

42. Letter signed W. S. Corderay, *Cherokee Advocate,* 6 June 1884, 1.

43. Curtis Act, 30 Stat. 495 (1898); "An Act To provide for the allotment of lands in severalty to Indians on the various reservations, and to extend the protection of the laws of the United States and the Territories over the Indians, and for other purposes," 8 February 1887, General Allotment Act/Dawes Act of 1887, 24 Statute L., 388; also see Miner, *Corporation and the Indian.*

44. For biographies of Benedict and Coppock, see *Illustrated Catalog: 1850–1905,* and Debo, *And Still the Waters Run,* 66–74.

45. Florence Wilson's "Great Leather-Bound Record Book," NSU; *Cherokee Advocate,* 9 September 1893, 2, and 14 March 1874, 2.

46. Wisdom to Jones, 17 September 1898, *ARCIA for 1898,* 55th Cong., 3rd sess., H. Exec. Doc. 5 (serial 3757), 157; W. A. Jones to Secretary of the Interior, 1 October 1900, *ARCIA for 1900,* 56th Cong., 2d sess., H. Exec. Doc. 5 (serial 4101), 240–41; Coppock to Benedict, 30 July 1902, *ARCIA for 1902,* 57th Cong., 2d sess., H. Exec. Doc. 5 (serial 4459), 240–41; Coppock to Benedict, 11 July 1901, *ARCIA for 1902,* 230.

47. Coppock to Benedict, 11 July 1901, *ARCIA for 1902,* pt. 2, 320.

48. Coppock to Benedict, 30 July 1902, *ARCIA for 1902,* 57th Cong., 2d sess., H. Exec. Doc. 5 (serial 4459), 240–41. Coppock to Benedict, 15 July 1902, *ARCIA for 1902,* 262; Coppock to Benedict, July 15, 1903, *ARCIA for 1903,* 58th Cong., 2d sess., H. Exec. Doc. 5 (serial 4646), pt. 2, 270–71.

49. Tinnin, "Educational Influences," 64; Owen to Atkins, 31 August 1885, *ARCIA for 1885–86,* 49th Cong., 1st sess., H. Exec. Doc. 1 (serial 2379), pt. 5, 329–34; Owen to Riley, *ARCIA for 1886–87,* 49th Cong., 2d sess., H. Exec. Doc. 1 (serial 2467), 5, 147.

50. Dr. Isabel Cobb, *Indian and Pioneer Histories,* vol. 65, 184–85; Etta Jane Scraper, excerpt from *TSA-LA-GI Columns* 8 (Spring 1984): 2.

51. Teachers Patsy Mayes and Mary Ann Duncan (Shelton) were seminary alumnae. Mary Llewelln Morgan graduated in 1894 and married William Lucullus Mayes. Ella Mae Covel graduated in 1899. See records of teacher payments in CHN 97 and CHN 99, Coppock to Benedict, 1899, *ARCIA for 1899,* 56th Cong., 1 st sess., H. Exec. Doc. 5 (serial 3915), pt. 2, 203; Report of W. A. Jones, 15 October 1901, *ARCIA for 1902,* 57th Cong., 1st sess., H. Exec. Doc. 5 (serial 4290), 135; Coppock to Benedict to Commissioner of Indian Affairs, 30 July 1902, *ARCIA for 1902,* 240. Minta Foreman, Dannie Ross, and Sallie G. Pendleton all attended the seminary.

52. J. Davis, "Belles of Tahlequah," 36; Evelyn Suagee Maheres interview,

#cLL 219.1; Bee McIntosh Fry and May McSpadden Poole interviews, #cLL 598.1, all in L. L. Coll., OHS.

53. "An Act in Relation to the Female Seminary," approved by Principal Chief T. M. Buffington, 4 December 1900, CHN 18, vol. 302, 77, also in CHN 99. The chiefs that served the Cherokee Nation during Wilson's tenure were Lewis Downing (November 1867 to November 1875), Charles Thompson (November 1875 to November 1879), Dennis Bushyhead (November 1879 to November 1888), Joel Mayes (January 1888 to December 1891), T. M. Buffington (5–23 December 1891, and November 1899 to November 1903), C. J. Harris (December 1891 to November 1895), S. H. Mayes (November 1895 to November 1899).

54. "An Act in Relation to the Female Seminary," CHN 18. An excerpt from the letter to Chief T. M. Buffington from J. George Wright, U.S. Indian Inspector for Indian Territory, 15 January 1901, regarding Senate Bill #22, D. 1612–1901, CHN 99, reads, "There would seem to be no difficulty in retaining Miss Wilson if her services be satisfactory to the Board of Education of the Cherokee Nation and the Superintendent of Schools in the Indian Territory, but it is believed to be unwise to establish the precedent of declaring that any person shall continue as a teacher of any school for life under all circumstances, and the act, therefore, appearing to be objectionable, it was recommended for disapproval." "An Act in Relation to the Female Seminary," 4 December 1900, CHN (microfilm), vol. 302, OHS.

55. Laura Gott (former student at Willie Halsell College), Muskogee, Oklahoma, to L. G. Bowers, 13 April 1947, and D. W. Hearon to L. G. Bowers, 31 March 1947, both in LGB Coll., NSU.

56. Maheres interview, #cLL 219.1, L. L. Coll., OHS; L. G. Bowers, "Traditions of Northeastern Given to Orientation Classes, 1937–1938," box 775, LGB Coll., NSU; Coppock to Benedict, 15 July 1902, ARCIA for 1902 (serial 4459), 263; Coppock to Benedict, ibid. (serial 4646), 273; Evelyn Suagee Maheres interview, #cLL 219.1, L. L. Coll., OHS; personal interview with Blanche Baker, 21 October 1988, Capital, Oklahoma. Rider's assistant teachers were seminary alumnae Mae Shelton, Flora Sabrina Lindsey, Lillian Alexander, Minta Foreman, Mineola Ward, Eldee Starr, Maymie Starr, Cherrie Adair, Beulah Benton Edmondson (remembered as "laughing, gay, and charming," and for her words of wisdom, such as "A hint to the wise is sufficient," and "Knowledge is the only jewel that will not decay"), and Janana Ballard (who possessed a "no-nonsense approach" to discipline and protocol); non-Cherokee teachers included Katherine Paine and Martha Lillian Williams. Flora Sabrina Lindsey taught from September 1901 to May 1902, when she died. Her sister Eldee took her position as fourth assistant teacher and remained until May 1902; Minneola Ward taught from 1901 to 1903. Beulah Benton Edmondson and Janana Ballard are profiled in Chapter 7;

57. Redd to Benedict, 1 August 1906, ARCIA for 1906, 59th Cong., 2d sess., H. Exec. Doc. 5 (serial 5118), 769; Statements of Poole and Alta Ward Nolton, #cLL 598.1, L. L. Coll., OHS.

58. Souvenir Catalog: 1850–1906; Statement of Mrs. Cecil Gibson Johnson,

student at the Female Seminary from 1906 to 1908, #cLL 219.2, L. L. Coll., OHS.

59. Coppock to Benedict, 11 July 1901, *ARCIA for 1902*, pt. 2, 319; Coppock to Benedict, 15 July 1902, ibid., 262.

60. *Northeastern State Normal School Catalog: 1909–1910*, 8, Archives, NSU; Governor Charles N. Haskell to the Oklahoma Legislature, 11 January 1909, in "Miscellaneous Documents," 67, Archives, NSU; Brad Agnew, "Northeastern: From Normal to University," *The Phoenix* 5 (1984): 3.

61. Cherokee Male Seminary Records of Grades, 1876–1909, Office of Admissions and Records, Administration Building, NSU; CHN 99, Cherokee *Schools: Female Seminary*, Documents 2865–2870, 1 July 1905–May 1909, OHS; Male Seminary Grade Book, NSU (for unknown reasons, many of the students are listed under two different grade levels during the same semester but were counted only once); C. M. Sanders, "After June 1909," 1, CNHS; idem, interview, #cLL 217.2, and Jack Brown interview, #cLL 213.1A, both in L. L. Coll., OHS.

62. *Cherokee Male Seminary*, 2870–A, OHS; personal interview with Blanche Baker.

63. Personal interview with Blanche Baker; Owen Covel interview, #cLL 216, L. L. Coll., OHS.

64. "Rules and Regulations: Male Seminary of the Cherokee Nation," compiled by teachers Herbert Taft Root, Robert C. Parks, and T. J. Adair, 13 February 1882, in Register of Cherokee Students, 1881–82, Records of the B.I.A., Record Group 75, 7RA 90/91, Federal Archives, Fort Worth, Texas; Brown interview, #cLL 608.2, L. L. Coll., OHS.

65. C. M. Sanders, "After 1909," 2; idem, interview, #cLL 217.2, L. L. Coll., OHS; J. Grover Scales, "Watching Seminary Burn," in "Life in the Cherokee Seminaries as Related by Former Students," ed. Roy Heffner, *May 7, 1973 Homecoming Brochure*, 1–2; James McSpadden interview, #cLL 215.2, L. L. Coll., OHS; Susie Martin Walker Alberty interview, #cLL 219.3, L. L. Coll., OHS; Ben Chandler interview, #cLL 215.1, James McSpadden interview, #cLL 215.2, and Jack Brown interview, #cLL 213.1A, all in L. L. Coll., OHS; personal interview with Roger Smith, 17 October 1988, Capital, Oklahoma.

66. *Preparing Indian Students to Meet the Challenges of the 80s* (Tahlequah: Northeastern State University, n.d.), 8 (this volume was a catalog provided for Indian students at Northeastern Oklahoma State University.); *Northeastern State University 1985–86 Students' Catalog* (Fort Worth: Evans Press, n.d.), 6–7. There is a question as to when the institution's name was changed officially from Northeastern State Normal School to Northeastern State Teachers College. According to written information provided by Delores Sumner, Special Collections Archivist at NSU, the Oklahoma Session Laws on 28 March 1923, refer to the school as Northeastern State Normal School, but by 1925 it was referred to as Northeastern State Teachers College in the appropriation documents; however, this was not an official change. Also, several issues of the school newspaper, *Northeastern News* (published in Tahlequah by the institution, now in Special Collections, NSU), further confuse the issue. The No-

vember 1920, vol. 5, issue refers to "Northeastern State Normal" on pages 1, 4; the March 1921, vol. 6, issue refers to "Northeastern State College" on page 1, "Northeastern State Normal School" on page 2, and "Northeastern Normal College" on page 3; the May 1921, vol. 6, issue calls the institution "Northeastern Teachers College" on page 1, and the November 1921, vol. 6, issue refers to "Northeastern Normal School" on page 1, and on page 2 calls the school "Northeastern State Normal."

67. Typescript provided by Delores Sumner, Special Collections Archivist, NSU.

68. G. Foreman, ed., *Indian and Pioneer Histories*, vol. 2, 32. Fite's statement also appears in the *Souvenir Catalog: 1850–1906*.

Chapter 5: Life at the Seminary

1. C. T. Foreman, *Park Hill*, 154, 160.

2. For a compilation of stores in the historic Tahlequah area, see Melody Lynn McCoy, "Location and Enterprise: A Review of Merchants in the Cherokee Nation, 1865–1907" (Master's thesis, Harvard University, 1981); West, *Tahlequah*, 61, 63, 102; receipts for wagon rental in "Account with Johnson Thompson," box 255A, John T. Drew Papers, in Special Collections, Northeastern State University, Tahlequah, Oklahoma; *Cherokee Advocate*, 21 October 1893, 2; Evelyn Suagee Maheres interview, #cLL 219.1, and Susie Martin Walker Alberty interview, #cLL 219.3, both in L. L. Coll., OHS; Tinnin, "Educational Influences," 60. The Cherokee National Prison was built in 1874 and still stands today in Tahlequah.

3. C. T. Foreman, *Park Hill*, 155; J. Strange, ed., "Seminaries," 5, typescript at CNHS, Tahlequah, Oklahoma; *Cherokee Advocate*, 22 April 1893, 2; Evelyn Suagee Maheres interview, #cLL 217.2, and Rosanna Harnage Daniel interview, #cLL 598.1, both in L. L. Coll., OHS; J. Strange, "Seminaries," 5; West, *Tahlequah*, 112; Ada, Anna, Elinor, and Ella Cookson all attended the seminary during the 1904–5 school year. According to Jack Brown (interview #cLL 213.1A, L. L. Coll., OHS), former student and teacher at the Male Seminary, the boys also had access to tennis courts, but considered it a "sissy sport." The teachers, however, played tennis often.

4. Bowers and Garrett, *A. Florence Wilson*, 6, 8, 22; *Cherokee Advocate*, 28 March 1877, 3; ibid., 10 December 1879; ibid., 31 August 1881; ibid., 14 September 181; ibid., 8 June 1882; ibid., 4 January 184; ibid., 22 April 1893, 2.

5. May McSpadden Poole (student at the Female Seminary from 1906 to 1907) interview, #cLL 598.1, L. L. Coll., OHS.

6. Eva Dameron Uhle interview, #cLL 215.3, L. L. Coll., OHS. The World's Fair at St. Louis was open from 30 April to 30 November 1904.

7. *Cherokee Advocate*, 2 December 1899, 2; Evelyn Suagee Maheres interview, #cLL 217.2, L. L. Coll., OHS; J. Strange, "Seminaries," 5.

160 Notes to Pages 75–77

8. Typescript of statement of Fannie Blythe Marks, 14 March 1942, "The Old Female Seminary," in the LGB Coll., NSU (Fannie Blythe graduated from the seminary in 1879); *Eufaula Indian Journal*, 28 June 1877; *Cherokee Advocate*, 11 July 1874, 2; ibid., 23 May 1884; Bowers and Garrett, *A. Florence Wilson*, 28; C. T. Foreman, *Park Hill*, 153–55, 160; Evelyn Suagee Maheres interview, #cLL 219.1, L. L. Coll., OHS; G. Foreman, ed., *Indian and Pioneer Histories*, vol. 43, 105. Anna Cora Archer graduated from the seminary in 1879 and married William Ross Shackleford. Mattie Bell, Nancy Robertson, and Arabella Nicholson attended the seminary for a few semesters, but did not graduate. The boat *Ada Archer* was owned by Riley Keys, Jr., and was named for Ada Archer, a student at the seminary during the 1876–77 school year; Archer graduated from the Kirkwood Seminary in 1882 and was a teacher at the Cherokee Female Seminary from 1883 to 1885.

9. Excerpt from manuscript of Hannah Worcester Hicks in the Alice M. Robertson Collection, McFarlin Library, Department of Special Collections, University of Tulsa.

10. *Cherokee Advocate*, 22 May 1885. Olive Heath was the elocution teacher at the seminary from February to June 1899; *Fort Smith Elevator*, 1 July 1892, 2; *The Tahlequah Arrow*, 24 May 1908, 4; ibid., 17 June 1908, 1. Also see Female Seminary Miscellaneous Box, Archives, NSU.

11. *1850–1909 Cherokee National Female Seminary Commencement Calendar*, Archives, NSU.

12. Ibid. For a short bibliographical sketch of Albert Sydney Wyly, see the *Souvenir Catalog: 1850–1906*.

13. *1850–1909 Seminary Commencement Calendar*.

14. Interview with Mrs. Rhoderick Dhu Richards (Grace Raper Wallace, a June 1903 graduate of the Female Seminary), *Indian and Pioneer Histories*, ed. G. Foreman, vol. 41, 437; "An Act amending the school law," 8 December 1883, in *Laws and Joint Resolutions of the Cherokee Nation Enacted During the Regular and Special Sessions of the Years 1881–3* (Tahlequah: E. C. Boudinot, Jr., Printer, 1884), reprinted in *CLAIT*, 6:121.

15. Tinnin, "Educational Influences," 63.

16. Bowersand Garrett, *A. Florence Wilson*, 14; C. T. Foreman, *Park Hill*, 158–59; *Cherokee Advocate*, 2 March 1881; D. W. Hearon to L. G. Bowers, 10 April 1947, L. G. B. to K. Garrett, December 19[47], Gonia Tinnin Edmondson to L. G. Bowers, n.d., LGB Coll., NSU; "General Rules of the Female Seminary of the Cherokee Nation," 13 February 1882, in Register of Cherokee Students, 7RA 90/91 (microfilm), Choctaw 1911 Payroll and Index; Register of Cherokee Students, 1881–1882, Federal Archives and Records Center, Fort Worth, Texas.

17. Arlie Rowe, tape I, Brad Agnew Collection, Archives, NSU.

18. Margaret Kidd, ibid.

19. C. M. Sanders, ibid. The students involved in the rendezvous were Mina Taylor, Susie Cobb, Paddy Mayes, and Owen Thornton.

20. Excerpt by Josephine Alice Crutchfield Dale in "Biographies of Members of the Class," in E. Starr, ed., *I Remember: Class of 1904, Commemorating the Fiftieth Anniversary of the Graduation Class of 1902*, 18–19, Archives, NSU.

21. Ibid.; Eva Dameron Uhle (student at the Female Seminary from 1901 to 1904) interview, #cLL 215.3, and Owen Covel interview, #cLL 216, both in L. L. Coll., OHS.

22. Typescript entitled "Orientations," LGB Coll., NSU; *Cherokee Advocate*, 16 September 1893, 2.

23. Gonia T. Edmondson to L. G. B., n.d., and L. G. B. to K. Garrett, 6 December 19[47], both in LGB Coll., NSU.

24. *Cherokee Male Seminary*, 2870–A, OHS; personal interview with Blanche Baker.

25. D. W. Hearon to L. G. Bowers, 31 March 1947, LGB Coll., NSU.

26. C. M. Sanders, Reminiscences, 3; J. Strange, "Seminaries," 7; Ruth Haynes Gerrard interview, #cLL 598.1, L. L. Coll., OHS; D. W. Hearon to L. G. Bowers, 10 April 1947, LGB Coll., NSU; also see photographs in the Anna Piburn Collection at the Western History Collection, Norman.

27. *Cherokee Advocate*, 23 September 1892, 2; typescript of Mrs. Fannie Blythe Marks, an 1879 graduate of the seminary, dated 14 March 1942, LGB Coll, NSU.

28. Gonia Edmondson Tinnin to L. G. Bowers, n.d., LGB Coll., NSU.

29. L. G. Bowers to K. Garrett, 6 December 19[47], LGB Coll., NSU.

30. *Cherokee Advocate*, 26 April 1888, 3.

31. Devon A. Mihesuah, "Too Dark to Be Angels: The Class System among the Cherokees at the Female Seminary," *American Indian Culture and Research Journal* 15 (1991): 32–33.

32. Compiled from Index to the Five Civilized Tribes, the Final Dawes Roll, M1186, roll 1, and Enrollment cards for the Five Civilized Tribes, 1898–1914, rolls 2–15, cards 1–11132, Federal Archives, Fort Worth branch.

33. Albert Sydney Wyly to John D. Benedict (1908), letter in Miscellaneous Female Seminary Box, archives, NSU.

34. Abbott, "Ann Florence Wilson."

35. Maggie Culver Fry, comp., *Cherokee Female Seminary Years: A Cherokee National Anthology by Many Tribal Authors* (Claremore, Okla.: Rogers State College Press, 1988), 83.

36. Ibid., 104–5.

37. Kate O'Donald Ringland to Abraham Knepler, 21 April 1938, cited in Knepler, "Education of the Cherokee Indians," 323.

38. Personal interview with Rodney Taylor, 27 December 1988, Midway, Texas.

39. *Cherokee Advocate*, 23 August 1873, 2.

40. *Kansas City Times*, 29 July 1889, 2. Stephen's comment almost echoes Thomas Jefferson's speech to Indians visiting Washington, D.C., in 1808, when he said, "You will unite yourselves with us, join in our great councils and form one people with us, and we shall all be Americans; you will mix with us by marriage, your blood will run in our veins, and will spread with us over this great continent." In Saul K. Padover, *Thomas Jefferson on Democracy* (New York: Mentor, New American Library, Appleton-Century, 1939), 106–7.

41. *Cherokee Advocate*, 4 February 1851, 2.

42. C. M. Sanders, Reminiscences.

43. For information on federal boarding schools, see Sally J. McBeth, *Ethnic Identity and the Boarding School Experience of West-Central Oklahoma American Indians* (New York: University Press of America, 1983); Robert A. Trennert, Jr., *The Phoenix Indian School: Forced Assimilation in Arizona, 1891–1935* (Norman: University of Oklahoma Press, 1988); Richard Henry Pratt, *Battlefield and Classroom: Four Decades with the American Indian, 1867–1904* (New Haven: Yale University Press, 1964); Wilbert H. Ahern, " 'The Returned Indians': Hampton Institute and its Indian Alumnae, 1879–1893," *Journal of Ethnic Studies* 10 (Winter 1983): 101–24; idem, "To Kill the Indian and Save the Man: The Boarding School and American Indian Education," in Larry Remele, ed., *Fort Totten: Military Post and Indian School, 1867–1959* (Bismark: State Historical Society of North Dakota, 1986), 23–59; idem, "Indian Education and Bureaucracy: The School at Morris, 1887–1909," *Minnesota History* 51 (Fall 1984): 83–98; Alban W. Hoopes, "Indian Education, 1879–1939," *Educational Outlook* 14 (January 1940): 49–63; Charles R. Kutzleb, "Educating the Dakota Sioux, 1876–1890," *North Dakota History* 32 (1965): 197–215; David Wallace Adams, "Schooling the Hopi: Federal Indian Policy Writ Small, 1887–1917," *Pacific Historical Review* 48 (August 1979): 335–56; Frederick E. Hoxie, "Beyond Savagery: The Campaign to Assimilate the Indians, 1880–1920" (Ph.D. diss., Brandeis University, 1977); also see Francis La Flesche, *The Middle Five: Indian Schoolboys of the Omaha Tribe* (Lincoln: University of Nebraska Press, 1963); Basil H. Johnson, *Indian School Days* (Norman: University of Oklahoma Press 1988).

44. Florence Wilson's "Great Leather-Bound Record Book," NSU.

45. Personal interview with Ellen Powers, 2 October 1988, Capital, Oklahoma.

46. Ibid.

Chapter 6: Medicine for the Rosebuds

1. For descriptions of some of the ailments that afflicted the seminary girls, see Annual Reports of the Medical Superintendent, Walter T. Adair, M.D., 10 November 1877, in CHN 100, *Schools: Medical Superintendent*, in Letters Sent and Letters Received and Other Documents, Cherokee Nation (Tahlequah), Undated and 22 November 1876 to 12 January 1901, OHS; ibid., 5 November 1878; ibid., 7 November 1881; ibid., 1 October 1886; W. T. Adair to the Cherokee National Council, 3 October 1885, Cherokee, vol. 403 (microfilm), 276–81, OHS; *Cherokee Advocate*, 4 April 1877, 2; ibid., 18 April 1877, 3; ibid., 9 May 1877, 3; C. T. Foreman, *Park Hill*, 154–55; Owen to Atkins, 31 August 1885, *ARCIA for 1885–86*, 49th Cong., 1st sess., H. Exec. Doc. 1 (serial 2379), pt. 5, 329–34; Owen to Riley, 1887, *ARCIA for 1886–87*, 147. For information on "hysteria," see Carroll Smith-Rosenberg, "The Hysterical Woman: Sex Roles and Role Conflict in Nineteenth-Century America," in Ester Katz and Anita

Rapone, *Women's Experience in America* (New Brunswick, N.J.: Transaction Books, 1980), 315–37.

2. *Cherokee Advocate*, 4 April 1877, 2; C. M. Ross to T. M. Buffington, Principal Chief, Cherokee Nation, 20 October 1900, in Official's Reports to the Principal Chief—Year 1899—Tahlequah, Cherokee Nation, Indian Territory, Cherokee, vol. 428, OHS, 336–38; Charlotte Mayes Sanders interview, Tape II, Brad Agnew Collection, NSU; Betsey Orwee died (d.) 5 September 1876; Indianola Hildebrand d. 21 March 1877; Angie Byers d. 15 April 1877; Martha W. Martin d. 7 December 1877; Laura Scales d. 9 November 1878; Eliza Mills d. August 1878; Jane Couch d. 18 November 1878; Lucinda Smith d. 1 August 1878; Sallie Locust d. 30 October 1883; Lou Landrum d. 29 October 1885; Lulu Crutchfield d. 4 March 1886; Philouri Scruggs d. 27 February 1886; Lizzie Thornton d. 8 April 1886; Ida Brown d. 1890; Mary McLemore d. 1893; Anna Klaus d. 28 October 1901; Winnie Ward d. March 1908.

3. Annual Report of W. T. Adair, 1 October 1886, in *Schools: Medical Superintendent*; Coppock to Benedict, 10 July 1900, *ARCIA for 1900*, 56th Cong., 1st sess., H. Doc. 5 (serial 4101), 167; Coppock to Benedict, 11 July 1901, *ARCIA for 1901*, 57th Cong., 1st sess., H. Doc. 5 (serial 4291), 318; Samuel Starr, comp., "Epidemic of Smallpox," excerpt from *I Remember: Class of 1904*, brochure commemorating the fiftieth anniversary of the graduating class of 1904 from the Cherokee National Seminaries, Special Collections, NSU.

4. Annual Report of Joseph M. Thompson, M.D., October 1890, in *Schools: Medical Superintendent*, OHS; Owen to Atkins, 31 August 1885, *ARCIA for 1885–86*, 49th Cong., 2d sess., H. Exec. Doc. 1 (serial 2379), pt. 5, 329–34; Owen to Riley, 1887, in ibid., *ARCIA for 1886–87*, 147; W. T. Adair to the Cherokee National Council, 3 October 1885, in *Official Reports, 1880–1885*, Cherokee volume 403, 276–81; *Cherokee Advocate*, 17 October 1884, 2.

5. Annual Report of W. T. Adair, 19 November 1877, in *Schools: Medical Superintendent*, OHS.

6. *Cherokee Advocate*, 4 April 1874, 2; Mrs. W. P. Ross, *William Potter Ross*, 197; Smith to Secretary of the Interior, 1 November 1874, *ARCIA for 1877–78*, 45th Cong., 2d sess., H. Exec. Doc. 1 (serial 1800), pt. 5, 505.

7. "An Act providing for a Medical Superintendent for the Male and Female High Schools," 22 November 1876, *CLAIT*, 5:7–8; "An Act making Walter T. Adair Medical Superintendent for the Male and Female Seminaries," 8 December 1876, ibid., 43.

8. Harry F. O'Bierne and Edward S. O'Bierne, "Walter Thompson Adair, M.D.," in *The Indian Territory: Its Chiefs, Legislators and Leading Men* (St. Louis: C. B. Woodward, 1893), 326–28.

9. Mabel Washbourne Anderson, *The Life of Stand Watie and Contemporary Cherokee History* (Pryor, Okla., 1931), 69.

10. Annual Report of W. T. Adair, 10 November 1877; ibid., 5 November 1878; Thomas Lee Ballenger, "Copies of Miscellaneous Cherokee Letters," Special Collections, NSU.

11. C. T. Foreman, *Park Hill*, 158; "An Act providing for a Medical Superintendent for the Male and Female Seminaries, Insane Asylum, and National

Prison," 18 November 1880, in *Complied Laws of the Cherokee Nation* (Tah-lequah, Indian Territory: National Advocate Print, 1881), reprinted in *CLAIT,* 9:326–27. See also Carl T. Steen, "The Home for the Insane, Deaf, Dumb, and Blind of the Cherokee Nation," *CO* 21 (December 1943): 402–19, and C. T. Foreman, "Captain David McNair and His Descendants," *CO* 36 (Autumn 1958): 278.

12. Narcissa Owen, *The Memoirs of Narcissa Owen* (Seattle: University of Washington Press, 1907), 89; Mrs. Cecil Gibson Johnson interview, #cLL 219.2, L. L. Coll., OHS.

13. Owen, *Memoirs,* 90.

14. Annual Report of W. T. Adair, 1 October 1886, in *Schools: Medical Superintendent;* An Act relating to the Male and Female Seminaries, 21 November 1884, *CLAIT,* 7:16.

15. Annual Report of W. T. Adair, 1 October 1886.

16. Annual Report of the Medical Superintendent of the Male and Female Seminaries, 7 November 1889, *Cherokee Nation Papers: Education,* M 943–1–10, box 4, folder 876, WHC.

17. Letter of charge from S. M. Whidden and E. P. Parris to Honorable Dennis W. Bushyhead, 16 December 1884. Affidavit of Daniel H. Ross, editor of *The Cherokee Advocate,* to Allen Ross, Clerk, Tahlequah District, Cherokee Nation, 29 December 1884, in CHN 101–14, Cherokee (Tahlequah), *Miscellaneous Schools,* 1 February 1884 to 30 December 1884, OHS; CHN 99 Cherokee (Tahlequah) *Schools: Female Seminary,* undated and 5 December 1874 to 15 January 1909; affidavit of C. P. Mayes to J. W. Ivy, Special Clerk of the Tahlequah District, Cherokee Nation, 22 December 1884.

18. Instructions to the sick-nurse at the Cherokee Female Seminary from W. T. Adair, 3 November 1884, 7 and 8 November 1884, and 29 December 1884, in CHN 101–14.

19. W. T. Adair to the Cherokee National Council, 3 October 1885, Cherokee, volume 403, 276–81.

20. Annual Report of W. T. Adair, 1 October 1886.

21. Ibid.

22. *Cherokee Advocate,* 27 November 1889, 1; O'Bierne and O'Bierne, "Joseph M. Thompson, M.D.," in *Indian Territory,* 403–4; J. G. Sanders, *Who's Who among Oklahoma Indians* (Oklahoma City: Trave Publishing Company, 1928), 95.

23. Annual Report of J. M. Thompson, 9 November 1889, in *Schools: Medical Superintendent.*

24. Isabel Cobb, M.D., Nursery and Childrens' Hospital, West New Brighten, Staten Island, New York, to Chief C. J. Harris, 29 October 1892, in CHN 99. Belle Cobb is profiled in Chapter 7.

25. Annual Report of the Medical Superintendent of Cherokee High Schools and Physician to the Insane Asylum and National Prison, Richard L. Fite, M.D., Tahlequah, Indian Territory, February 189[3] (first page of report missing) to August 1894 in Lela K. Canada, R.N., *History of the Student Health Center,*

a bound volume in Special Collections, NSU; *Souvenir Catalogue: 1850-1906*, 37.

26. Annual Report of Medical Superintendent, Joseph M. Thompson, 9 November 1889, in *Schools: Medical Superintendent*; R. F. Wyly to C. J. Harris, 24 November 1893, in CHN 99; *Cherokee Advocate*, 27 November 1889, 1; ibid., 26 May 1900, 2; Coppock to Benedict, 15 July 1902, *ARCIA for 1902*, 57th Cong., 2d sess., H. Doc. 5 (serial 4459), 262; Coppock to Benedict, 15 July 1903, *ARCIA for 1903*, 58th Cong., 2d sess., H. Doc. 5 (serial 4646), pt. 2, 272.

27. O'Bierne and O'Bierne, "Dr. Charles M. Ross," in *Indian Territory*, 154; Duane H. King, "The Great Tahlequah Fire of 1895," *TSA-LA-GI Columns* 10 (1987): 2; *Cherokee Advocate*, 17 November 1900, 2.

28. Charles M. Ross to Principal Chief, Cherokee Nation, 10 October 1899, in Officials' Reports to the Principal Chief—Year 1899, 315-16; *Cherokee Advocate*, 26 May 1900, 2; Coppock to Benedict, 9 November 1904, vol. 26, box 49, 632-3, G. Foreman Coll., Gilcrease Institute, Tulsa, Oklahoma; Zoe McSpadden Whitehill to L. G. Bowers, 26 April 1957, LGB Coll., NSU; Sec. 558 of "An Act Relating to Education," *CLAIT*, 10:281.

29. Lola Garrett Bowers, excerpt from Alice Bershire, ed., *History of Physical Education, Northeastern State College, Presented to the State Educational Historical Commission, 23 June 1952*, Special Collections, John Vaughan Library, NSU; Dora Wilson Hearon, Denver, Colorado, to L. G. Bowers, 10 April 1947, in LGB Coll., NSU; Etta Jane Scraper, "Reminiscences of the Cherokee Female Seminary," *TSA-LA-GI Columns* 8 (Spring, 1984): 2; *Souvenir Catalogue, 1850-1906*, 5.

30. *Cherokee National Papers: Education*, M 943-1-10, box 2, folder 63; ibid, box 3, folder 70; CHN 97, *Cherokee Schools: Female Seminary*, Docs. 2735-2777, Letters Sent and Letters Received and Other Documents, 11 May 1887-December 1902, OHS: ibid., 31 December 1902 to 29 June 1905, Docs. 2775-2864, CHN 98; *Indian-Pioneer Histories*, vol. 41, 436; CHN 99; "An Act Relative to High Schools and Orphan Asylums," 12 December 1885, *CLAIT*, 7:31.

31. Interview with Patric Stevens, 12 August 1988, Trinity, Texas; Fry, *Seminary Years*, 128.

32. Strange, ed., excerpt from *TSA-LA-GI Columns* (August 1982-January 1983): 7; J. Davis, "Belles of Tahlequah," 37; Bowers and Garrett, *A. Florence Wilson*, 12; E. J. Scraper, "Reminiscing," in the seminaries' 7 May 1971 homecoming program entitled *Life in the Cherokee Seminaries as Related by Former Students*, 4-7; Joseph F. Robertson, "Tamale Mischief" in ibid., 1; Susie Martin Walker Alberty interview, #cLL 219.3, L. L. Coll., OHS.

33. Annual Report, Medical Superintendent of Male and Female Seminaries, 7 November 1879, Cherokee Nation Papers, M 943-1-10, box 4, F876, WHC.

34. See Virginia E. Allen, " 'When We Settle Down, We Grow Pale and Die; Health in Western Indian Territory,' " *Oklahoma State Medical Association Journal* 70 (June 1977): 227-32.

Chapter 7: Farewell to the Seminary

1. See N. B. Johnson, "The Cherokee Orphan Asylum," *CO* 44 (Autumn 1966): 275–280.

2. The students' home districts were compiled from the 1880 Cherokee Census and Index, Schedules 1–6, 7RA-07, rolls, 1–4, and the 1890 Cherokee Census (no index), Schedules 1–4, 7RA-08, rolls 1–4, at Federal Archives and Records Center, Forth Worth, Texas; Wilson's Grade Book; Mary Stapler's Class Book; *Catalog of the C.N.F.S., 1896 and Announcements for 1897 and 1898*, 3–6; *Souvenir Catalog: 1850–1906*; "Register and Accounts of Female Seminary Primary and Boarding School Students" (bound ledger), all in Archives, NSU.

3. The following families had at least three of their members enrolled in the seminary at the same time: Abbott, Ballard, Barnes, Bean, Benge, Blackstone, Brewer, Chamberlain, Christie, Cobb, Cookson, Crutchfield, Cunningham, Daniels, Dougherty/Dougherity, Downing, Duckworth, Duncan, Eaton, Edmondson, England, Eubanks, Fields, Foreman, Freeman, French, Frye, Garrett, Ghormley, Gunter, Hare, Harland, Harnage, Harris, Hawkins, Heinrichs/Heindricks, Henry, Hicks, Hill, Holland, Horn, Jackson, Kidd, Landrum, Lindsey, Lowrey/Lowry, Lynch, McDaniel, McGhee, McNair, McSpadden, Martin, Mayes, Mayfield, Melton, Miller, Morgan, Morris, Musgrove, Nash, Nicholson, Nidiffer, Osage, Paden, Parris, Philips, Prather, Price, Pyeatte, Rattlinggourd, Rider, Riley, Roach, Roberts, Rogers, Ross, Sanders, Schrimcher, Scott, Scraper, Sevier, Shelton, Sixkiller, Sloan, Smith, Spears, Starr, Sunday, Swimmer, Taylor, Thompson, Thornton, Vann, Walker, Walkingstick, Ward, Welch, West, Wetzel, Williams, Wilson, Wolfe, Woodall, Woods, Wyly.

4. The parents' literacy rates were compiled from the 1880 Cherokee Census and Index, Schedules 1–6, 7RA-07, rolls 1–4, and the 1890 Cherokee Census (no index), schedules 1–4, 7RA-08, rolls 1–4, at Federal Archives, Fort Worth branch.

5. *Cherokee Advocate*, 9 September 1893, 2; ibid., 16 September 1893, 2; ibid., 30 September 1893, 2; ibid., 7 October 1893, 2; ibid., 14 October 1893, 2; Coppock to Benedict, 11 July 1901, *ARCIA for 1901*, 57th Cong., 1st sess., H. Doc. 5 (serial 4291), 318–19; CHN 97, *Cherokee Schools: Female Seminary Documents 2735–2777*, 11 May 1887–December 1902, at OHS.

6. Florence Wilson's "Great Leather-Bound Record Book," NSU.

7. Cherokee 1880 and 1890 Census Records; Final Dawes Roll; Enrollment Cards for the Five Civilized Tribes; Wardell, *Political History*; Louis Thompson, "A Cross Section in the Life of a Missionary Teacher among the Indians," *CO* 17 (March-December 1939): 329–23.

8. K. Tsianina Lomawaima, "Oral Histories From Chilocco Indian Agricultural School, 1920–1940," *American Indian Quarterly* 11 (Summer 1987): 241–54.

9. See Devon A. Mihesuah, "'Out of the Graves of the Polluted Debauches': The Boys of the Cherokee Male Seminary," *American Indian Quarterly* 15 (Fall 1991): 503–21.

10. The years in which males outnumbered females enrolled in Cherokee schools were 1872, 1877, and 1900. Ballenger, *Lists of Seminary Students*; Wilson's Grade Book; *ARCIA* for the following years: *1872* (serial 1560), 387; *1873* (serial 1601), 336-37; *1875* (serial 1680), 110-11 (same data as for 1874); *1876* (serial 1749), 212-13; *1877* (serial 1800), 234-35, 294-95; *1884* (serial 2287), 270-71; *1888* (serial 2637), 118; *1899* (serial 3915), 92; *1899* (serial 3916), 203; *1900* (serial 4101), 113, 168; *1902* (serial 4458), 124; idem, *1902* (serial 4291), 293, 319; *1902* (serial 4459), 263; *1903* (serial 4645), 79; *1903* (serial 4646), 269; *1904* (serial 4798), 94; *1906* (serial 4959), 113; *1907* (I20.1: 907), 97; Summary of the 1880 Census of the Cherokee Nation, 11, WHC.

11. "A Valedictory Address by a Cherokee Lady of the Class of 1856," in NSU Archives.

12. *ARCIA for 1879*, 42d Cong., 2d sess., H. Doc. 1 (serial 1505), 599.

13. *Wreath of Cherokee Rose Buds*, 14 February 1855, 8; also see Anne Firor Scott, "Women's Perspective on the Patriarchy in the 1850s," *Journal of American History* 61·(June 1974): 52-64.

14. See Appendix B for a list of early alumnae who taught.

15. C. T. Foreman, "Aunt Eliza of Tahlequah," *CO* 9 (March 1931): 43-55.

16. "Special Message of Honorable D. W. Bushyhead, Principal Chief, May 9, 1879," box 4, file 470, D. W. Bushyhead Collection, Special Collections, NSU.

17. Ann Firor Scott, "The Ever-Widening Circle: The Diffusion of Feminist Values From the Troy Female Seminary, 1822-1872," *History of Education Quarterly* 19 (Spring 1979): 3-25.

18. *Tahlequah Arrow*, 7 June 1902, 1, 4.

19. Tinnin, "Educational Influences," 64; Pocahontas Club members interview, #cLL 598.1, L. L. Coll., OHS.

20. Compiled from Starr, *History of the Cherokee Indians*, 489-680; Sanders, *Who's Who*.

21. Starr, *History of the Cherokee Indians*, 655, 494-95; Sanders, *Who's Who*, 188; *Muskogee Daily Phoenix and Times Democrat*, 2 November 1988, 9; G. Foreman, ed., *Indian and Pioneer Histories*, vol. 43, 105.

22. Muriel H. Wright, "Rachel Caroline Eaton," *CO* 10 (March 1932): 8; Sanders, *Who's Who*, 18; Starr, *History of the Cherokee Indians*, 666. Martha Pauline Eaton graduated in 1897 and John Merrit Eaton graduated in 1899.

23. Sanders, *Who's Who*, 18.

24. Starr, *History of the Cherokee Indians*, 489; Sanders, *Who's Who*, last page; manuscript of Belle Cobb in *Indian and Pioneer Histories*, ed. G. Foreman, vol. 65, 184-218; *The Record-Democrat* (Wagoner, Oklahoma), 14 August 1947, 1.

25. Sanders, *Who's Who*, 19, 26, 28, 45, 77; Starr, *History of the Cherokee Indians*, 679.

26. Sanders, *Who's Who*, 19.

27. Ibid., 90; Starr, *History of the Cherokee Indians*, 424.

28. Sanders, *Who's Who*, 45.

29. Ibid., 90, 185.

30. See Appendix C.

31. See Appendices D and E.

32. Personal interview with Edward Morgan, 18 October 1988, Capital, Oklahoma.

33. Thomas J. Harrison, "Carlotta Archer: 1865–1946," *CO* 25 (Spring-Winter 1947–48): 158–60; *Cherokee Seminaries Homecoming Program for May 7, 1958*, Archives, NSU; Starr, *History of the Cherokee Indians*, 666, 678–79; Wright, "Rachel C. Eaton."

34. See transcript cards of all the Northeastern State Normal School students in the Archives of NSU. These cards give the date enrolled, courses and grades, hometown, student's age, number of months taught, parents' names, and previous education.

35. Peggy Pascoe, *Relations of Rescue: The Search for Female Moral Authority in the American West, 1874–1939* (New York: Oxford University Press, 1990), 54–56, 115–22, 123–27, 142–43.

36. Frazier, *Black Bourgeoisie*.

37. Joyce Antler, "After College, What?: New Graduates and the Family Claim," *American Quarterly* 32 (Fall 1980): 409–34; Robert Conley's short story "Wickliffe," one of his eighteen excellent essays in *The Witch of Goingsnake and Other Stories* (Norman: University of Oklahoma Press, 1988), 71–79, illustrates the wide gulf between the values of the mixed-bloods and fullblood Cherokees and the cultural confusion many Cherokees faced (and still face).

38. Derived from the 1880 Cherokee Census and Index, Schedules 1–6, 7RA-07, rolls 1–4, and the 1890 Cherokee Census (no index), schedules 1–4, 7RA-08, rolls 1–4, and Index to the Five Civilized Tribes, the Final Dawes Roll, M1186, roll 1, and the Enrollment Cards for the Five Civilized Tribes, 1898–1914, M1186, rolls 2–15, cards 1–11132, at the Federal Archives, Fort Worth branch. The blood quantums of the graduates are given in Appendix A. Most of the girls of seven-eighths or more Cherokee blood graduated prior to 1880.

39. Compiled from Starr, *History of the Cherokee Indians*, 489–672; Sanders, *Who's Who*; Paul W. Dewitz, *Notable Men of Indian Territory at the Beginning of the 20th Century, 1904–1905* (Muskogee, Indian Territory: Southwest Historical Company, 1905); Littlefield and Parins, *Bibliography of Native American Writers*; O'Bierne and O'Bierne, *Indian Territory*; various issues of the *Chronicles of Oklahoma*, *The Cherokee Advocate*, and Female and Male Seminary yearly catalogs and homecoming brochures.

40. See Appendix F.

41. Cherokee Censuses for 1880 and 1890; Final Dawes Roll and Enrollment Cards for the Five Civilized Tribes.

42. It is noteworthy that descendants of the seminarians are exceedingly defensive about their ancestors, and that defensiveness is quite revealing. One individual objected to any of the alumnae being referred to as "elitist." Yet her letter to me read, "The people I knew were not elitist, but they did consider themselves to be elite. I was always taught that the mixed-blood Cherokees

were the only true aristocrats in this country. There was a real sense of noblisse oblige [sic] among the members of my family of that age."

43. See the seminaries' Students Association programs and correspondence in box of same name, group 30, correspondence, in Archives, NSU. It is quite possible that the reputation of the graduates accounts for the "Cherokee grandmother" phenomenon. If a white American were to claim Indian lineage, why not an educated, Christian, civilized, and therefore "safe" tribe, as opposed to a supposed "wild" and heathenistic one? See also Rayna Green, "The Tribe Called Wannabee: Playing Indian in America and Europe," *Folklore* 99 (1988): 30–55.

44. Personal interview with Blanche Baker, 21 October 1988, Capital, Oklahoma.

45. Fry, *Female Seminary Years*, 157.

46. For discussions on Indian identity, race, and culture, see W. David Baird, "Real Indians in Oklahoma?" *CO* 68 (Spring 1990): 4–23; William T. Hagan, "Fullblood, Mixed-blood, Generic, and Ersatz: The Problem of Indian Identity," *Arizona and the West* 27 (Winter 1985): 309–26; Robert Jarvenpa, "The Political Economy and Political Ethnicity of American Adaptations and Identities," *Ethnic and Racial Studies* 8 (January 1985): 29–48; Gossett, *Race*; Reginald Horsman, *Race and Manifest Destiny: The Origins of American Racial Anglo-Saxonism* (Cambridge, Mass.: Harvard University Press, 1981); James A. Clifton, ed., *Being and Becoming Indian: Biographical Studies of North American Frontiers* (Chicago: Dorsey Press, 1989). Chapter 1 of the latter is rather cynical and insulting to mixed-bloods, but thought-provoking nonetheless.

47. *ARCIA for 1852* (serial 673), 407; Summary of the Census of the Cherokee Nation for 1880, 11; *ARCIA for 1899* (serial 3916), 203; *ARCIA for 1903* (serial 4646), 271; Ballenger, *Lists of Seminarians*; Wilson's Grade Book.

48. Personal interview with Michael Hammond, 18 October 1988, Capital, Oklahoma.

Epilogue

1. See Paula Gunn Allen, *The Sacred Hoop: Recovering the Feminine in American Indian Traditions* (Boston: Beacon Press, 1986); Gretchen Bataille and Kathleen Mullen Sands, *American Indian Women: Telling Their Lives* (Lincoln: University of Nebraska Press, 1984); Rayna Green, *Native American Women: A Contextual Bibliography* (Bloomington: Indiana University Press, 1983).

2. See Rayna Green, "The Pocahontas Perplex: The Image of Indian Women in American Culture," *Massachusetts Review* 16 (1975): 698–714.

3. Gerda Lerner, "Placing Women in History: Definitions and Challenges," *Feminist Studies* 3 (Fall 1975): 5–14.

Appendixes

1. I have compiled appendixes A through C from information in: Starr, *History of the Cherokee Indians*, 232–39, 243, 305–466, 489–680; Index to the Five Civilized Tribes, the Final Dawes Roll, M1186, roll 1, and the Enrollment Cards for the Five Civilized Tribes, 1898–1914, rolls 2–15, cards 11132, Federal Archives, Fort Worth branch; Cherokee Census and Index, Schedules 1–6, 7RA-07, rolls 1–4; 1890 Cherokee Census (no index), Schedules 1–4, 7RA-08, rolls 1–4, at Federal Archives and Records Center, Fort Worth, Texas; Ballenger, *Lists of Seminary Students*; Cherokee Male and Female Seminary Student Association catalogs for various years, at Archives, NSU.

Appendixes D and E were compiled from: Florence Wilson's "Great Leather-Bound Record Book," NSU; G. Foreman, ed., *Indian and Pioneer Histories*, vol. 2, 36; vol. 2, 37; vol. 3, 15; vol. 8, 133; vol. 41, 434; vol. 43, 105, 257; vol. 65, 215.

Selected Bibliography

Manuscripts

Fort Worth, Texas. Federal Archives.
M1186. Roll 1. Index to the Five Civilized Tribes. Final Dawes Roll.
M1186. Enrollment Cards for the Five Civilized Tribes, 1898–1914, Rolls
    1–15, Cherokees by blood, 1–11, 132.
M685. Roll 1. General Index to Eastern Cherokee Applications, Vols. 1 and
    2. Records Relating to Enrollment of Eastern Cherokees by Guion Miller.
7RA-07. Cherokee Census of 1880:
    7RA07–1. Roll 1. Index.
    7RA07–2. Roll 2. Canadian, Cooweescoowee, Delaware, and Flint Dis-
        tricts.
    7RA07–3. Roll 3. Goingsnake, Illinois, Saline, Sequoyah, and Tahlequah
        Districts.
7RA08–1. Cherokee Census of 1890:
    7RA8–1. Roll 1. (No index.) Canadian and Coowescoowee Districts.
    7RA8–2. Roll 2. Delaware and Flint Districts.
    7RA8–3. Roll 3. Goingsnake, Saline, and Illinois Districts.
    7RA8–4. Roll 4. Sequoyah and Tahlequah Districts.
    7RA8–5. Roll 5. Schedules 2–5.
    7RA8–6. Roll 6. Schedule 6.
7RA024. Index to Rejected Applicants of the Final Roll of the Five Civilized
    Tribes—Dawes Roll of 1906–7.
7RA-90/91. Choctaw 1911 Payroll and Index; Register of Cherokee Students,
    1881–82.

Norman, Oklahoma. Western History Collection.
Althea Bass Collection
Anne Ross Piburn Collection
Cherokee Nation Papers

Dennis Wolfe Bushyhead Papers
Thomas Lee Ballenger Collection

Oklahoma City, Oklahoma. Oklahoma Historical Society. Indian Archives Division.
Alice Robertson Papers
Ann Augusta Robertson Moore Papers
Cherokee Female Seminary Vertical File 10
Grant Foreman Collection
Indian and Pioneer History Collection
Joseph B. Thoburn Collection
Cherokee National Records (microfilm):
    CHN 012, Vol. 273. Senate and Council, 1887–88.
    CHN 013, Vol. 278. Council and Senate, 1800–1883.
    CHN 015, Vol. 284. Council and Senate, 1884–88.
    CHN 016, Vol. 290. Senate, 1886–87.
    CHN 018, Vol. 302. Senate and Council, 1892–95; 1900–1902.
    CHN 097. Cherokee-*Schools: Female Seminary*, Documents 2735–2777, 11 May 1887–Dec. 1902.
    CHN 098. Cherokee-*Schools: Female Seminary*, Documents 2778–2864, 31 December 1902–29 June 1905.
    CHN 099. Cherokee-*Schools: Female Seminary*, Documents 2865–2870, 1 July 1905–May 1909; Cherokee (Tahlequah)-*Schools: Female Seminary*, Undated and 5 December 1874–16 January 1909.
    CHN 100. Letters Sent and Letters Received and Other Documents. Cherokee (Tahlequah)-*Schools: Medical Superintendent*, Undated and 22 November 1876–12 January 1901.
    CHN 101. Letters Sent and Letters Received and Other Documents. Cherokee-*Schools: Miscellaneous*, Documents 3007–3292, 2 June 1890–10 June 1913; Cherokee (Tahlequah)-*Schools: Miscellaneous*, Undated and 16 December 1841–30 December 1884.
    CHN 102. Cherokee (Tahlequah)-*Schools: Miscellaneous*, 21 January 1885–20 March 1911.
Cherokee National Records (bound ledgers):
    Cherokee, Vol. 403. Officials' Reports, 1880–85.
    Cherokee, Vol. 428. Officials' Reports to Principal Chief, 1899.
    Cherokee, Vol. 726. Officers' Reports to the Principal Chief, 1901–4; 1903 Report of the Medical Superintendent of Schools.
Living Legends Oral History Collection:
    #cLL 213.1 A, Jack Brown
    #cLL 213.1 B, Jack Brown
    #cLL 213.1 C, Jack Brown
    #cLL 213.2, Rosanna Harnage Daniel
    #cLL 215.1, Ben Chandler
    #cLL 215.2, James McSpadden

#cLL 215.3, Eva Dameron Uhle
#cLL 216.0, Cherokee Male Seminary Alumnae
#cLL 217.2, Charlotte Mayes Sanders
#cLL 219.1, Evelyn Suagee Maheres
#cLL 219.2, Mrs. Cecil Gibson Johnson
#cLL 219.3, Susie Martin Walker Alberty
#cLL 219.4, R. S. "Bob" Duncan
#cLL 598.1, Pocahontas Club Members
#cLL 608.2, Jack Brown

South Hadley, Massachusetts. Mount Holyoke College, Williston Memorial
    Library/Archives.
    Cherokee Collection
    Alumnae Files
    Cherokee Female Seminary File: Uncatalogued Letters,
        Manuscripts, Articles
    Student Papers File

Tahlequah, Oklahoma. Northeastern State University, Archives, John Vaughan
    Library.
    Brad Agnew Audio-Visual Collection
    Thomas Lee Ballenger Collection
    Lola Garrett Bowers Collection
    Cherokee Seminary Students Association Correspondence
    Cherokee Seminaries Homecoming Brochures
    Cherokee Male Seminary Catalogs 1883, 1884, 1888, 1896
    John T. Drew, Jr., Papers
    R. Lee Fleming Collection
    Northeastern State Normal School Students Transcripts
    Albert Sydney Wyly Collection
    Records of Primary, Boarding, and Beneficiary Students of the Cherokee
        Female Seminary, 1877–87
    "Time Capsule" Collection (from cornerstone of the seminary building)

Tahlequah, Oklahoma. Northeastern State University, Special Collections, John
    Vaughan Library.
    Northeastern State University/Seminaries Vertical File
    Annual Messages of Chief Dennis Bushyhead

Tahlequah, Oklahoma. Northeastern State University, Office of Admissions
    and Records, Administration Building.
    Cherokee Female Seminary Records of Grades, 1876–1903
    Cherokee Male Seminary Records of Grades, 1876–1903
    1909–10 Student Rolls, Cherokee Male Seminary

Tulsa, Oklahoma. University of Tulsa. McFarlin Library, Department of Special
Collections.
Alice M. Robertson Collection

Tulsa, Oklahoma. Thomas Gilcrease Institute of American History and Art
Library.
Grant Foreman Collection
Orr Papers
Dr. James Greene Walker Collection
Samuel Austin Worcester Papers

Washington, D.C., Smithsonian Institution, Museum of Natural History, National Anthropological Archives.

Government Documents

The Constitution and Laws of the American Indian Tribes. Vols. 1–10. Wilmington,
Del.: Scholarly Resources, 1973, 1975.
*Fifth Annual Report of the Bureau of Ethnology to the Secretary of the Smithsonian
Institution, 1883–1884.* Washington, D.C.: U.S. Government Printing Office,
1884.
Kappler, Charles J. *Indian Affairs: Laws and Treaties.* Vols. 1–4. Washington,
D.C.: Government Printing Office, 1902.
Morse, Rev. Jedidiah. *A Report to the Secretary of War of the United States on
Indian Affairs, Comprising a Narrative of a Tour Performed in the Summer of
1820.* New Haven: South Converse, 1822.
Prucha, Francis Paul, ed. *Documents of United States Indian Policy.* Lincoln:
University of Nebraska Press, 1975.
Richardson, James D. *A Compilation of the Messages and Papers of the Presidents,
1789–1897.* Vol. 2. Washington, D.C.: Government Printing Office, 1896–99.
*Sixth Annual Report of the Commissioner to the Five Civilized Tribes to the
Secretary of the Interior for the Fiscal Year Ended June 30, 1899.* Washington,
D.C.: Government Printing Office, 1899.
United State Congress. House Executive Documents. *Annual Reports of the
Commissioner of Indian Affairs.*
28th Cong., 1st sess., 1843, serial 439.
28th Cong., 2d sess., 1844, serial 463.
29th Cong., 2d sess., 1846, serial 497.
30th Cong., 1st sess., 1847, serial 503.
32d Cong., 2d sess., 1852, serial 673.
33d Cong., 1st sess., 1853, serial 710.
37th Cong., 3d sess., 1862, serial 1157.
38th Cong., 3d sess., 1863, serial 1182.
38th Cong., 2d sess., 1864, serial 1220.

39th Cong., 1st sess., 1865, serial 1248.
41st Cong., 3d sess., 1870, serial 1449.
42d Cong., 2d sess., 1871–72, pt. 5, serial 1505.
42d Cong., 3d sess., 1872–73, pt. 5, serial 1560.
43d Cong., 1st sess., 1873, pt. 5, serial 1601.
43d Cong., 2d sess., 1874–75, pt. 5, serial 1639.
44th Cong., 2d sess., 1876–77. pt. 5, serial 1749.
45th Cong., 2d sess., 1877–78, pt. 5, serial 1800.
46th Cong., 3d sess., 1880, serial 1959.
49th Cong., 1st sess., 1885–86, pt. 5, serial 2379.
49th Cong., 2d sess., 1887, pt. 5, serial 2467.
50th Cong., 2d sess., 1888–89, pt. 5, serial 2637.
51st Cong., 1st sess., 1889–90, pt. 5, serial 2725.
51st Cong., 2d sess., 1890–91, pt. 5, serial 2841.
55th Cong., 3d sess., 1898, serial 3757.
56th Cong., 1st sess., 1899, pt. 1, serial 3915.
56th Cong., 1st sess., 1899, pt. 2, serial 3916.
56th Cong., 2d sess., 1900, serial 4101.
57th Cong., 1st sess., 1901, pt. 1, serial 4290.
57th Cong., 2d sess., 1902, pt. 1, serial 4459.
58th Cong., 2d sess., 1903, pt. 2, serial 4798.
58th Cong., 3d sess., 1904, pt. 2, serial 4799.
59th Cong., 1st sess., 1906, serial 4959.
59th Cong., 2d sess., 1906, serial 5118.
United States Congress. Department of the Interior. *Annual Report of the Commissioner of Indian Affairs*, 1907.
United States Congress. Senate Executive Documents. *Annual Report of the Commissioner of Indian Affairs*:
25th Cong., 2d sess., 1837, serial 314.
30th Cong., 1st sess., 1847, serial 503.
33d Cong., 2d sess., 1854, pt. 1, serial 746.
34th Cong., 1st sess., 1855, pt. 1, serial 810.
34th Cong., 3d sess., 1856, pt. 1, serial 875.
35th Cong., 1st sess., 1857, pt. 1, serial 919.
35th Cong., 2d sess., 1858, pt.1, serial 974.
36th Cong., 1st sess., 1859, pt. 1, serial 1023.
U.S. Department of the Interior. *Historical American Buildings Survey.* "Cherokee Female Seminary ('Seminary Hall')." June–August 1975.
Washburn, Wilcomb E. *The American Indian and the United States.* Vols. 1–4. New York: Random House, 1973.
Washington, D.C. Office of the Commissioner of Indian Affairs. "The Cherokee Question." Washington, D.C., June 1866; Reprint edition: "The Cherokee Question," edited by Joseph B. Thoburn, *Chronicles of Oklahoma* 2 (June 1924): 141–242.

Newspapers

Arkansas Democrat
Arkansas Gazette
Cherokee Advocate
Cherokee Phoenix
Cherokee Rose Buds
Columbian Star
Eufaula Indian Journal
Fort Smith Herald
Kansas City Times
Little Rock Gazette
Northeastern News
Sequoyah Memorial
Tahlequah Arrow
Wreath of Cherokee Rose Buds

Books, Theses, Dissertations, and Catalogs

Abbott, Devon I. "Cultivating the Rose Buds: The Administration of the Cherokee Female Seminary, 1846–1907." Master's thesis, Texas Christian University, 1986.
———. "History of the Cherokee Female Seminary: 1851–1910." Ph.D. diss., Texas Christian University, 1989.
Adair, James. *The History of the American Indians.* 1775.
Adams, Evelyn C. *American Indian Education: Government Schools and Economic Progress.* Morningside Heights, N.Y.: King's Crown Press, 1946.
Agnew, Brad. *Fort Gibson: Terminal on the Trail of Tears.* Norman: University of Oklahoma Press, 1980.
Albers, Patricia, and Beatrice Medicine. *The Hidden Half: Studies of Plains Indian Women.* Washington, D.C.: University Press of America, 1983.
Allen, Paula Gunn. *The Sacred Hoop: Recovering the Feminine in American Indian Traditions.* Boston: Beacon Press, 1986.
Anderson, Mabel Washbourne. *The Life of Stand Watie and Contemporary Cherokee History.* Pryor, Okla., 1931.
Anderson, Rufus. *Memoir of Catherine Brown, A Christian Indian of the Cherokee Nation.* Boston: Samuel T. Armstrong, Croker, and Brewster, 1825.
Anderson, William L., ed. *Cherokee Removal: Before and After.* Athens: University of Georgia Press, 1991.
An Illustrated Souvenir Catalog of the Cherokee National Female Seminary: 1850–1906. Chilocco, Okla.: Indian Print Shop, 1906.
Aptheker, Herbert, ed. *The Correspondence of W. E. B. Du Bois.* Amherst: University of Massachusetts Press, 1973–78.
Babcock, Sydney Henry, and John Y. Bryce. *History of Methodism in Oklahoma:*

Story of the Indian Mission Annual Conference of the Methodist Episcopal Church, South. Oklahoma City: Times Journal Publishing Company, 1937.

Bahr, Howard, Bruce Chadwick, and Robert C. Day. *Native Americans Today: Sociological Perspectives.* New York: Harper and Row, 1972.

Baillett, Samuel C. *Historical Sketches of the Mission of the American Board.* Religion in America Series 2. Reprint edition. New York: Reno Press, 1972.

Bailyn, Bernard. *Education in the Forming of American Society.* Chapel Hill: University of North Carolina Press, 1960.

Ballenger, Thomas Lee. *Around Tahlequah Council Fires.* Muskogee, Okla.: Motter Bookbinding Company, 1935.

———. "Lists of Students of Cherokee Male and Female Seminaries, Tahlequah, Oklahoma, from 1876 to 1904." Special Collections, John Vaughan Library, Northeastern State University.

———, ed. *Copies of Miscellaneous Papers.* Special Collections, John Vaughan Library, Northeastern State University.

Balyeat, Frank Allen. "Education in Indian Territory." Ph.D. diss., Stanford University, 1927.

Basham, Robert H. "A History of Cane Hill College in Arkansas." D.Ed. diss., University of Arkansas, 1969.

Bass, Althea. *A Cherokee Daughter of Mount Holyoke.* Muscatine, Iowa: Prairie Press, 1937.

———. *Cherokee Messenger.* Norman: University of Oklahoma Press, 1936.

Bataille, Gretchen, and Kathlen Mullen Sands. *American Indian Women: Telling Their Lives.* Lincoln: University of Nebraska Press, 1984.

Beadle, J. H. *The Undeveloped West: Five Years in the Territories.* Chicago: National Publishing Company, 1873.

Beecher, Catharine, and Harriet Beecher Stowe. *The American Woman's Home.* American Life Foundation, 1869.

Benedict, John Downing. *Muskogee and Northeastern Oklahoma.* Chicago: S. J. Clarke Publishing Company, 1922.

Benson, Henry C. *Life among the Choctaw Indians and Sketches of the Southwest.* Cincinnati: L. Swormstedt and A. Poe, 1860.

Berg, Barbara J. *The Remembered Gate: Origins of American Feminism, The Woman and the City, 1800–1860.* New York: Oxford University Press, 1978.

Berkhofer, Robert F. *Salvation and the Savage: An Analysis of Protestant Missions and American Indian Response, 1787–1862.* Lexington: University of Kentucky Press, 1965.

Berkin, Carol Ruth, and Mary Beth Norma, eds. *Women of America: A History.* Boston: Houghton Mifflin, 1979.

Bershire, Alice. *History of Physical Education, Northeastern State College, Presented to the State Physical Education Historical Commission, June 23, 1952.* Bound volume in Special Collections, John Vaughan Library, Northeastern State University.

Bieder, Robert E. *Science Encounters the Indian, 1820–1880.* Norman: University of Oklahoma Press, 1986.

Boudinot, Elias. *An Address to the Whites, Delivered in the First Presbyterian Church, May 26, 1826.* Philadelphia: W. F. Geddes, 1826.

————. *Letters and Other Papers Relating to Cherokee Affairs; Being in Reply to Sundry Publications Authorized by John Ross.* Athens, Ga.: Office of the "Southern Banner," 1837.

Bowden, Henry Warner. *American Indians and Christian Missions: Studies in Culture Conflict.* Chicago: University of Chicago Press, 1981.

Bowers, Lola Garrett, and Kathleen Garrett. *A. Florence Wilson: Friend and Teacher.* Tahlequah, Okla.: Rockett's Printers and Publishers, 1951.

————. *The Journal of Ellen Whitmore.* Tahlequah, Okla.: Northeastern State College, 1953.

Brown, John. *Old Frontiers.* Kingsport, Tenn.: Southern Publishers, 1938.

Brown, Nettie Terry. "The Missionary World of Ann Eliza Worcester Robertson." Ph.D. diss., North Texas State University, 1978.

Brownlee, W. Elliot, and Mary Brownlee, eds. *Women in the American Economy: A Documentary History, 1675–1927.* New Haven: Yale University Press, 1976.

Burstall, Sara A. *The Education of Girls in the United States.* New York: Arno Press, 1971.

Butler, Nicholas Murray, ed. *Education in the United States.* Salem: N. W. Ayer Company, 1969.

Caldwell, Charles. *Thoughts on the Original Unity of the Human Race.* New York: E. Bliss, 1830.

Canada, Lela K. *History of the Student Health Center.* Bound volume in Special Collections, John Vaughan Library, Northeastern State University.

Carselowey, James Manford. *Cherokee Pioneers.* Adair, Okla.: By the Author, 1961.

Catalogue of the Cherokee National Female Seminary: 1886–1887. St. Louis: Levison and Blythe Stationery Company, 1887.

Catalogue of the Cherokee National Female Seminary: 1896 and Announcements for 1897–1898.

Chafe, William Henry. *Women and Equality: Changing Patterns in American Culture.* New York: Oxford University Press, 1977.

Cherokee National Female Seminary Commencement Calendar: 1906.

Cherokee National Female Seminary 1850–1909 Commencement Calendar.

Church, Robert L., and Michael W. Sedlak. *Education in the United States: An Interpretive History.* New York: Free Press, 1976.

Clifton, James A., ed. *Being and Becoming Indian: Biographical Studies of North American Frontiers.* (Chicago: Dorsey Press, 1989).

Clinton, Catherine. *The Other Civil War: American Women in the Nineteenth Century.* New York: Hill and Wang, 1984.

Cole, Arthur C. *A Hundred Years of Mount Holyoke College.* New Haven: Yale University Press, 1940.

Coleman, Michael C. *Presbyterian Missionary Attitudes toward American Indians 1837–1893.* Jackson: University of Mississippi Press, 1985.

Collier, Peter. *When Shall They Rest: The Cherokees' Long Struggle with America.* New York: Holt, Rinehart, and Winston, 1973.

Conley, Robert J. *The Witch of Goingsnake and Other Stories.* Norman: University of Oklahoma Press, 1988.

Corkran, David H. *The Cherokee Frontier: Conflict and Survival, 1740–1762.* Norman: University of Oklahoma Press, 1962.

Cott, Nancy F. *Bonds of Womanhood: Women's Sphere in New England, 1780–1835.* New Haven: Yale University Press, 1977.

———. *The Grounding of Modern Feminism.* New Haven: Yale University Press, 1987.

———, ed. *A Heritage of Her Own: Toward a New Social History of American Women.* New York: Simon and Schuster, 1979.

Couch, Nevada. *Pages from Cherokee Indian History as Identified with Samuel Austin Worcester, D.D.: A Paper Read at the Commencement of the Worcester Academy at Vinita, Indian Territory, June 18, 1884.* St. Louis: R. P. Studley and Company, Printers, 1884.

Dale, Edward Everett, and Jessie L. Radar. *Cherokee Cavaliers: Forty Years of Cherokee History as Told in the Correspondence of the Ridge-Watie-Boudinot Family.* Norman: University of Oklahoma Press, 1939.

———. *Readings in Oklahoma History.* Evanston, Ill.: Row, Peterson, 1930.

Danziger, Edmund Jefferson, Jr. *Indians and Bureaucrats: Administering Policy during the Civil War.* Urbana: University of Illinois Press, 1974.

Davis, Allen F. *Spearheads for Reform: The Social Settlements and the Progressive Movement: 1890–1914.* New York: Oxford University Press, 1967.

Dearborn, Ned Harland. *The Oswego Movement in American Education.* New York: Arno Press, 1969.

Debo, Angie. *And Still the Waters Run: The Betrayal of the Five Civilized Tribes.* Reprint. Norman: University of Oklahoma Press, 1989.

———. *The Rise and Fall of the Choctaw Republic.* Norman: University of Oklahoma Press, 1986.

———. *The Road to Disappearance: A History of the Creek Indians.* Norman: University of Oklahoma Press, 1941.

Delamont, Sara, and Lorna Duffin, eds. *The Nineteenth-Century Woman: Her Cultural and Physical World.* New York: Barnes and Noble, 1978.

Deutrich, Mabel E., and Virginia C. Purdy. *Clio Was a Woman: Studies in the History of American Women.* Washington, D.C.: Howard University Press, 1980.

Dewitz, Paul W. *Notable Men of Indian Territory at the Beginning of the 20th Century, 1904–1905.* Muskogee, Indian Territory: Southwest Historical Company, 1905.

DuBois, Ellen Carol, et al. *Feminist Scholarship: Kindling in the Groves of Academe.* Urbana: University of Illinois Press, 1987.

Eastman, Charles A. *From the Deep Woods to Civilization.* Lincoln: University of Nebraska Press, 1977.

Eaton, Carolyn Rachel. *John Ross and the Cherokee Indians.* Menasha, Wis.: George Banta, 1914.

Edmunds, R. David. *American Indian Leaders: A Study in Diversity.* Lincoln: University of Nebraska Press, 1980.

Evans, Sara M. *Born for Liberty: A History of Women in America.* New York: Free Press, 1989.

Everett, Diana. *The Texas Cherokees: A People between Two Fires, 1819–1840.* Norman: University of Oklahoma Press, 1990.

Felton, Harold W. *Nancy Ward, Cherokee.* New York: Dodd, Mead, 1975.

Ferguson, Mrs. Tom B. *They Carried the Torch.* Kansas City: Burton Publishing Company, 1937.

Foner, Eric, ed. *The Other Civil War: American Women in the Nineteenth Century.* New York: Hill and Wang, 1984.

Foreman, Carolyn Thomas. *Oklahoma Imprints.* Norman: University of Oklahoma Press, 1936.

———. *Park Hill.* Muskogee, Okla.: Star Printery, 1948.

Foreman, Grant. *Five Civilized Tribes.* Norman: University of Oklahoma Press, 1934.

———. *Fort Gibson: A Brief History.* Norman: University of Oklahoma Press, 1936.

———. *Indian Removal: The Emigration of the Five Civilized Tribes of Indians.* Norman: University of Oklahoma Press, 1932.

———. *Sequoyah.* Norman: University of Oklahoma Press, 1938.

———, ed. *A Traveler in Indian Territory: The Journal of Ethan Allen Hitchcock, Late Major-General in the U.S. Army.* Cedar Rapids: Torch Press, 1930.

Fraser, Walter J., R. Frank Saunders, Jr., and Jon L. Wakelyn, Jr. *The Web of Southern Social Relations: Essays on Family Life, Education, and Women.* Athens: University of Georgia Press, 1985.

Frazier, E. Franklin. *Black Bourgeoisie.* Glencoe, Ill.: Free Press, 1957.

French, Lawrence. *Psychocultural Change and the American Indian: An Ethnohistorical Analysis.* New York: Garland, 1987.

Fritz, Henry E. *The Movement for Indian Assimilation: 1860–1890.* Philadelphia: University of Pennsylvania Press, 1963.

Fry, Maggie Culver, comp. *Cherokee Female Seminary Years: A Cherokee National Anthology by Many Tribal Authors.* Claremore, Okla.: Rogers State College Press, 1988.

Fuchs, Estelle, and Robert J. Havighurst. *To Live on This Earth: American Indian Education.* Albuquerque: University of New Mexico Press, 1972.

Fullerton, Eula E. "Some Social Institutions of the Cherokees: 1820–1906." Master's thesis, University of Oklahoma, 1931.

Gabriel, Ralph Henry. *Elias Boudinot, Cherokee, and His History.* Norman: University of Oklahoma Press, 1941.

Gaines, W. Craig. *The Confederate Cherokees: John Drew's Regiment of Mounted Rifles.* Baton Rouge: Louisiana State University Press, 1989.

Gearing, Fred. *Priests and Warriors: Social Structures of Cherokee Politics in the 18th Century.* Memoir 93, The American Anthropological Association, vol. 54, no. 5, pt. 2, October 1962.

Gibson, Arrell, M. *American Exiles: Indian Colonization in Oklahoma.* Oklahoma City: Oklahoma Historical Society, 1976.

———. *Oklahoma: A Student's Guide to Localized History.* New York: Columbia University Press, 1950.

Gilchrist, Beth Bradford. *The Life of Mary Lyon.* Boston: Houghton Mifflin, 1910.

Goodsell, Willystine, ed. *Pioneers of Women's Education in the United States.* New York: AMS Press, 1970.

Goodwin, Gary C. *Cherokees in Transition: A Study of Change, Culture, and Environment Prior to 1775.* Chicago: University of Chicago Press, 1977.

Gossett, Thomas F. *Race: The History of an Idea in America.* Dallas: Southern Methodist University, 1963.

Graham, Patricia Albjerg. *Community and Class in American Education: 1865–1918.* New York: John Wiley and Sons, 1974.

Green, Elizabeth Alden. *Mary Lyon and Mount Holyoke, Opening at the Gates.* Hanover, N. H.: University Press of New England, 1979.

Green, Rayna. *Native American Women: A Contextual Bibliography.* Bloomington: Indiana University Press, 1983.

Haliburton, R., Jr., *Red Over Black: Black Slavery among the Cherokee Indians.* Westport, Conn.: Greenwood, 1977.

Hargrett, Lester. *The Gilcrease-Hargrett Catalogue of Imprints.* Norman: University of Oklahoma Press, 1972.

Harlan, Louis R. *Booker T. Washington: The Making of a Black Leader, 1856–1901.* New York: Oxford University Press, 1972.

———. *Booker T. Washington: The Wizard of Tuskegee, 1901–1915.* New York: Oxford University Press, 1983.

Hawkins, Hugh, ed. *Booker T. Washington and His Critics: The Problem of Negro Leadership.* Boston: D.C. Heath and Company, 1962.

Healy, William J. *Women of Red River.* Winnipeg: Women's Canadian Club, 1923.

Heilbrun, Carolyn G. *Writing a Woman's Life.* New York: Norton, 1988.

Henry, Jeanette, ed. *The American Indian Reader: Education.* 2 vols. San Francisco: Indian History Press, 1972.

Hewes, Leslie. *Occupying the Cherokee Country of Oklahoma.* University of Nebraska Studies, New Series, No. 57. Lincoln: University of Nebraska Press, 1978.

Hinsley, Curtis. *Savages and Scientists: The Smithsonian Institution and the Development of American Anthropology, 1846–1910.* Washington, D.C.: Smithsonian Institution Press, 1981.

Horsman, Reginald. *Race and Manifest Destiny: The Origins of American Racial Anglo-Saxonism.* Cambridge, Mass.: Harvard University Press, 1981.

Hoxie, Frederick. "Beyond Savagery: The Campaign to Assimilate the Indians, 1880–1920." Ph.D. diss., Brandeis University, 1977.

Hudson, Charles M. *Four Centuries of Southern Indians.* Athens: University of Georgia Press, 1975.

Jackson, Joe. "History of Education in Eastern Oklahoma from 1898 to 1915." Ed.D. thesis, University of Oklahoma, 1950.

Jacobs, Mary. *Women Writing and Writing about Women.* New York: Barnes and Noble, 1979.

Johnson, Basil H. *Indian School Days*. Norman: University of Oklahoma Press 1988.

Jordan, H. Glenn, and Thomas M. Holm, eds. *Indian Leaders: Oklahoma's First Statesmen*. Oklahoma City: Oklahoma Historical Society, 1979.

Jordan, Janet Etheridge. "Politics and Religion in a Western Cherokee Community: A Century of Struggle in a White Man's World." Ph.D. diss., University of Connecticut, 1975.

Katz, Esther, and Anita Rapone. *Women's Experience in America*. New Brunswick, N.J.: Transaction Books, 1980.

Kaufman, Polly Welts. *Women Teachers on the Frontier*. New Haven: Yale University Press, 1984.

Kelly, Mary, ed. *Women's Being, Women's Place: Female Identity and Vocation in American History*. Boston: G. K. Hall, 1979.

Kilpatrick, Jack Frederick. "The Wahnenauhi (Lucy Lowrey Keys) Manuscript: Historical Sketches of the Cherokees." Bureau of American Ethnology Bulletin 196; Anthropological Papers #77. Washington, D.C.: Smithsonian Institution, 1966.

Kilpatrick, Jack Frederick, and Anna Gritts Kilpatrick, eds. *The Shadow of Sequoyah: Social Documents of the Cherokees, 1862–1964*. Norman: University of Oklahoma Press, 1965.

——. *New Echota Letters: Contributions of Samuel A. Worcester to the Cherokee Phoenix*. Dallas: Southern Methodist University, 1968.

Knepler, Abraham Eleazer. "Digest of the Education of the Cherokee Indians." Ph.D. diss., Yale University, 1939.

La Flesche, Francis. *The Middle Five: Indian Schoolboys of the Omaha Tribe*. Lincoln: University of Nebraska Press, 1963.

Lasser, Carol, ed. *Educating Men and Women Together: Coeducation in a Changing World*. Urbana: University of Illinois Press, 1987.

Layman, Martha. "A History of Indian Education in the United States." Ph.D. diss., University of Minnesota, 1942.

Liberty, Margot. *American Indian Intellectuals*. St. Paul: West Publishing Company, 1978.

Linton, Ralph. *Acculturation in Seven American Indian Tribes*. New York: D. Appleton-Century, 1940.

Littlefield, Daniel F., Jr., and James W. Parins. *A Bibliography of Native American Writers, 1772–1924*. Metuchen, N.J.: Scarecrow Press, 1981.

Long, E. B. *The Civil War Day by Day: An Almanac, 1861–1865*. Garden City: Doubleday, 1971.

Loomis, Augustus W. *Scenes in the Indian Country*. Philadelphia, 1859.

McBeth, Sally J. *Ethnic Identity and the Boarding School Experience of West-Central Oklahoma American Indians*. New York: University Press of America, 1983.

McCoy, Melody Lynn. "Location and Enterprise: A Review of Merchants in the Cherokee Nation, 1865–1907." Master's thesis, Harvard University, 1981.

McLoughlin, William G. *Champions of the Cherokees: Evan and John B. Jones*. Princeton: Princeton University Press, 1990.

————. *The Cherokee Ghost Dance: Essays on the Southeastern Indians, 1789–1861.* Macon, Ga.: Mercer University Press, 1984.

————. *Cherokee Renascence in the New Republic.* Princeton: Princeton University Press, 1986.

————. *Cherokees and Missionaries: 1789–1839.* New Haven: Yale University Press, 1984.

Malone, Henry Thompson. *Cherokees of the Old South: A People in Transition.* Athens: University of Georgia Press, 1956.

Marshall, Mrs. A. James. *The Autobiography of Mrs. A. J. Marshall.* Pine Bluff, Ark.: Adams-Wilson Printing Company, 1897.

Mays, Samuel Edward. *Genealogy of the Mays Family to 1929.* Plant City, Fla., 1929.

Milling, Chapman, J. *Red Carolinians.* Chapel Hill, N.C.: University of North Carolina Press, 1940.

Miner, Craig H. *The Corporation and the Indian: Tribal Sovereignty and Indian Civilization in Indian Territory, 1867–1907.* Columbia: University of Missouri Press, 1976.

Mooney, James. *Historical Sketch of the Cherokee.* Chicago: Aldine, 1975.

————. *Myths of the Cherokees and Sacred Formulas of the Cherokees.* Nashville: Charles and Randy Elder, 1982.

Moore, J. H. *The Political Condition of the Indians and the Resources of Indian Territory.* St. Louis: Southwestern Book and Publishing Company, 1874.

Morris, John W., Charles R. Goins, and Edwin C. McReynolds. *Historical Atlas of Oklahoma.* 3d ed. Norman: University of Oklahoma Press, 1986.

Morton, Samuel George. *Crania Americana; or, A Comparative View of the Skulls of Various Aboriginal Nations of North and South America to Which Is Prefixed an Essay on the Varieties of the Human Species.* Philadelphia: J. Dobson, 1839.

Moulton, Gary E. *John Ross Cherokee Chief.* Athens: University of Georgia Press, 1978.

————, ed. *The Papers of Chief John Ross.* Vols. 1 and 2. Norman: University of Oklahoma Press, 1984, 1985.

Nutall, Thomas. *Journal of Travels into the Arkansas Territory, etc.* Philadelphia, 1821.

O'Bierne, Harry F., and Edward S. O'Bierne. *The Indian Territory: Its Chiefs, Legislators, and Leading Men.* St. Louis: C. B. Woodward, 1892.

100th Anniversary of the Opening of the Cherokee National Seminaries: 1851–1951. Tahlequah, Okla.: Northeastern State College, 1951.

Owen, Narcissa. *The Memoirs of Narcissa Owen.* Seattle: University of Washington Press, 1907.

Padover, Saul K. *Thomas Jefferson on Democracy.* New York: Mentor, New American Library, Appleton Century Company, 1939.

Parins, James W. *John Rollin Ridge: His Life and Works.* Lincoln: University of Nebraska Press, 1991.

Pascoe, Peggy. *Relations of Rescue: The Search for Female Moral Authority in the American West, 1874–1939.* New York: Oxford University Press, 1990.

Payne, Betty, and Oscar Payne. *A Brief History of Old Dwight Cherokee Mission: 1820–1953.* Tulsa: Dwight Presbyterian Mission, 1954.

Perdue, Theda. *Cherokee Editor: The Writings of Elias Boudinot.* Knoxville: University of Tennessee Press, 1983.

————. *Slavery and the Evolution of Cherokee Society: 1540–1866.* Knoxville: University of Tennessee Press, 1979.

Phillips, Clifton J. *Protestant America and the Pagan World: The First Half Century of the American Board of Commissioners for Foreign Missions, 1810–1860.* Cambridge, Mass.: Harvard University Press, 1969.

Pratt, Richard Henry. *Battlefield and Classroom: Four Decades with the American Indian, 1867–1904.* New Haven: Yale University Press, 1964.

Priest, Loring B. *Uncle Sam's Stepchildren: The Reformation of United States Indian Policy, 1865–1887.* New Brunswick: Rutgers University Press, 1942.

Prucha, Francis Paul. *American Indian Policy in the Formative Years: The Indian Trade and Intercourse Acts, 1790–1834.* Lincoln: University of Nebraska Press, 1962.

————. *Americanizing the American Indian: Writings by the Friends of the Indians, 1880–1900.* Cambridge, Mass.: Harvard University Press, 1973.

————. *The Churches and the Indian Schools: 1888–1912.* Lincoln: University of Nebraska Press, 1979.

————. *The Dawes Act and the Allotment of Indian Land.* Norman: University of Oklahoma Press, 1973.

Pumphrey, Stanley. *Indian Civilization: A Lecture by Stanley Pumphrey of England.* Philadelphia: Bible and Tract Distributive Society, 1877.

Reid, John P. *A Law of Blood: The Primitive Law of the Cherokee Nation.* New York: New York University Press, 1970.

Riegal, Robert. *American Feminists.* Greenwood, Mo.: Greenwood Press, 1980.

Riley, Glenda. *Inventing the American Woman: A Perspective on Women's History.* Arlington Heights, Ill.: Harlan Davidson, 1986.

Rogin, Michael Paul. *Fathers and Children: Andrew Jackson and the Subjugation of the American Indian.* New York: Knopf, 1975.

Ronda, James P. and James Axtell. *Indian Missions: A Critical Bibliography.* Bloomington: Indiana University Press, 1978.

Ross, Mrs. William Potter. *Life and Times of William Potter Ross.* Fort Smith, Ark.: Weldon and Williams, Printers, 1893.

Rothman, Sheila. *Women's Proper Place: A History of Changing Ideals and Practices, 1870 to the Present.* New York: Basic Books, 1978.

Royce, Charles C. *The Cherokee Nation of Indians.* Chicago: Aldine, 1975.

Rudolph, Frederick. *The American Colleges and Universities.* New York: Knopf, 1962.

Ruskin, Gertrude McDaris. *John Ross: Chief of an Eagle Race.* Tahlequah, Okla.: John Ross House Association, 1963.

Sanders, J. G. *Who's Who among Oklahoma Indians.* Oklahoma City: Trave Publishing Company, 1928.

Satz, Ronald. *American Indian Policy in the Jacksonian Era.* Lincoln: University of Nebraska Press, 1975.

Savage, William W., Jr. *The Cherokee Strip Livestock Association: Federal Regulation and the Cattleman's Last Frontier.* Columbia: University of Missouri Press, 1973.

Schwarze, Edmund. *History of the Moravian Missions among the Southern Indian Tribes of the United States.* Bethlehem, Pa.: Times Publishing Company, 1923.

Scott, Anne Firor. *The Southern Lady: From Pedestal to Politics, 1830–1930.* Chicago: University of Chicago Press, 1970.

Skelton, Robert H. "A History of the Educational System of the Cherokee Nation, 1801–1910." Ph.D. diss., University of Arkansas, 1970.

Sklar, Katherine Kish. *Catharine Beecher: A Study in American Domesticity.* New York: Norton, 1976.

Smith, Timothy. *Revivalism and Social Reform in the Mid-Nineteenth Century America.* New York: Abingdon, 1957.

Smith, W. R. L. *The Story of the Cherokees.* Cleveland, Tenn.: Church of God Publishing House, 1928.

Spencer, Samuel R., Jr. *Booker T. Washington and the Negro's Place in American Life.* Boston: Little, Brown, 1955.

Spicer, Edward H. *Perspectives in American Indian Culture Change.* Chicago: University of Chicago Press, 1961.

Starkey, Marion Lena. *The Cherokee Nation.* New York: Knopf, 1946.

Starr, Edward C. *A History of Cornwall, Connecticut: A Typical New England Town.* New Haven: Tuttle, Morehouse, and Taylor, 1941.

Starr, Emmet. *History of the Cherokee Indians and Their Legends and Folk Lore.* Oklahoma City: Warden, 1979.

Stewart, Dora Ann. "The Government and Development of Oklahoma Territory." Ph.D. diss., University of Oklahoma, 1933.

Stow, Sarah D. Locke. *History of Mount Holyoke Seminary, South Hadley, Massachusetts, during Its First Half Century, 1837–1887.* 2d ed. South Hadley, Mass.: Mount Holyoke Seminary, 1887.

Strickland, Rennard. *Fire and Spirits: Cherokee Law from Clan to Court.* Norman: University of Oklahoma Press, 1975.

Szasz, Margaret Connell. *Indian Education in the American Colonies, 1607–1783.* Albuquerque: University of New Mexico Press, 1988.

Thoburn, Joseph B., and Muriel H. Wright. *Oklahoma: The State and Its People.* New York: Lewis Historical Publishing Company, 1929.

Thomas, Clarence Lot. *Annotated Acts of Congress: Five Civilized Tribes and the Osage Nation.* Columbia, Mo.: E. W. Stephens, 1913.

Thomas, Howard K. "Origin and Development of the Redbird Smith Movement." Master's thesis, University of Oklahoma, 1933.

Thompson, Eleanor Wolf. *Education for Ladies, 1830–1860: Ideas on Education in Magazines for Women.* New York: King's Crown Press, 1947.

Thornton, Russell. *American Indian Holocaust and Survival: A Population History since 1492.* Norman: University of Oklahoma Press, 1987.

———. *The Cherokees: A Population History.* Lincoln: University of Nebraska Press, 1990.

Thurman, Melvina. *Women in Oklahoma: A Century of Change.* Oklahoma City: Oklahoma Historical Society, 1983.

Tracy, Joseph, ed. *History of American Missions to the Heathen, from Their Commencement to the Present Time.* Worcester, Mass.: Spooner and Howland, 1940.

Trennert, Robert A., Jr. "Educating Indian Girls at Nonreservation Boarding Schools, 1878–1920." In Roger L. Nicols, ed. *The American Indian, Past and Present,* 218–31. 3d ed. New York: Knopf, 1986.

————. *The Phoenix Indian School: Forced Assimilation in Arizona: 1891–1935.* Norman: University of Oklahoma Press, 1988.

Tyler, Alice Felt. *Freedom's Ferment: Phases of American Social History to 1860.* 1944.

Tyner, Howard Q. "The Keetoowah Society in Cherokee History." Master's thesis, University of Tulsa, 1949.

Unrau, William E. *Mixed-Bloods and Tribal Dissolution: Charles Curtis and the Quest for Indian Identity.* Lawrence: University of Kansas Press, 1989.

Van Avery, Dale. *Disinherited: The Lost Birthright of the American Indian.* New York: Morrow, 1966.

Van Kirk, Sylvia. *Many Tender Ties: Women in Fur Trade Societies in Western Canada, 1670–1830.* Norman: University of Oklahoma Press, 1983.

Walker, Robert Sparks. *Torchlights to the Cherokees: The Brainerd Mission.* New York: Macmillan, 1931.

Walsh, Mary Roth. *Doctors Wanted: No Women Need Apply—Social Barriers in the Medical Profession, 1835–1975.* New Haven: Yale University Press, 1977.

Wardell, Morris J. *Political History of the Cherokee Nation, 1830–1907.* Norman: University of Oklahoma Press, 1938.

Washburn, Wilcomb E. *The Assault on Indian Tribalism: The General Allotment Law (Dawes Act) of 1887.* Philadelphia: Lippincott, 1975.

West, Clarence William. *Among the Cherokees: A Biographical History of the Cherokees Since the Removal.* Muskogee, Okla.: Muskogee Printing, 1981.

————. *Tahlequah and the Cherokee Nation: 1841–1941.* Muskogee, Okla.: Muskogee Publishing Company, 1978.

White, Richard. *The Roots of Dependency: Subsistence, Environment, and Social Change Among the Choctaws, Pawnees, and Navajos.* Lincoln: University of Nebraska Press, 1988.

Wilkins, Thurman. *Cherokee Tragedy: The Story of the Ridge Family and the Decimation of a People.* New York: Macmillan, 1970.

Wilson, Raleigh Archie. "Negro and Indian Relations in the Five Civilized Tribes from 1865 to 1907." Ph.D. diss., University of Iowa, 1949.

Wood, Mary I. *The History of the General Federation of Women's Clubs.* New York: Norwood, 1912.

Woodward, Grace Steele. *The Cherokees.* Norman: University of Oklahoma Press, 1963.

Woody, Thomas. *A History of Women's Education in the United States.* Vol. 1. New York: Science Press, 1929.

Worcester, Sarah Alice. *The Descendants of Reverend William Worcester, with a*

Brief Notice of the Connecticut Wooster Family. 2d ed. Boston: E. P. Worcester, Publisher, Hudson Printing Company, 1914.

Wright, Muriel. *Springplace: Moravian Mission and the Ward Family of the Cherokee Nation.* Guthrie, Okla.: Cooperative Publishing Company, 1940.

Zak, Michele Wender, and Patricia Moots. *Women and the Politics of Culture: Studies in the Sexual Economy.* New York: Longman, 1983.

Articles and Typescripts

Abbott, Devon I. "Ann Florence Wilson: Matriarch of the Cherokee Female Seminary." *Chronicles of Oklahoma* 67 (Winter 1989–90): 426–37.

———. "Commendable Progress: Acculturation at the Cherokee Female Seminary." *American Indian Quarterly* 11 (Summer 1986): 187–201.

———. "Medicine for the Rosebuds: Health Care at the Cherokee Female Seminary, 1876–1909." *American Indian Culture and Research Journal* 12 (1988): 59–71.

Adams, David Wallace. "Schooling the Hopi: Federal Indian Policy Writ Small, 1887–1917." *Pacific Historical Review* 48 (August 1979): 335–56.

Agnew, Brad. "Northeastern: From Normal to University." *The Phoenix* 5 (1984): 3–9.

Ahern, Wilbert H. "Indian Education and Bureaucracy: The School at Morris, 1887–1909." *Minnesota History* 51 (Fall 1984): 83–98.

———. " 'The Returned Indians': Hampton Institute and Its Indian Alumni, 1879–1893," *Journal of Ethnic Studies* 10 (Winter 1983): 101–24.

———. " 'To Kill the Indian and Save the Man': The Boarding School and American Indian Education." In *Fort Totten: Military Post and Indian School, 1867–1959,* ed. Larry Remele. Bismarck: State Historical Society of North Dakota, 1986.

Allen, Virginia R. " 'When We Settle Down, We Grow Pale and Die': Health in Western Indian Territory." *Oklahoma State Medical Association Journal* 70 (June 1977): 227–32.

Antler, Joyce. "After College, What?: New Graduates and the Family Claim." *American Quarterly* 32 (Fall 1980): 409–34.

Autry, Stephen T., and R. Palmer Howard, M.D. "Health Care in the Cherokee Seminaries, Asylums and Prisons: 1851–1906." *Oklahoma State Medical Association Journal* 65 (December 1972): 495–502.

Babcock, James M. "History of the Oklahoma State Medical Association." *Journal of the Oklahoma State Medical Association* 49 (May 1956): 147–89.

Baird, W. David. "Real Indians in Oklahoma?" *Chronicles of Oklahoma* 68 (Spring 1990): 4–23.

———. "Spencer Academy, Choctaw Nation, 1842–1900." *Chronicles of Oklahoma* 45 (Spring 1967): 25–43.

Baker, Donna. "Color, Culture and Power: Indian-White Relations in Canada and America." *Canadian Review of American Studies* (1972): 8–20.

Ballenger, Thomas Lee. "A College Tour to Points of Historic Interest." *Chronicles of Oklahoma* 9 (September 1931): 265–67.
——. "Colored High School of the Cherokee Nation." *Chronicles of Oklahoma* 30 (Winter 1952–53): 454–62.
——. "The Cultural Relations between Two Pioneer Communities." *Chronicles of Oklahoma* 34 (Autumn 1956): 286–95.
——. "Joseph Franklin Thompson." *Chronicles of Oklahoma* 30 (Autumn 1952): 285–91.
——. "The Life and Times of Jeff Thompson Parks: Pioneer, Educator, Jurist." *Chronicles of Oklahoma* 30 (Summer 1952): 173–99.
Balyeat, Frank A. "Education of White Children in the Indian Territory." *Chronicles of Oklahoma* 15 (June 1937): 191–97.
Bass, Althea. "William Schenk Robertson." *Chronicles of Oklahoma* 37 (1959): 28–34.
Bass, Dorothy C. "Gideon Blackburn's Mission to the Cherokees: Christianization and Civilization." *Journal of Presbyterian History* 52 (Fall 1973): 203–26.
Bloom Leonard. "The Acculturation of the Eastern Cherokee: Historical Aspects." *North Carolina Historical Review* 19 (October 1942): 323–58.
——. "The Cherokee Clan: A Study in Acculturation." *American Anthropology* 41 (1939): 266–68.
Boydston, Jeanne. "To Earn Her Daily Bread: Housework and Antebellum Working Class Subsistence." *Radical History Review* 35 (1986): 7–25.
Bryce, J. Y. "About Some of Our First Indian Schools in the Choctaw Nation." *Chronicles of Oklahoma* 6 (September 1928): 354–94.
Bunkle, Phillida. "Sentimental Womanhood and Domestic Education, 1830–1870." *History of Education Quarterly* 14 (Spring 1974): 13–31.
Carr, Sarah J. "Bloomfield Academy and Its Founder." *Chronicles of Oklahoma* 2 (1924): 365–79.
Caywood, Elzie Ronald. "The Administration of William Rogers, Principal Chief of the Cherokee Nation, 1903–1907." *Chronicles of Oklahoma* 30 (Spring 1952): 29–37.
Champagne, Duane. "Cherokee Social Movements: A Response to Thornton." *American Sociological Review* 50 (February 1985): 124–30.
"Cherokee National Museum—A Dream Becomes a Reality." *TSA-LA-GI Columns* 7 (25 October 1983): 8–10.
Clark, J. Stanley. "The Principal Chiefs of the Cherokee Nation." *Chronicles of Oklahoma* 15 (September 1937): 253–70.
Conway, Jill. "Women Reformers and American Culture: 1870–1930." *Journal of Social History* 5 (1971–72): 164–77.
Cunningham, Hugh T. "A History of the Cherokee Indians." *Chronicles of Oklahoma* 8 (September 1930): 291–314.
Curti, Merle. "American Philanthropy and the National Character." *American Quarterly* 10 (Winter 1988): 420–37.
Dale, Edward E. "The Cherokee Strip Livestock Association." *Proceedings of*

the Fifth Annual Convention of the Southwestern Political and Social Science Association, 1924.

Davis, Caroline. "Education of the Chickasaws: 1856–1907." *Chronicles of Oklahoma* 16 (March 1938): 415–48.

Davis, John Benjamin. "The Life and Work of Sequoyah." *Chronicles of Oklahoma* 8 (June 1930): 149–80.

———. "Public Education among the Cherokee Indians." *Peabody Journal of Education* 7 (November 1929): 168–73.

Davis, Junetta. "The Belles of Tahlequah." *Oklahoma Today* 35 (March-April 1985): 34–38.

Doran, Michael. "Population Statistics of 19th-Century Indian Territory." *Chronicles of Oklahoma* 35 (Winter 1975–76): 492–515.

Duncan, James. "The Keetoowah Society." *Chronicles of Oklahoma* 4 (1926): 251–55.

Eakes, Lon H. "Reverend Amory Nelson Chamberlin." *Chronicles of Oklahoma* 12 (March 1934): 98–99.

Evans, E. Raymond. "Highways to Progress: Nineteenth-Century Cross Roads in the Cherokee Nation." *Journal of Cherokee Studies* (Fall 1977): 394–400.

Evarest, Emma E. "Famous Women: Mrs. A. E. W. Robertson, Ph.D." *Chaperone Magazine* 9 (1894): 445–48.

Foreman, Carolyn Thomas. "Aunt Eliza of Tahlequah." *Chronicles of Oklahoma* 9 (March 1931): 43–55.

———. "Captain David McNair and His Descendants." *Chronicles of Oklahoma* 36 (Autumn 1958): 270–81.

———. "The Cherokee Gospel Tidings of Dwight Mission." *Chronicles of Oklahoma* 12 (December 1934): 454–69.

———. "The Coodey Family of Indian Territory." *Chronicles of Oklahoma* 25 (Spring-Winter 1947/1948): 323–41.

———. "An Early Account of the Cherokees." *Chronicles of Oklahoma* 34 (Summer 1956): 141–58.

———. "Education Among the Chickasaw Indians." *Chronicles of Oklahoma* 16 (March 1938): 139–65.

———. "Gustavis Loomis: Commandant of Ft. Gibson and Ft. Towson." *Chronicles of Oklahoma* 18 (March-December 1940): 219–27.

———. "Miss Sophia Sawyer and Her School." *Chronicles of Oklahoma* 32 (Winter 1954–55): 395–413.

———, ed. "Journal of a Tour in the Indian Territory." *Chronicles of Oklahoma* 10 (June 1932): 219–56.

Foreman, Grant. "The Honorable Alice M. Robertson." *Chronicles of Oklahoma* 10 (1932): 11–17.

———. "A Survey of Tribal Records in the Archives of the United States Government in Oklahoma." *Chronicles of Oklahoma* 11 (March 1933): 625–34.

———, comp. "Early Post Offices of Oklahoma." *Chronicles of Oklahoma* 6 (March-December 1928): 4–25.

————, ed. "Notes of a Missionary Among the Cherokees." *Chronicles of Oklahoma* 16 (June 1938): 171–89.

————. "Notes of a Missionary [Reverend Carles Cutler Torrey] Among the Cherokees." *Chronicles of Oklahoma* 16 (June 1938): 171–89.

Freeman, Charles R. "Reverend Thomas Bertholf: 1810–1817." *Chronicles of Oklahoma* 11 (December 1933): 1018–24.

Fullerton, Eula. "Joseph Augustus Lawrence, 1856–1938." *Chronicles of Oklahoma* 17 (March-December 1939): 122–23.

Garrett, Kathleen. "Music on the Indian Territory Frontier." *Chronicles of Oklahoma* 33 (Autumn 1955): 339–49.

Gordon, Jean. "American Women and Domestic Consumption: 1800–1920." *Journal of American Culture* 8 (Fall 1985): 35–46.

Green, Rayna. "The Tribe Called Wannabee: Playing Indian in America and Europe." *Folklore* 99 (1988): 30–55.

————. "The Pocahontas Perplex: The Image of Indian Women in American Culture." *Massachusetts Review* 16 (1975): 698–714.

Hafen, LeRoy R. "Cherokee Goldseekers in Colorado: 1849–1850." *Colorado Magazine* 15 (May 1938): 101–9.

Hagan, William T. "Full Blood, Mixed-Blood, Generic, and Ersatz: The Problem of Indian Identity." *Arizona and the West* 27 (Winter 1985): 309–26.

Hagler, D. Harland. "The Ideal Woman in the Antebellum South: Lady or Farmwife?" *Journal of Southern History* 46 (August 1980): 405–18.

Halliburton, Rudy, Jr. "Northeastern's Seminary Hall." *Chronicles of Oklahoma* 51 (Winter 1973–74): 391–98.

Hammond, Sue. "Socioeconomic Reconstruction in the Cherokee Nation, 1865–1870." *Chronicles of Oklahoma* 56 (Summer 1978): 158–70.

Hansen, Klaus J. "The Millennium, the West, and Race in the Antebellum American Mind." *Western History Quarterly* 3 (October 1972): 373–90.

Harrison, Thomas J. "Carlotta Archer: 1865–1946." *Chronicles of Oklahoma* 25 (Spring-Winter 1947–48): 158–60.

Hendrick, Irving G. "Federal Policy Affecting the Education of Indians in California, 1849–1934." *History of Education Quarterly* 16 (Summer 1976): 163–85.

Hewes, Leslie. "The Eastern Border of the Cherokee Country of Oklahoma as a Cultural 'Fault Line.' " *Chronicles of Oklahoma* 32 (March 1942): 120–21.

————. "The Oklahoma Ozarks as the Land of the Cherokees." *Chronicles of Oklahoma* 32 (April 1942): 269–81.

Hicks, Hannah Worcester. "The Diary of Hannah Hicks." *American Scene* 13 (1972): 5–21.

Holland, Reid A. "Life in the Cherokee Nation, 1855–1860." *Chronicles of Oklahoma* 49 (Autumn 1971): 284–301.

Holway, Hope. "Ann Eliza Worcester Robertson as a Linguist." *Chronicles of Oklahoma* 37 (Spring 1959): 35–44.

Hoopes, Alban W. "Indian Education: 1879–1939." *Educational Outlook* 14 (January 1940): 49–63.

Horsman, Reinald. "Scientific Racism and the American Indian in the Mid-Nineteenth Century." *American Quarterly* 27 (May 1975): 152–68.

Howard, R. Palmer, and Virginia Allen. "Stress and Death in the Settlement of Indian Territory." *Chronicles of Oklahoma* 54 (Fall 1976): 352–59.

Jackson, Joe C. "Schools among the Minor Tribes in Indian Territory." *Chronicles of Oklahoma* 32 (1954): 58–69.

Jarvenpa, Robert. "The Political Economy and Political Ethnicity of American Indian Adaptations and Identities." *Ethnic and Racial Studies* 8 (January 1985): 29–48.

Johnson, N. B. "The Cherokee Orphan Asylum." *Chronicles of Oklahoma* 44 (Autumn 1966): 275–80.

Knepler, Abraham E. "Education in the Cherokee Nation." *Chronicles of Oklahoma* 21 (December 1943): 378–401.

———. "18th-Century Cherokee Educational Efforts." *Chronicles of Oklahoma* 20 (March 1942): 55–61.

Knight, Oliver. "Cherokee Society Under the Stress of Removal: 1820–46." *Chronicles of Oklahoma* 32 (Winter 1954–55): 414–28.

———. "History of the Cherokees: 1830–1846." *Chronicles of Oklahoma* 34 (Summer 1956): 159–82.

Kutzleb, Charles R. "Educating the Dakota Sioux: 1876–1890." *North Dakota History* 32 (October 1965): 197–215.

Lauderdale, Virginia E. "Tullahassee Mission." *Chronicles of Oklahoma* 26 (Autumn 1948): 285–300.

Laurence, Robert. "Indian Education: Federal Compulsory School Attendance Law Applicable to American Indians: The Treaty-Making Period: 1857–1871." *American Indian Law Review* (1977): 393–413.

Lerner, Gilda. "The Lady and the Mill Girl: Changes in the Status of Women in the Age of Jackson, 1800–1840." *Midcontinent American Studies Journal* 10 (Spring 1969): 5–14.

———. "Placing Women in History: Definitions and Challenges." *Feminist Studies* 3 (Fall 1975): 5–14.

Littlefield, Daniel, and Lonnie Underhill. "Timber Depredations and Cherokee Legislation: 1864–1881." *Journal of Forest History* 18 (April 1974): 4–13.

———. "Utopian Dreams of the Cherokee Fullbloods: 1890–1934." *Journal of the West* 10 (July 1971): 404–27.

Lomawaima, K. Tsianina. "Oral Histories from Chilocco Indian Agricultural School, 1920–1940." *American Indian Quarterly* 11 (Summer 1987): 241–54.

McClary, Ben Harris. "Nancy Ward: The Last Beloved Woman of the Cherokees." *Tennessee Historical Quarterly* 21 (December 1962): 352–64.

McLoughlin, Virginia, ed. "Letters and Reports of Oswald Langdon Woodford, 1827–1870." Unpublished typescript, Williston Memorial Library/Archives, Mount Holyoke College.

McLoughlin, William G. "Civil Disobedience and Evangelism among the Missionaries to the Cherokees: 1829–30." *Journal of Presbyterian History* 51 (Summer 1973): 116–39.

————. "Indian Slaveholders and Presbyterian Missionaries: 1837–1861." *Church History* 42 (December 1973): 535–51.

————. "Red Indians, Black Slavery, and White Racism: America's Slaveholding Indians." *American Quarterly* 26 (October 1974): 367–85.

McLoughlin, William G., and Walter H. Conser, Jr. "The Cherokees in Transition: A Statistical Analysis of the Federal Cherokee Census of 1835." *Journal of American History* 64 (December 1977): 678–703.

Malone, Henry Thompson. "The Early Nineteenth-Century Missionaries in the Cherokee Country." *Tennessee Historical Quarterly* 10 (June 1951): 127–39.

Martin, Robert G., Jr. "The *Cherokee Phoenix*: Pioneer of Indian Journalism." *Chronicles of Oklahoma* 25 (Summer 1947): 102–18.

Melder, Keith. "Mask of Oppression: The Female Seminary Movement in the United States." *New York History* 55 (July 1974): 261–79.

Meserve, John Bartlett. "Chief John Ross." *Chronicles of Oklahoma* 8 (December 1935): 421–37.

Mihesuah, Devon A. " 'Out of the Graves of the Polluted Debauches': The Boys of the Cherokee Male Seminary." *American Indian Quarterly* 15 (Fall 1991): 503–21.

————. "Too Dark to Be Angels: The Class System among the Cherokees at the Female Seminary." *American Indian Culture and Research Journal* 15 (1991): 29–52.

Moulton, Gary R. "Chief John Ross during the Civil War." *Civil War History* 19 (December 1973): 314–33.

Murchison, A. H. "Intermarried Whites in the Cherokee Nation." *Chronicles of Oklahoma* 6 (September 1928): 302–27.

Palmer, Marcus. "Extracts of a Letter of Dr. Palmer Dated at Fairfield, February 15, 1831." *Missionary Herald* 27 (July 1831): 212–13.

Penton, Emily. "Typical Women's Schools in Arkansas before the War of 1861–1865." *Arkansas History Quarterly* 4 (Winter 1945): 325–39.

Perdue, Theda. "Cherokee Women and the Trail of Tears." *Journal of Women's History* 1 (Spring 1989): 14–30.

————. "The Conflict Within: The Cherokee Power Structure and Removal." *Georgia Historical Quarterly* 73 (Fall 1989): 467–91.

————. "The Traditional Status of Cherokee Women." *Furman Studies* (1980): 1–25.

Prucha, Francis Paul. "Andrew Jackson's Indian Policy: A Reassessment." *Journal of American History* 56 (December 1969): 527–39.

Riley, Glenda. "Origins of the Argument for Improved Female Education." *History of Education Quarterly* 9 (Winter 1969): 455–70.

Riley, Sam G. "A Note of Caution—The Indian's Own Prejudice as Mirrored in the First Native American Newspaper." *Journalism History* 6 (Summer 1979): 44–47.

Ross, William Potter. "Public Education among the Cherokee Indians." *American Journal of Education* 1 (August 1855): 120–22.

Routh, E. C. "Early Missionaries to the Cherokees." *Chronicles of Oklahoma* 15 (December 1937): 449–65.

Savage, William W. "Barbed Wire and Bureaucracy: The Foundation of the Cherokee Strip Livestock Association." *Journal of the West* 8 (July 1968): 405–14.

Scott, Anne Firor. "The Ever-Widening Circle: The Diffusion of Feminist Values from the Troy Female Seminary, 1822–1872." *History of Education Quarterly* 19 (Spring 1979): 3–25.

———. "Women's Perspective on the Patriarchy in the 1850s." *Journal of American History* 61 (June 1974): 52–64.

Scraper, Etta Jane. "Excerpt from *TSA-LA-GI Columns*" 8 (Spring 1984): 1–2.

Sharpes, Donald K. "Federal Education for the American Indian." *Journal of American Indian Education* 19 (October 1979): 19–32.

Social Science Research Council Summer Seminar on Acculturation. "Acculturation: An Exploratory Formulation." *American Anthropologist* 56 (December 1954): 973–1002.

Stahl, Wayne K. "The U.S. and Native American Education: A Survey of Federal Legislation." *Journal of American Indian Education* (May 1979): 28–32.

Starr, Samuel. "Epidemic of Smallpox." Excerpt from *I Remember the Class of 1904.* Brochure commemorating the fiftieth anniversary of the graduating classes of 1904.

Steen, Carl T. "The Home For the Insane, Deaf, Dumb and Blind of the Cherokee Nation." *Chronicles of Oklahoma* 21 (December 1943): 402–19.

Sterns, Bertha Monica. "Reform Periodicals and Feminist Reformers, 1830–1860." *American History Review* 37 (1937): 678–99.

Strange, John. Excerpt from *TSA-LA-GI Columns* 6 and 7 (August 1982–January 1983): 7.

Thompson, Louis. "A Cross Section in the Life of a Missionary Teacher among the Indians." *Chronicles of Oklahoma* 17 (March-December 1939): 329–23.

Thornton, Russell. "Nineteenth-Century Cherokee History: Comment on Champagne." *American Sociological Review* 50 (February 1985): 124–30.

Tinnin, Ida Wetzel. "Educational and Cultural Influences of the Cherokee Seminaries." *Chronicles of Oklahoma* 37 (Spring 1959): 59–67.

Tracy, Joseph. "History of the American Board of the Commissioners for Foreign Missions." In *History of American Missions to the Heathen, from Their Commencement to the Present Time.* Worcester, Mass.: Spooner and Howland, 1940.

Travis, V. A. "Life in the Cherokee Nation a Decade after the Civil War." *Chronicles of Oklahoma* 4 (March 1926): 16–30.

Tucker, Norma. "Nancy Ward, Ghighau of the Cherokees." *Georgia Historical Quarterly* 53 (June 1969): 192–200.

Van Kirk, Sylvia. "The Role of Native Women in the Fur Trade Society of Western Canada, 1670–1830." *Frontiers* 7 (1984): 9–13.

Wahrhaftig, Albert L. "Institution Building among Oklahoma Traditional Cherokees." In *Four Centuries of Southern Indian,* ed. Charles M. Hudson. Athens: University of Georgia Press, 1975.

Wahrhaftig, Albert L., and Robert K. Thomas. "Renaisssance and Repression: The Oklahoma Cherokee." In Ed Bahr, Howard Chadwick, and Robert C. Day, *Native Americans Today: Sociological Perspectives.* New York: Harper and Row, 1972.

Wax, Murray. "American Indian Education as a Cultural Transaction." *Teachers College Record* 64 (May 1963): 693–704.

Wein, Roberta. "Women's Colleges and Domesticity, 1875–1918." *History of Education Quarterly* 14 (Spring 1974): 31–47.

Welter, Barbara. "Cult of True Womanhood: 1820–1860." In *Woman's Experience in America: An Historical Analogy*, ed. Esther Katz and Anita Rapone. New Brunswick, N.J.: Transaction Books, 1980.

———. "The Feminization of American Religion, 1800–1860." In *Clio's Consciousness Raised*, ed. Mary Hartman and Lois Banner. New York, 1974.

Williams, Samuel C. "Christian Missions to the Overhill Cherokees." *Chronicles of Oklahoma* 12 (March 1934): 66–73.

Wilms, Douglas C. "Cherokee Acculturation and Changing Land Use Practice." *Chronicles of Oklahoma* 56 (Fall 1978): 331–43.

Worcester, Samuel. "Letter From Mr. Worcester to the Corresponding Secretary, July 4, 1827." *Missionary Herald* 23 (July 1827): 275–77.

Wright, Muriel H. "Rachel Caroline Eaton." *Chronicles of Oklahoma* 10 (March 1932): 8.

———. "Samuel Austin Worcester: A Dedication." *Chronicles of Oklahoma* 37 (Spring 1959): 2–21.

———. "Wapanucka Academy, Chickasaw Nation." *Chronicles of Oklahoma* 12 (December 1934): 402–31.

Index